PASTURES OF
THE EMPTY PAGE

CHARLES N. PROTHRO TEXANA SERIES

PASTURES OF THE EMPTY PAGE

Fellow Writers on the Life and Legacy of
Larry McMurtry

GEORGE GETSCHOW

EDITOR

UNIVERSITY OF TEXAS PRESS

AUSTIN

The following essays were previously published: Skip Hollandsworth, "The Larry McMurtry I Knew," reprinted with permission from *Texas Monthly*; Geoff Dyer, "Ranging across Texas," first published by the *Times Literary Supplement* (TLS) of the *London Times*; Oscar Cásares, "Snakes in a River," reprinted with permission from *Texas Monthly*; and Sarah Bird, "Finding Home," first published on the *Texas Highways* website in March 2021.

Requests for permission to reproduce material from this work should be sent to:
Permissions
University of Texas Press
P.O. Box 7819
Austin, TX 78713-7819
utpress.utexas.edu

∞ The paper used in this book meets the minimum requirements of ANSI/NISO Z39.48-1992 (R1997) (Permanence of Paper).

Library of Congress Cataloging-in-Publication Data
Names: Getschow, George, 1950– editor. | McMurtry, Larry, honoree.
Title: Pastures of the empty page : fellow writers on the life and legacy of Larry McMurtry / George Getschow, editor.
Description: First edition. | Austin : University of Texas Press, 2023.
Identifiers: LCCN 2022052900 (print) | LCCN 2022052901 (ebook)
    ISBN 978-1-4773-2787-6 (hardcover)
    ISBN 978-1-4773-2788-3 (pdf)
    ISBN 978-1-4773-2789-0 (epub)
Subjects: LCSH: McMurtry, Larry. | McMurtry, Larry—Friends and associates. | McMurtry, Larry. Works. Selections. | McMurtry, Larry—Characters. | Western stories—History and criticism. | LCGFT: Essays.
Classification: LCC PS3563.A319 Z79 2023 (print) | LCC PS3563.A319 (ebook) | DDC 813/.54—dc23/eng/20221125
LC record available at https://lccn.loc.gov/2022052900
LC ebook record available at https://lccn.loc.gov/2022052901

doi:10.7560/327876

Contents

Acknowledgments

GEORGE GETSCHOW

This book is dedicated to Larry McMurtry. Larry touched us all. He shaped us. He defined us. And his stories became so deeply embedded in us that they are now a part of who we are, the way we think, the way we see each other. So when Larry died, on March 25, 2021, a piece of us died too. But there was no funeral. No memorial service. No opportunity to commemorate and celebrate the epic life of Texas's literary titan.

That's why my literary sidekick and the administrator of the Archer City Writers Workshop, Kathy Floyd, and I decided to host a tribute to Larry in his hometown. We summoned a dozen prominent writers, mostly from Texas, to write about the mark Larry left on them. Their essays were read to a convocation gathered at the storied Royal Theater, where the adaptation of Larry's book *The Last Picture Show* was shown later that night. Our event, which we titled, in Larry's own words, "Larry McMurtry: Reflections on a Minor Regional Novelist," became a catalyst for the luminous collection of essays you now hold in your hand.

You, our readers, should know that the thirty-eight writers in this collection, including Kathy and me, wrote out of our deep respect—even reverence—for Larry and his immortal body of work. Which is why we're dedicating royalties from the sale of this book to a nonprofit foundation called the Archer City Writers Workshop: A Living Legacy to Larry McMurtry.

Our hope, and the hope of Larry's sisters, brother, and other family members, is that proceeds from the collection will help create and support a monument to Larry's storytelling legacy—a permanent writing center in Archer City to serve countless students and professional writers who have flocked to Larry's hometown over the last two decades hoping to channel Larry as their muse.

Our readers should also know that this book and our plans for the writing center would not have happened were it not for Kathy Floyd. She worked closely with Jerry Phillips and the Wichita Falls Area Community Foundation to obtain grants from the Royal C. "Bingo" Kinder fund, which enabled us to host our literary tribute at the Royal Theater and to conduct writing workshops in Archer City.

Underneath Kathy's shy and self-effacing personality lurks a lioness who, I've learned, is relentless in her pursuit of noble literary objectives. Looking over the hundreds of emails and texts we exchanged while putting together this collection, I'm reminded that Kathy never balked—not even once—no matter how high I stacked her plate with time-consuming tasks that I felt had to be done immediately. If our readers don't find any ghastly errors in grammar, spelling, or punctuation, it's because of Kathy's diligence and exacting standards. Simply put, Kathy has been an indispensable player on my team.

Same for Steve Harrigan. He wrote a splendid essay for this collection, solicited prominent writers as contributors, and spent many, many hours helping me navigate around some rocky shoals I encountered as the editor of this collection. At times of uncertainty and doubt, Steve served as my North Star.

Steve, a generous soul, even put Kathy and me in touch with his editor at UT Press, Casey Kittrell. From the get-go, we were thrilled to hear that Casey fully embraced our book idea. But transforming our idea into a book proved far more challenging than we anticipated. Fortunately, from beginning to end, Casey kept us on track, coaching us on how to clear all the hurdles that stood in the path of publishing. With Casey cheering us on, we cleared the last hurdle feeling like we had run the good race.

In assembling and editing this collection, I've been fortunate to work with, and become friends with, our highly accomplished contributors. Scan their bios at the end of each essay. I think you'll be as impressed with their literary careers as I am. One of them, Stephen Graham Jones, provided a tender foreword to our collection that still makes me tear up. When he was a young, aspiring novelist, Stephen recalls spotting Larry inside his giant bookstore in Archer City.

> Larry McMurtry looked right down the heart of that aisle and into my future, and what I thought then, what I want to have been true, was that he could see me now, twenty-six years later, still looking back at him, and holding my breath, trying to make this moment last.

I'm sitting in my living room, staring at a bookcase I fashioned out of solid hickory. It houses all of Larry's novels, essay collections, biographies, and memoirs. My lovely bookcase is a shrine to Larry's literary achievements and to his warm inner core. Each book is inscribed "To George, In Friendship." The book you're now holding in your hand is my way of returning the favor.

Foreword

STEPHEN GRAHAM JONES

"Sam the Lion."

Every time I start a new novel, I say this to myself. It's a reminder. What it tells me is that this world I'm about to start creating, that I'm already dreaming up, it's not shiny and new, it's not created from nothing. No, if it's to be real, if it's to be something the reader can engage with, invest in, *live* in, believe in, then it has to have a past. Like Sam the Lion.

A lot of readers find Holden Caulfield at that important part of their lives. Or Jude the Obscure.

I found *The Last Picture Show*.

At the time, I was still living those Friday nights Larry McMurtry talks about. Friday nights with nothing to do in the vast nothing of West Texas.

In his later years, Louis L'Amour would talk about what he called "the Yondering." It's that restlessness to head out, your saddlebags slung over your shoulder, your boots down at heel, maybe two dimes and a nickel in your pocket.

That yondering is what so many of Larry McMurtry's books are made of. It's what I connect with in his stories, his characters—I want to say "his worlds," but, really? The Texas he wrote about so much, it's the same Texas that's in me, and that I'm pretty sure is in all the writers in these pages, each of whom also feels a connection to Larry McMurtry, or owes him a debt, or just wants to pay homage with the best thing they have: their words.

As for me, after seeing "the Yondering" and my Texas in *The Last Picture Show*, man, I was hooked. There was *Horseman, Pass By*, which I could never understand why he disowned. *Lonesome Dove*, of course, and its sequel that had no right to be so good—has any sequel ever stood on its own as well as *Streets of Laredo*?

And on and on down the bookshelf and into television and film . . . if there was a story that Larry McMurtry couldn't tell and tell well, then I haven't heard of it.

He came at fiction in a way we don't get to read very much. He was dismissive of attempts to intellectualize his work, to drag it into the academy—counting on that for validation is never the best bet—but what he was doing wasn't the kind of commercial we used to see on spinner racks, either.

I think Larry McMurtry just wanted to tell a good story, and to hell with people who wanted him to be part of this movement or that era, and to hell with genre distinctions as well. I can imagine him saying that if it works, it works, so what's all the blather about?

That doesn't mean you can't learn from him, though.

What I learned was "Sam the Lion."

After reading about Sam, and how he used to be before *The Last Picture Show*, I found myself considering my uncles and great-uncles differently. I wondered what untold stories their pasts held. Because they hadn't always been like they were now.

So?

So I started hanging around, listening to the lies they would tell about being young, and when I could keep myself from believing in them all the way, I could sometimes get the briefest glimmer of the way it actually might have been. And I could guess at why they were telling this story *this* way now, not some other way.

They became people, I'm saying. Broken and wonderful, hurt and proud, and moving still, in spite of what they were dragging behind them.

Every time I sit down to write something, I remind myself of this—that these characters have been shaped by their experiences. And that just because they're not spouting those experiences, it doesn't mean the past isn't there all the same.

In graduate school, in a class on Robert Browning, the professor slowed a poem down to show us the grime and rust on a roomful of implements, grime and rust that meant this room had existed for decades before the story walked into it.

I already knew that, though.

I'd come up reading Larry McMurtry, I mean.

Even more than that, the year before I read that Robert Browning poem, I'd trekked over to Archer City to catch a glimpse of Larry McMurtry.

I was in Denton at the time, attending the University of North Texas, and my wife had to pack me a cold lunch because we didn't have money for me to be stopping anywhere to eat, but . . . I saw him.

For many of the writers in this collection, that won't be a big thing. Larry McMurtry was in the world, he was available to see, maybe even to talk to, or to sit at a table with.

Not to me, though.

To me at twenty-three, he was made of Other Stuff. He was some higher order.

Word was, back then, that the downtown of Archer City, which he'd turned into a sprawling bookstore, would sometimes be haunted by him. That if you hung around long enough, you might could see him.

I cruised the science fiction, I cruised the thrillers, I ran my fingers down the spines of row after row of books, some of them probably by the people in this book you're holding, and then, finally, way down at the end of one aisle, there he was.

He was guiding a book dolly, and he stopped for a moment like he'd sensed me. What I told myself was that we were making a connection. I was writing fiction by then, and knew I was destined to reach the same literary heights he already had, so I imagined a taut string of awareness connecting the two of us.

It is grandiose, yeah. Is there any other way to think when you're twenty-three, though? If you don't think like that, then the world swallows you. Thinking like that's self-defense, almost.

So he looked up, Mr. McMurtry looked up. Larry McMurtry looked right down the heart of that aisle and into my future, and what I thought then, what I want to have been true, was that he could see me now, twenty-six years later, still looking back at him, and holding my breath, trying to make the moment last, to never have it end.

Thank you, sir.

I'm still in your bookstore. All of us listed in the table of contents, we're bunched down at the end of that aisle, and we don't really want to leave. Even after you nod once, push your book dolly back into the shadows, we're still looking into the space you just filled.

It's filled yet.

STEPHEN GRAHAM JONES is the Ivena Baldwin Professor of English, as well as a Professor of Distinction, at the University of Colorado Boulder. He is the author of more than twenty-five books, including *The Only Good Indians* and *My Heart Is a Chainsaw*. Jones has been an NEA Fellow and a Texas Writers League Fellow. He won the Texas Institute of Letters Award for Fiction, the Independent Publishers Multicultural Award, the Bram Stoker Award, four This Is Horror Awards, and he was a Shirley Jackson Award finalist and a Colorado Book Award finalist.

PASTURES OF
THE EMPTY PAGE

Larry McMurtry as a boy on his family's ranch, sitting on his first pony.

Introduction

IDIOT RIDGE—It looks like any other cattle gate in rural Texas—as crude and rough as the ranch behind it. A rusted stirrup, the ranch brand, is mounted on top, and its white paint is as rigid and cracked as the ground beneath.

But this is no ordinary gate. It marks the entry to the McMurtry ranch, a scruffy plateau bordered by the rocky ledges known by locals as Idiot Ridge. It's the place where stories were told and passed around even before Larry McMurtry was born in 1936. He would become one of the most influential Western writers of the twentieth century, shooting holes in romantic portrayals of the Old West.

Beyond the cattle gate, a dirt road leads up to a mesquite-covered hill. Here, over a hundred years earlier, Larry's grandparents unhitched their wagon and made a life, and it's the spot where Larry's life as a storyteller began. Throughout his life, before starting work on any one of his novels, Larry felt impelled to walk the perimeter of the McMurtry ranch, gazing upon that hill that would shape his literary destiny. "To this day," Larry wrote many years later in an autobiographical essay, "if I attempt a rural setting, I invariably produce the contours of the hill where I first walked."

Growing up on Idiot Ridge, he felt the power of the big Western sky, the empty plains and endless horizon breaking over the ridge and stretching north all the way to Montana. Riding out in the early dawn through dewy grassland, watching the sunlight turn the prairie gold, enthralled him. He later wrote: "The hold the landscape had on me was so powerful that I couldn't imagine living long in any other place."

Larry lived on the raw edge of a frontier gasping its last breaths. Raised in the shadow of pioneering grandparents, he heard story after story of free-spirited McMurtry cowmen running cattle on the open range. By the time he was born, the open ranges had been cut up into fenced pastures.

But his grandfather kept two longhorns on the ranch, wild and powerful beasts that had once roamed freely across the southern plains of Texas, reminders of early days on the vast frontier. The power of its previous inhabitants, the Comanches and the Kiowa, had been broken a decade before the McMurtrys' arrival in Archer County in 1888, but fear of their return remained.

As he grew older the young cowboy saw the deep blue sky and rolling prairie that had once enchanted turn treacherous. Tornadoes barely missed the barn, grass fires licked at the homestead, and sandstorms and cloudbursts buried the ranch in dust and mud. His horse, Polecat, dragged him through a mesquite briar, ripping his skin to shreds. He was swept up in stampedes, hurled off his horse when a steer panicked in a lightning storm, and trapped "on the wrong side" of the surging Little Wichita River, as he recalled it, "stuck on a weak horse in a world of mud." He saw cowboys crushed under their horses, a teenager decapitated by a drilling rig, his father's unending battle against the mesquite that choked the precious grass on the hill.

As he watched, a split developed in Larry's Western soul. Year by year the young cowboy became increasingly disenchanted with romantic notions of cowboy life and with the traditional frontier values that governed his own family. As his sister Sue Deen observed, "Larry saw the loneliness and futility in their lives."

His father, Jeff Mac, believed in cowboying the old-fashioned way. Working cattle dawn to dusk, he disallowed even a cup of ice water. Warm water from a canteen was sufficient. With so much to do, no one dared leave the homeplace without good reason. And so Jeff Mac came unglued whenever his wife, Hazel, went off to play bridge at the local Amity Club meetings. "It grated on Dad's nerves that other people might have the time to socialize a little," says Larry's brother, Charlie. "Dad thought of Mom as hopelessly irresponsible."

One morning Larry watched his grandmother, a fiercely independent woman who had raised twelve children on the frontier, slap his mother hard across the face when she tried to make herself useful in the kitchen. Jeff Mac, standing nearby, said nothing. Larry later observed in an essay, "My father could not forgive my mother for having an easier life than his mother had."

That slap in the kitchen changed Larry's world. Jeff Mac began expecting less and less of his wife and more and more of young Larry. The list of duties and obligations grew longer: cleaning out the barn, hauling hay, mending fences, fixing the windmill, feeding the chickens, and clearing out the ever-invading horde of prickly pear and mesquite.

As Larry put it in *Paradise*, "I began to feel bound, in my small way, to hold the world together long enough for my father to run over to Odessa and watch the steer-roping for an afternoon."

His grandfather, his father, and his uncles had taught him that the only thing in the world that mattered was ranching. The family motto was "McMurtry means beef." But Larry was feeling more and more detached from the ranch, more and more drawn by the world outside.

Instead of sitting on the front porch listening to the old tales, he would climb the steps of the windmill and sit on the platform beneath the blades, looking out across the dim lights strung across the tops of oil derricks, listening to the roar of cars on the highway that ran alongside the pasture, watching the headlights of the eighteen-wheelers pointed toward Fort Worth, Dallas, and beyond. He remembered afterward hearing the roar of the nightly train, the *Texas Zephyr*, fly by with passengers headed to Amarillo, Denver, Los Angeles, and points in between.

As a cowboy on Idiot Ridge, young Larry didn't have the vaguest notion yet that he would end up a writer. All he knew "was that I would have to deal with cowboying, either successfully or unsuccessfully, because there was nothing else in sight."

His life changed the day a cousin, heading to boot camp and World War II, dropped off a box of books. This small stable of books gave Larry a feeling of independence, freedom. "Literature, as I saw it then, was a vast open range, my equivalent of the cowboy's dream."

He continued to ride across Idiot Ridge, moving cattle, mending fences. But his head was elsewhere. Reading became "the central and stable activity of my life," he would write in an essay. "Making a living would have to be made to fit in somehow, but if I could help it, it would not involve cows."

When he decided to attend the Rice Institute, now Rice University, in the fall of 1954, Larry left the ranch, torn and conflicted, unsure whether he could abandon his heritage. But the moment the eighteen-year-old cowboy stepped into the Rice library, his conflicts dissolved like heat after a hard rain. "I felt that I had found my intellectual home and began to relax in ways that had not been possible on the ranch," he wrote many years later.

In the copious Rice library, he rode the "vast open range" of literature, reading literary journalists such as H. L. Mencken and Edmund Wilson, who directed him to books he had never heard of by Victorian, Edwardian, and early-twentieth-century English writers. Soon he was exploring outside the library in used bookshops, hunting for the books he intended to take back with him to Idiot Ridge as "my support group." He still assumed he would return to Archer County to saddle up again.

As Larry read, he wondered whether he could write too. He began by imitating the writers he was reading. But his days at Rice were short lived. Feeling defeated after failing a math class, he transferred to North Texas State, now the University of North Texas. In Denton, he hoped, as he wrote in his undergraduate "Abridged Autobiography," "to make some weird combination of writer-rancher-professor out of myself."

And so he wrote fiction, poetry, and essays about everything but the ranching life he had escaped. He wrote fifty-two short stories that he felt were so bad he burned them. Reluctantly, he returned to his cowboy roots. "That first life had not quite died in me—not quite," he recalled later. "Not long after I entered the pastures of the empty page I realized that the place where all my stories start is the heart faced suddenly with the loss of its country, its customary and legendary range."

He wrote a short story about the destruction of a diseased cattle herd, then another dealing with the death of a Texas cattle rancher. He expanded the short stories into a novel about a venerable rancher facing the loss of his blood country and a way of life dating back to the Texas frontier. The autobiographical novel, *Horseman, Pass By*, explores the deep conflicts between the urban and rural values of the changing West, the tragic consequences for families caught up in the conflict, the loss of the open range, and the emergence of the oil patch with its materialistic values.

He had discovered the themes that would occupy him the rest of his writing life.

Those themes not only echoed in his books but also translated with stunning effect to an entirely different medium: movies. In *Hud*, the film adaption of *Horseman, Pass By*, Paul Newman portrays the title character, a thinly disguised rogue hell-bent on seizing his elderly father's most prized possession: his cattle ranch. Filmed in black-and-white, the 1963 movie is faithful to Larry's spare yet eloquent prose and the bareness and beauty of the Texas prairie. *Hud* quickly achieved critical and commercial success. Nominated for seven Academy Awards, it won three.

Larry collaborated with Peter Bogdanovich on the film adaptation of *The Last Picture Show*. Released in 1971, the black-and-white film remains perhaps the best movie ever made about the seamy side of small-town life in Texas. *The Last Picture Show* was nominated for eight Academy Awards, including Best Adapted Screenplay, and marked a breakthrough in Larry's career as a screenwriter and Bogdanovich's career as a "New Hollywood" director.

After his debut as the co-screenwriter for *The Last Picture Show*, Larry went on to a long and celebrated career adapting some of his own books and the work of other writers for the screen. What distinguished him from other screenwriters was his gift for writing dialogue, with all its quirkiness, unexpectedness, and authenticity.

That's why critics were surprised that in adapting Annie Proulx's short story "Brokeback Mountain" to the screen, Larry and his partner, Diana Ossana, often used silence rather than dialogue to express the unrequited love and heartbreak of two homosexual cowboys working on a Wyoming sheep ranch in the 1960s. In the 2005 film adaptation, it's what's left unsaid that most poignantly expresses the lonely cowboys' anguish and despair. *Brokeback Mountain* was universally acclaimed as a cinematic masterpiece, earning Larry and Diana an Academy Award for Best Adapted Screenplay.

Larry's screenwriting success, of course, still lay in an unimagined future when *Horseman, Pass By* was published in 1961. The book was quickly dubbed a "classic" and created a stir in the literary world, launching Larry's career as a writer. "Never before had a writer portrayed the contemporary West in conflict with the Old West in such stark, realistic, unsentimental ways," raved the publisher.

Set on Idiot Ridge, it reveals Larry's deep reverence for the land and the old cowboys who devoted themselves to it. Like Larry's grandfather, Homer Bannon, the old ranch owner of the novel, keeps two rangy longhorns on Idiot Ridge "for old time's sake," to remind him of the days when cattle roamed free and a rancher's heritage meant something.

The novel also reveals Larry's distaste for the violence, the sentimentality, and the small-mindedness of the ranching ethos that produced in him, as he later described it in a collection of essays, *In a Narrow Grave*, "an ambivalence as deep as the bone."

During a dance at the annual rodeo, the biggest event of the year, Lonnie (Larry's alter ego) lies across the bed of a pickup near the outdoor dance floor listening to an old Hank Williams song that expresses his disillusionment with the cowboy way of life.

> All of them wanted more and seemed to end up with less; they wanted excitement and ended up stomped by a bull or smashed against a highway; or they wanted a girl to court; and anyway, whatever they wanted, that was what they ended up doing without.

In the novel Lonnie leaves Idiot Ridge the next day in search of a life that's more exciting, more civilized, more fulfilling than cowboying. He takes a few clothes and a few of his paperbacks with him and drives to Thalia (Archer City). He spies a red cattle truck parked at the filling station, heading for New Mexico, and bums a ride.

> We rode through the outskirts of Thalia. The sun was going into the great western canyons, the cattleland was growing dark. I saw the

road and the big sky melt together in the north, above the rope of highway. I was tempted to do like Jesse once said: to lean back and let the truck take me as far as it was going.

Lonnie leaves, but Larry stayed in Texas to write five more novels exploring his strained, ambivalent attitude toward his blood country. In 1969, feeling he was "sucking air" after exhausting the central themes of his frayed connections to his homeplace, he left Texas, moving to Virginia in search of a fresh story. Yet even as he was cutting his Texas ties, he continued to pierce "the cowboy myth" in newspaper and magazines articles, such as his piece for *Atlantic Monthly* in 1975:

> Texas was built on the myth of self-reliant individualism. . . . In a culture long on work and short on the kind of discourse that creates community, a deep sense of isolation and valuelessness seizes and blights many personalities just at the point at which they finally mature. Men and women seem no longer able to recognize themselves, either in their works or in their lives; they suffer, drink, do crazy things, to a degree go mad, not merely because they have no one to talk to, but because even if they did they would feel it was wrong to talk.

Larry concluded that he no longer felt any connection to his homeplace. After living in the wooded landscape of Virginia, he claimed, he was now "rooted differently."

"That really hurt Daddy," says his sister Sue.

Two years later, after working a full day in the pastures, Jeff Mac died of a heart attack. A card was found in his wallet, written in his own hand. It asked, "If worse came to worse and in the end there was no grass, what would you do?" His father's death caused Larry to do some serious soul-searching. He traveled to Archer City in the summer of 1980 to reexamine his connections to home. In an eighty-three-page essay written in Archer City, *Walter Benjamin at the Dairy Queen*, Larry found himself reconsidering his views about his homeplace.

In the end, my father's career and my own were not as different as I had once thought. He cattle ranched in a time he didn't much like, and I word ranched, describing the time he longed to live in and the kind of cowboys he would have liked to know.

In 1981, Larry moved back to Idiot Ridge, back to the place of his heritage, asking his sister Sue to get someone to clear the mesquite that was taking over the hill, a painful reminder of his father's lifelong struggle against the invasive shrub.

Once again, he was gazing over the hill to the long horizon stretching northward. Inspired in part by his father's frustrated ambition to be a trail driver, Larry began working on a trail-drive novel that he had started as a screenplay.

As he was writing *Lonesome Dove*, a novel about a harrowing trail drive from Texas to Montana, he felt very much at home. "[I] didn't feel that I was writing about the Old West, in capital letters—I was merely writing about my grandfather's time, and my uncles', none of whom seemed like men of another time to me."

Lonesome Dove earned Larry a Pulitzer Prize and international fame. His one regret was that his father never knew that his dream to drive cattle across the Great Plains "had found its way into one of my books."

Larry found himself drawn back to his ranching instincts in other ways. Shortly after his trail-drive novel was published, he began herding more and more books into Archer City, making the former cowboy a big-time book rancher. In a place he once disparaged as "a bookless town in a bookless part of the state," Larry filled the entire town with books, more than four hundred thousand of them—"my equivalent of the King Ranch," he called it.

"Larry grew up a herdsman, and he's still a herdsman," says Sue.

In an essay for *Esquire*, he attempted to understand his recurring desire to drive back and forth across America's interstate highways. He hadn't escaped his cowboying days at all. "What was I doing, proceeding north on I-35, but driving the trucks and cars ahead of me up to their northern pastures?" he wrote. "My driving was a form of nomadism, and the vehicles ahead of me were my great herds."

If Larry's father had a religion, it was grass. After his father's death, it became Larry's. When a neighboring rancher and close friend of Jeff Mac's died, the rancher's family invited Larry to give his eulogy. Larry spoke so eloquently about the majesty and grandeur of grass that "everyone was in tears," says Sue. "Daddy had instilled in Larry a reverence for the grass. It's something that's sacred to him."

In his sixties, Larry made a road trip to the high plains of the Panhandle, where his uncles had built their own cattle kingdoms. His kinsmen who had settled on the grassy plateaus of the Panhandle— every one of whom had only a few decades before proudly posed for a family reunion photograph, resolute and determined to stay put on their patch of prairie no matter what—were now gone.

Alas, as Larry mused in *Roads*, "the grass is there still but the McMurtrys are gone."

At times Larry cursed his uncles for what he called their "religious allegiance" to the myth of the cowboy god and their belief in the "divinity of the range." For them, Larry said, "the good Lord is the name of rain and grass."

Yet even after moving to Houston—"the metropolis of the muses," Larry called it—and writing three novels preoccupied with the excitement, melancholy, struggles, and passions of urban life, in his deepest affections he could not turn loose of Old Texas. Like those of his uncles before him, his heart remained in his blood country.

As I reflect on the empty pastures Larry has left to us, an old song, "The Cowboy's Lament," about the passing of the cowboy, plays in my mind:

> I'm going to leave Old Texas now;
> They've got no use for the longhorn cow.
> They've plowed and fenced my cattle range
> And the people there are all so strange.

Now the longhorns are gone. The cowboys are gone. Old Texas is gone. And Larry McMurtry, the preeminent Western writer of the twentieth century, is gone. But his influence will endure for as long as literature endures. Larry's books, which scrutinize and filter the myths of the Old West through his hard-bitten experiences as a cowboy, forged a new brand of literature and a new generation of writers captivated by his clear-eyed vision and unvarnished realism about Texas and the American West.

Which is why all the writers in this collection felt it essential that we examine Larry's titanic influence on the literature of Texas, and on us. Larry never professed a calling, but his entire body of work pointed toward it: to strip Texas and the West of its myths, sentimentality, clichés, and prosaic prose that "makes one want to grind one's teeth."

What Larry wrote didn't always sit well with his family, his community, or even his fellow writers. But he kept writing and writing and writing, filling the pastures of the empty page with stories of the heart, stories of his blood country, stories of loss and longing, strife and struggle, dreams fulfilled and dreams denied. Stories that remain embedded in our bones. And he kept writing until his death on March 25, 2021.

There isn't a writer in this collection who could ever fill that empty space, that empty pasture, the way Larry McMurtry did. He broke trail. And thanks to the trail he left to us, wide and luminous, we won't be groping in the dark. As Steve Harrigan puts it in his essay, "We could never hope to measure up, but we could dare to press on, because he showed us how."

GEORGE GETSCHOW, a Pulitzer Prize finalist, worked for the *Wall Street Journal* as a reporter, bureau chief, and Mexico correspondent. He was a Pulitzer Prize jurist in 2017 for General Nonfiction and for Feature Writing in 2013 and 2014. He was inducted into the Texas Institute of Letters in 2012 for "distinctive literary achievement." As writer-in-residence at the Mayborn Literary Nonfiction Conference at the University of North Texas, Getschow oversaw the 2006 publication of *Spurs of Inspiration*, a collection of stories about Larry McMurtry and his hometown. This introduction contains excerpts from his story about Larry's life as a rancher and writer.

NATIVE GROUND

Larry's ancestors on Idiot Ridge, circa 1920s.

In Awesome Wonder

From *Tom and Big Boy*

Dad was already a wiry, grouchy, set-in-his-ways, fifty-year-old rancher when I was born. And my arrival didn't alter any of those things. I started going with Dad to feed cattle when I was two, sitting up high on the truck seat and a box with a pillow on it. I remember going in the Mobil filling station when I was four or five, and hearing men tell Dad that he'd almost waited too long to raise his own cowboys.

My brother, Larry, had already left for college by the time that I started going horseback with Dad every day. Over the next twenty years, Larry returned only occasionally, not nearly often enough to help with much of the ranch work, so Dad had no intention of letting another son slip away.

I started going with Dad every Saturday and six days a week in the summer when I was seven years old, though that is not a particularly early age for cowboys to begin their training. I had a big bay horse named Pee Wee, who was too big for me to get on by myself. So Dad always had to swing me up onto his back. I wanted a Shetland pony so that I could get on and off whenever I wanted, but Dad wouldn't hear of it.

"Hell no! You're not getting any damned Shetland pony," he'd say every time that I would ask for one.

Excerpts from *In Awesome Wonder*, a collection of essays written by Larry McMurtry's younger brother, William Charlie McMurtry, for his 1996 doctoral dissertation.

"They can't keep up with the grown horse, and they're meaner than hell," Dad said. "Larry had one named Polecat, and the son of a bitch tried to drag him off under every mesquite limb he could find."

I remember looking off across the mesquite-covered pasture and thinking Larry must have had a hell of a time of it. Maybe that was why he didn't want to be a cowboy.

From *Triumph*

God, I'll never forget the summer Dad and I built the roping arena behind our house in town. We did it partly so that we could have some fun in the evenings and partly for educational purposes. I don't have any idea why either of us thought we could have fun building or using anything, but I remember why we began the project in the first place. We were on our way home late one afternoon after a day of calf branding. I'd been doing some of the roping, but I hadn't done a very good job of it.

"You're going to have to learn to rope better, or nobody's going to let you take a turn," Dad said.

I didn't see any need answering that statement. Dad was driving and I was sulking. He'd hollered at me every time I'd missed a loop.

"Did you hear me?" Dad asked, looking over at me.

"Yes, I heard you," I replied. "What do you want me to say? I'm learning as fast as I can."

I was sixteen years old and had only started learning to rope six months earlier. Roping cattle was an art that took quite a bit of skill. Nobody learned without lots of practice, and I'd had practically none. But Dad expected me to be an expert the first time I picked up a rope.

"Well, you could offer some excuse, at least," Dad said.

"I haven't had much practice, you know?" I said.

"At making excuses or roping?" Dad said, his tone solemn.

"Roping," I said. "I've had plenty of practice at the other."

From *Snakes*

"I want you to go down to the ranch and clean out the hayloft," Dad said, puffing on his pipe a little. "Clean all the old hay out, just kick it out the end doors, and get things good and clean. I may buy a load of hay while I'm gone."

I didn't say anything. I figured there was more to come, and there was.

"While you're down there, you might as well clean out the saddle room too," Dad added. "When you get that done, you better straighten up the hallway of the barn and then sharpen your shovel and cut the broom weeds around all the corrals. I don't want to step on a damn rattlesnake one of these days."

"Don't you think those are the kind of chores where there ought to be two of us?" I asked.

"Yeah, probably, but you're old enough to look out for yourself," Dad said. "Just watch what you're doing. . . . You still remember Larry dragging that rattler out of the barn that morning, don't you? Well, it was dark that morning."

"Yeah, it sure was," I said. I could still remember the morning, clearly.

Dad, my big brother Larry, and myself had gotten out of Dad's old truck one morning about 4:30. I couldn't have been over eight years old at the time. We had to catch our horses early to go help a neighbor do some cow work. Larry had come home that summer from college, and he went with us sometimes.

The evening before, Larry and I had put our saddles just inside the big sliding barn door. There was always some hay scattered there in the hallway. We didn't have any barn light back then, and Dad had turned the truck lights off when he stepped out of the truck. Larry and I could see pretty good by the moonlight, so we grabbed the barn door and slid it open. Larry had reached inside, grabbed his saddle, and dragged it toward us. A rattlesnake came with it, and we couldn't see the bastard, but we could sure hear him. He must have been right at our feet, and he was mad as hell at our having disturbed him in his warm hiding place. Larry and I both hollered and jumped back, and Dad turned the truck lights back on and came running with the shovel. Neither of us had been bitten, but the incident scared the hell out of me, and I'd never forgotten it.

From *The Windfall*

Dad came from a long line of ranchers, and he did not disgrace the line at all. He was considered one of the best ranchers and managers in our part of North Texas. By the time I was sixteen, he owned and leased over four thousand acres of rangeland and ran upwards of 250 cows. That was a fair amount of land and cattle for our part of the country.

In addition to those holdings, Dad partnered with some insurance men on another ranch of three hundred cows and five thousand acres. They provided the land, and Dad provided the know-how. I had worked for Dad on all of his ranches since I turned seven. I wanted to be a cowboy. Before I was sixteen, and at Dad's insistence, I borrowed some money and leased a couple of small pastures of my own and ran thirty or so cows and calves. Dad wanted me to be a cowman, and he explained the difference to me one day.

"Son," he said, "anybody can be a cowboy. It doesn't take many smarts, just mostly a weak mind and a willing back."

"That doesn't make it bad, does it?" I asked. "I kind of like being a cowboy."

"I didn't say it was bad," Dad replied. "I'm trying to tell you why you should be more of one than the other, that's all."

I didn't tell him that I had more fun cowboying with other people's cattle than I did with my own. That would have pissed him off.

"So what are you getting at?" I asked.

"I'm getting at the fact that cowboys work for other people," Dad said, "and these other people are cowmen. If you can make money for the other man, you can make money for yourself."

I thought about that for a while. My best friend was a cowboy for a neighboring ranch, and the happiest man I knew. I longed to be like him, both in ability and every other way.

"Why are you telling me this?" I asked. "What do you mean?"

"Son," Dad said, "I'm getting too old to run as much country as I have. I might want you to run some of it for me someday."

Dad was sixty-six that year, but he hadn't slowed down any. He worked twelve-hour days, like always. I worked them too, and I thought that I was helping him run his country. . . .

"I don't think you take enough interest in your own damn cattle, much less mine," Dad said. "You don't think about them enough."

I knew what he meant. We'd had plenty of arguments about my not knowing my cows. Dad thought a cowman ought to know each and every cow by her markings. He was forever saying, "Cattle are just like people. There's not any two that looks exactly alike." When we worked my cattle and some were missing, I didn't know which ones were gone, but he did.

That just aggravated the hell out of him.

"Dad, we've been through this before," I said. "I know that I don't know my cows, but I'm learning as fast as I can."

Actually, I was learning every bit as fast as I wanted to.

"By God, it's not fast enough," Dad said.

After he quit the ranching life to pursue his creative yearnings, **WILLIAM CHARLIE MCMURTRY** attended graduate school at the University of North Texas, where he wrote eighteen short stories for his dissertation and earned a PhD in 1996. Upon graduation, he took a job as a lecturer in the English Department at Angelo State University in San Angelo, Texas. At Angelo, he taught creative writing and developmental reading and writing for ten years. By 2006, Charlie McMurtry says, he was "burned out" and set up a welding shop in Archer City, where he worked until he retired in 2019 because of his failing vision.

The Boy with the Lamp

IN '09 LARRY MCMURTRY took an option on my novel *The Color of Lightning* to write a screenplay based on the story. He was writing it on spec. The novel is a fictionalized account of the life and death of Britt Johnson, a Black frontiersman who lived in Young County. McMurtry did not manage to sell the screenplay to that amorphous and somewhat incoherent tribal entity called "Hollywood." There are several steps that led up to this not-selling of the script. The point of this rather inconsequential anecdote is McMurtry's solid footing in his own community, his own people, and his own raising in Archer County. He was deeply rooted in North Texas, and his best work was drawn from the people and the landscape of that country.

This story has to do with not finding Britt's grave as well as with not selling a script.

Britton Johnson was a historical character. The novel is the only time I have written a story with a real person as its protagonist, so accuracy was important, even though the available details of Britt's life are scarce and sometimes contradictory. He was born into slavery, probably in the early 1840s but maybe the mid-1830s. He was "owned" by a Johnson family in either Tennessee or Alabama, and some say they were from Kentucky. They all came to Texas probably in the 1850s, to Elm Creek near Graham. Britt seemed to be a free man with a free wife and either three or four children. At any rate, in a combined raid in 1864, Kiowa and Comanche attacked the Elm Creek settlements, killing eleven people, including Britt's oldest son, and taking his wife and two other children and several other white settlers captive.

Britt went alone into Indian Territory and by some miraculous means got them all back except one. I found him an amazing figure, courageous and also relentless. Finally, he and two Black companions in his freighting business, Dennis Cureton and Paint Crawford, were ambushed and killed in 1871 by a Kiowa raiding party. And that's the story.

So when I was in the middle of writing *The Color of Lightning*, I drove up to those northern counties and into Oklahoma to visit the land and the valley of the Red River, the crossings and the gallery forests, and to talk to people up there. That would be Archer, Young, Montague, and Wichita Counties. I asked a friend to go with me, June Chism. Her husband, Wayne Chism, is the one who told me about his great-grandfather, Caesar Aloysius Kidd, called Captain Kidd, who went around North Texas doing readings from newspapers.

So in November of '07, June and I drove north in my aging pickup. It seemed like I drove that rust bucket *forever* through endless stretches of a landscape I found entrancing and beautiful and ever changing in its sounds and tones and color values. We stayed with and met yet more Chisms and friends of Chisms, and they were all very kind. We were taken to Fort Belknap and down to the Red River, to Spanish Fort, to the old crossing at Rock Bluff. Then June and I started out to look for Britt's grave. He and Dennis and Paint are buried where they fell; there are not many graves about which you can say that.

I had a photo of his gravestone from a genealogical website about "graves in Young County" that gave directions on how to find it.

June and I climbed an oil-field fence and struck out into the brush and the rolling plains. We walked and searched and went back to check the directions and then walked and searched some more. By this time the norther that had been under construction in the northwest was building up, and as we pushed through the brush and tall grass the temperature dropped by many degrees. At least ten, maybe fifteen, I don't know, but the wind was very strong and neither of us had brought a warm coat. There were those weird-looking clouds that resemble lenses or alien spaceships, perfectly oval with clean, hard edges, sailing along underneath the heavier cloud cover. This means high winds and hard weather. We gave up and ran for the pickup. It blew for days.

By the time McMurtry and I were writing back and forth about the script I mentioned earlier, I had searched for Britt's grave and been unable to find it. He wrote back:

> (14 May 09) By chance last week in Archer City who should plop down beside me but Jack Loftin, the county historian and also my nearest country neighbor, as he has been my whole life. I mentioned Britt and he said he himself has placed Britt's grave marker and that he had set it about forty feet from where Britt's remains actually [are.] To discourage vandals? I'm not sure. He offered to take us to it—maybe we'll go someday; but I'm sure he'd take you. Jack has plugged away, a county historian with [very] little interest from any-one and when he gets a chance to talk he doesn't waste it.

So that's why we couldn't find it.

I also searched for a face to put to my characters; it seems the characters live somehow in the faces of old photos. No matter who they were, they become iconic, more than themselves, invested with a strange kind of meaning, or life. Looking for Tissoyo, Britt's Comanche friend, I came upon *Comanches in the New West 1895–1908* and began flipping through the pages in search of him. I found him, on page 67, a splendidly decorated young man with a beautiful face named Wockneahtooah, whom I renamed Tissoyo and put in the novel.

I also discovered that McMurtry had written the foreword to the book. There he mentioned one of the most remarkable photos in the collection—the next-to-last one, a photo of a young man demonstrating a kerosene lamp to a collection of cowboys and ranchers. The lighting is poor, even though it's outdoors. It's a cloudy day, so things don't seem to have edges and all the tones blur out to an amorphous equality except for the shirt fronts, which are glaring white. It is initially hard to find the young man with the lamp in his hand, but finally there he is, with short light hair, oddly dressed in some kind of peculiar circus tights. It's a strange and absorbing photograph once you start in on

A historical photograph of a boy demonstrating a kerosene lamp to a crowd of cowboys, soldiers, and Indians.

a close inspection of the rough crowd of cowboys and a few soldiers intent on the boy and his lamp. Since I was assigning other identities to the people in these photos, the more I studied it the more I realized that here was McMurtry himself.

He is the boy with the lamp. He lifts it to reveal his characters, his imaginary people, and they are all there, regarding him and his magic lantern with an intent gaze, Call and Gus and Newt and Deets and Pea Eye and Lorena—all of them. He brought them to light and into being with the illumination of his creative mind. He never left that country, no matter whether he lived in New York or Tucson. It was a loyalty that could not be revoked or abandoned. This was him, then: dressed in an acrobat's flashy tights, holding up his lamp to bring that extraordinary country and its people out of the shadows and into literature.

PAULETTE JILES is a novelist, memoirist, and poet. Her best-selling novels include *Enemy Women*, *Stormy Weather*, and *The Color of Lightning*. Her book *News of the World* was a National Book Award finalist and was made into a film, starring Tom Hanks, in 2020. She has won Canada's highest award for poetry, the Governor General's Award. Her next book, *Chenneville*, will be released in 2023. Jiles graduated from the University of Missouri with a degree in Romance languages. She lives near San Antonio, Texas.

The Larry McMurtry I Knew

I caught my first glimpse of the *Lonesome Dove* author on the streets of Archer City when I was a kid. It was an encounter that shaped the rest of my life.

In 1970, when I was a junior high school student living in Wichita Falls, I rode one afternoon with a friend and his older brother to Archer City, a town located twenty-five miles away. At the time, Peter Bogdanovich was shooting a movie called *The Last Picture Show*, about some teenagers trying to find happiness in a desolate Texas town. Rumor had it that one of the actresses in the film, Cybill Shepherd, was going to be filming a nude scene that day. My friend's older brother told us we had to be there.

When we arrived in Archer City, the three of us gathered with other onlookers at the end of the street. We watched as the film crew moved equipment from one building to another. For the next hour, nothing else happened. Cybill Shepherd did not appear. We figured our trip was a waste of time. But just before we headed back to our car in defeat, several adults in the crowd began buzzing. One of them pointed at a thin young man quickly crossing the street. He had thick, tousled black hair and wore Buddy Holly–style glasses.

"That's Larry McMurtry!" a woman exclaimed. Seeing the baffled looks on our faces, she explained that McMurtry was an Archer City rancher's son and had written the novel on which the movie was based.

"Hey, Larry!" someone else yelled. McMurtry turned and gave us a brief wave. I was amazed. I had no idea that a writer could be famous.

I went home, came across a worn-out paperback edition of *The Last Picture Show*, and devoured it. I was floored by the characters Mc-Murtry had created, who were just like people I knew in real life. They talked the same way. They had the same problems. They stood around on Friday nights trying to think of something to do to entertain them-selves. And most incredible was the fact that the novel—about Ar-cher City, Texas, of all places—was being hailed as a major work of literature.

By college, I was an unabashed McMurtry fanboy. I wrote papers about him for my English classes in which I always pointed out that he and I were, more or less, neighbors. During my trips back to Wichita Falls, I made regular excursions to Archer City, hoping to run into him. In my early twenties, I decided to compose my own McMurtrian novel about a boy coming of age in rural Texas. "How hard could it be?" I asked, leafing through *The Last Picture Show* for the hundredth time. After learning that McMurtry wrote five double-spaced pages of fiction on his manual typewriter every day of the week, just after breakfast I vowed that I would do the very same thing each morning before going off to my job as a reporter at a Dallas newspaper. I never got past the second chapter. How, I wondered, did McMurtry do it?

McMurtry, who was eighty-four, died of congestive heart failure. He spent his final days surrounded by Ossana; her daughter, Sara; his wife, Faye Kesey; his son, James; his grandson, Curtis; and Ossana's three dogs, all of whom adored McMurtry. Just before he died, Ossana sent me an email. "I keep walking through my house and remembering so many things he did, where he'd sit, typing at the counter, staring out at the mountains for hours at a time," she wrote. "I know I'll sur-vive, but at the same time, I don't know how I'll survive. This feels like someone is sawing off one of my limbs."

————————

McMurtry was not always the friendliest man. In 2016, when I visited him in Tucson and Archer City for a *Texas Monthly* story I was writing, he always seemed bored and changed the subject whenever I asked him about his accomplishments. He grunted at my queries about his "writing process." When I called him to ask follow-up questions, he got so tired of talking with me that he hung up the phone without saying goodbye. Not once did I ever hear him laugh out loud.

But Lord, he was a lot of fun to be around. At dinners, he'd get wound up and talk about everything from eighteenth-century Russian poetry to the joys of Dr Pepper and Fritos. He passed on juicy gossip about movie directors, politicians, and best-selling authors. I felt cheated when he said it was time for me to leave because, of course, he had to get up early the next morning to write.

Day after day he churned out the pages. The Archer City boy who grew up in a ranch house with no books turned out to be one of the most prolific writers in American letters. He published some thirty novels and fourteen books of nonfiction, wrote or cowrote more than forty screenplays and teleplays, and produced reams of book reviews, magazine essays, and forewords to other texts. "Larry is like an old cowboy who has to get up in the morning and do some chores," Ossana told me in 2016. "He has to get up and write. I don't think he would know what to do with himself if he didn't have something to write."

I haven't come close to reading all of McMurtry's work. The only person I know who's accomplished that Herculean task is Mark Busby, an English professor at Texas State University. Busby argues that McMurtry, more than anyone else, has shaped the way people see Texas. His novels about the fictional town of Thalia (*Duane's Depressed*; *Horseman, Pass By*; *The Last Picture Show*; and *Texasville*, among others) are pitch-perfect depictions of the realities—and hilarities—of small-town Texas life. (When we spoke in 2016, Busby went so far as to compare the Thalia novels to William Faulkner's great Southern novels about Yoknapatawpha County.) And the novels McMurtry wrote in the seventies about Houston, including *All My Friends Are Going to Be Strangers* and *Terms of Endearment*, are, in Busby's words, "brilliant and moving domestic dramas, something that no one was expecting from him."

And then there's *Lonesome Dove*, his 1985 novel about two retired Texas Rangers leading a brutal cattle drive from Texas to Montana in the 1870s. McMurtry had spent years railing against writers who produced clichéd novels about the Old West. He swore he would never stoop to writing a Western. But he did, and the novel he produced gripped the public's imagination. *Lonesome Dove* won the Pulitzer Prize and sold nearly three hundred thousand copies in hardcover and more than a million copies in paperback. It spawned a sequel as well as pre-quels and was adapted to television to become one of the most popular miniseries of all time, starring Tommy Lee Jones and Robert Duvall. To Texans, went one joke, *Lonesome Dove* was the third-most-import-ant book in publishing history, right behind the Bible and the Warren Commission Report.

Even when McMurtry was writing novels set in Los Angeles or Las Vegas or Washington, DC, Texans were always a part of the narra-tive. He wrote of a former rodeo cowboy who became a womanizing antiques dealer (*Cadillac Jack*) and an erstwhile University of Texas football player who later became a Hollywood striver (*Somebody's Dar-ling*). Just before he fell ill, he was working on two more Texas-based stories—one a Western based on the life of the cattleman Charles Goodnight, and the other a modern-day novel of manners about a Fort Worth socialite. (He never published them.) For all of the acerbic criticism of mundane Texas life and literature that marked his essays, the man loved Texans, big and small.

McMurtry took his knocks for writing too much and not editing what he had written, but even his fiercest critics admitted that he had a Dickensian ability to spin a yarn. Besides the Pulitzer, he won an Academy Award with Ossana in 2006 for *Brokeback Mountain*, their adapted screenplay based on Annie Proulx's story about two gay ranch hands. (McMurtry famously wore blue jeans to the ceremony and had a less than ecstatic response while accepting the Oscar.) When he wasn't writing, he served as the president of PEN America, the association of prominent writers. He operated a massive secondhand bookstore that, at its peak, spread across four buildings in downtown Archer City.

Periodically—this is one of my favorite details about him—he'd rent a Lincoln Continental, drive across the country, visit a friend or two, drop off the car at a rental facility whenever he got tired of driving, pay the exorbitant drop-off charge, and then fly home. I asked him what he did with all his dirty clothes on those excursions. Would he stop at a laundromat and clean them? Oh, hell no, he said. He'd stuff the clothes in a Federal Express box and ship them back to his house.

When I went to see him in 2016, he seemed weary. He had had a couple of heart attacks. He stumbled a few times. His memory slipped. "Old age comes on apace to ravage all the clime," he said at one point, quoting the eighteenth-century Scottish poet James Beattie. "And old age is doing what it can to ravage me."

I tried to get McMurtry to reflect on the end of his life. I asked him how he felt about the inevitable day that was approaching when he would no longer be around to write his five pages. But he was having none of it. I changed the subject slightly and asked where he wanted to be buried. He said he had bought a plot at a Wichita Falls cemetery, but he recently had begun thinking about cremation and keeping his ashes in an urn. "I expect there will be a little memorial service of some kind, and then my ashes will be placed unobtrusively on a shelf in one of the bookstores in Archer City," he said.

"Your ashes forever among books?" I asked, hoping my question might spur McMurtry to say something sentimental. Predictably, he refused to rise to the bait.

"Well," he said, "maybe people will want to come up to Archer City and stare at my urn. And maybe they'll buy more books."

SKIP HOLLANDSWORTH has been a staff writer at *Texas Monthly* since 1989. In 2010, he won the National Magazine Award for feature writing for "Still Life," his story about a young man who, after suffering a crippling football injury in high school, spent the next thirty-three years in his bedroom, unable to move. His 2016 book, *The Midnight Assassin*, a true-crime historical thriller, became a *New York Times* bestseller. Hollandsworth and Richard Linklater cowrote the 2012 movie *Bernie*, which was based on his 1998 *Texas Monthly* story "Midnight in the Garden of East Texas," about a peculiar murder mystery. Hollandsworth lives with his family in Dallas.

The Master Geologist
of Archer County

I WAS TRAVELING through the northern part of Michigan with my friend Grahame Larson last summer. Dr. Larson is a professor of geology (emeritus) at Michigan State, and as we drove down the coast of Lake Michigan he pointed out the glacial cuts, the sand dunes, the cigar-shaped hills (called drumlins) that define the shore.

That led me to ask him about north-central Texas, where I would be going in a few months for a celebration of the life of Larry McMurtry. He told me that a long time ago—600 million years ago—north-central Texas was covered by marine waters.

"And what about Archer County?" I asked, describing its location near the Oklahoma border. "Have you ever heard of *Archeria*?" Graham replied. It turns out that *Archeria* was an aquatic predator, with chisel-shaped teeth, that flourished 210 million years ago in Archer County—hence its name, *Archeria*.

The work of writers is often shaped by the terrain in which they were raised. Down where I live in coastal South Carolina, the novelist Pat Conroy wrote, "The island land where I grew up was a fertile semitropical archipelago that gradually softened the ocean for the grand surprise of the continent that followed."

Hemingway similarly found material for his first stories in northern Michigan, where he spent his teenage summers: "They stood together, looking out across the country, down over the orchard, beyond the road, across the lower fields and the woods of the point, to the lake."

In the same way that Pat Conroy studied and assayed the landscape of South Carolina and Hemingway that of northern Michigan, Larry became the master geologist of Archer County, peeling back the surface of the land and its history, layer by layer, in both his fiction and his nonfiction. "Most of our pastures consisted of rolling country—from the rises and ridges of all of them I could see Archer City," he wrote in *Walter Benjamin at the Dairy Queen: Reflections at Sixty and Beyond*. He said the effect was reminiscent of a Thomas Hardy novel. "The village or manor, where we returned every night, was never long out of sight."

Larry didn't populate his landscape with the marine amphibian *Archeria*, or even *Dimetrodon incisivus*, a pre–Republic of Texas lizard with a nasty personality and spikes on his back. But he spawned plenty of other peculiar creatures slinking along the cracked sidewalks and sunbaked lawn surrounding Archer City's courthouse. "Sonny had watched the two shoot so many times that it held no interest for him, so he took his week's wages and walked across the dark courthouse lawn to the picture show."

I remember my first trip to Archer City, about twelve years ago. There was the courthouse, the Spur Hotel, the Royal Theater movie house, the old jail, even the blinking stoplight in the middle of town. *All the world's a stage*, I thought to myself, quoting from Shakespeare, and so it was in Archer City. As I walked late at night through these streets, it seemed to me that the characters from Larry's books and films had just recently departed. The props had been left standing, unchanged by time.

Larry wrote about how the stage had been set. Take Archer's museum, for instance. "The museum is housed in the old jail, and the county history was written by my lifelong neighbor Jack Loftin, who long ago took it upon himself to establish historical markers at spots about the county where notable events had occurred."

With a broad brush, Larry described the museum's prize artifacts, including "a few ancient tractors, a gas pump, various fragments of oil field equipment, a few harrows, my grandfather's last saddle, and a few well-rusted tools, all of which would have been seized by the garage-salers had they materialized a few years earlier."

Another artifact of sorts is the Spur Hotel. It opened in 1929, just in time for the stock market to crash, which wiped out its first board of directors, and turned the place, or at least the bottom floor, alternately into a shoe store, a domino parlor, and a newspaper office. Abby Abernathy and his sister renovated the hotel in 1990.

Abby is credited with shooting the bobcat that snarls by the fireplace and Mitch Green shot the elk whose head hangs nearby. One travel website describes the Spur as a "boutique hotel." Another notes that travelers must find their room key themselves, behind the reception desk. A third mentions that the Spur is NOT "within 15 miles of a beach." Well, of course not. Nor is it fifteen miles from any "Major Pilgrimage Place." But that's misleading, because within fifteen miles is Archer City's sweetest cathedral, the Dairy Queen.

It was in the late 1960s, Larry explains, that Dairy Queens began to appear in "the arid little towns of West Texas," and they performed an essential function: "Certainly, if there were places in west Texas where stories might sometimes be told, those places would be the local Dairy Queens: clean, well-lighted places open commonly from 6 A.M. until ten at night."

The Archer City Dairy Queen combined the functions of a tavern, café, and general store:

> The oilmen would be there at six in the morning; the courthouse crowd would show up about ten; cowboys would stop for lunch or a midafternoon respite; roughnecks would jump out of their trucks or pickups to snatch a cheeseburger as their schedules allowed; and the women of the villages might appear at any time, often merely to sit and mingle for a few minutes; they might smoke, sip, touch themselves up, have a cup of coffee or a glass of iced tea, sample the gossip of the moment, and leave.

Larry noted that local gossip soon goes stale—and so regular attendance is necessary: "Most local scandals were flogged to death within a day or two; only the steamiest goings-on could hold the community's attention for as long as a week."

Last, and most important, is the movie house. Larry's attention to the theater seems to have been piqued by a personal experience: Larry's father went to Wichita Falls in 1917 to see his first film. It was a comedy, Larry wrote, and his father had to be carried out of the theater, he was laughing so hard.

The Archer City theater depicted in *The Last Picture Show* had *Storm Warning* on its marquee that summer night in the 1950s, along with posters announcing films by Doris Day, Ronald Reagan, Steve Cochran, and Ginger Rogers. Finally, the characters strolled onto the stage.

"It was past 10 P.M.," Larry wrote in *The Last Picture Show*, "and Miss Mosey, who sold tickets, had already closed the window; Sonny found her in the lobby cleaning out the popcorn machine. She was a thin little old lady with such bad eyesight and hearing that she sometimes had to walk halfway down the aisle to tell whether the comedy or the newsreel was on."

The connection between Larry's novel and the real Archer City became even more obvious when the film was made. "A little more than half a century after my father saw that pie thrower," Larry wrote, "a movie company arrived in Archer City to film a novel of mine called *The Last Picture Show*."

All the set pieces were there, in living black-and-white: the Spur, the corner gas station, the courthouse on the square, the old county jail. And now there were Ben Johnson, Cloris Leachman, and Cybill Shepherd coming along the streets. It was a far cry from *Dimetrodon incisivus* dragging his tail around town.

The Last Picture Show wasn't the last film to use the streets as its stage. There came the sequel, *Texasville*, and then a documentary about the making of both films. "That made—in all—three movies and two novels set in the same small Texas town, adding onionlike layers of fiction to what was already the somewhat complex facts," Larry noted.

One of the most salient characteristics of Larry's fiction is his representation of the land of West Texas as hard and unforgiving. It was a lonely land too. Larry said that the only beauty in his birthplace could be found by looking into the sky. "One of the things I've been doing," he once wrote, "is filling that same emptiness, peopling it." These weren't imagined characters. "They were the real people, living their lives, unaware that it might be one day reflected in art."

Plopping real people into his novels and screenplays, Larry acknowledged in a book-length, semi-autobiographical essay written in Archer City, *Walter Benjamin at the Dairy Queen*, caused some problems. "The townspeople at times seemed understandably confused, as parts of their own lives leaked into the film and parts of the film leaked back into their lives . . . as time went on it became harder and harder to say where fiction started or fact left off."

Yet Larry seemed surprised that in using real characters from the town he created more than a few cases of mistaken identity. "I recently learned to my amazement that several impeccable matronly local women now think that they were the model for Charlene, the gum-chewing teenager who hangs her bra from the pickup's rearview mirror in *The Last Picture Show*."

Understandably, Larry didn't go out of his way to point out to his publicists or reviewers that *The Last Picture Show* was based on Archer City. He called the fictional town Thalia, in fact, and the copyright page declares, "This book is a work of fiction. . . . Any resemblance to actual events or locales or persons, living or dead, is entirely coincidental."

But anyone within a hundred miles knew it was Archer. After all, Archer City is a thirty-minute drive from Wichita Falls, just as Thalia is in the book. And Archer has a single stoplight in town. And a museum and a café. Sure, a few other Texas towns have that. But what other town is thirty minutes from Wichita Falls *and* has a picture house right across the street from the county courthouse? None. The clincher came when Larry confessed in print: "*The Last Picture Show* is lovingly dedicated to my hometown."

Many Americans live in towns that have changed dramatically over the last few years, with layer upon layer of commercial sediment settling on top of what was once there. Take Orlando: Once there were orange groves and modest mom-and-pop stores. Now chain restaurants, souvenir shops, condos, and shopping centers have buried the original place beyond recognition. Austin, Texas, is going through the same process. It's even happening in Charleston, South Carolina.

But Archer City is *less* today than it was in 1966 when Larry's novel was released, and less than when the movie was filmed. Gone is the Goodyear tire store, the Cole-Ellis appliance store, McWhorter's Food, and Holder's Jewelry. Gone is the movie theater. It's a starker place than it was. This decline in the economy is of no comfort to the citizens here. The shuttered buildings spark fear and anxiety among residents that Archer City could someday crumble into the prairie like so many other small towns surrounding it.

But to an out-of-town writer attempting to adopt Larry's gift for peeling back the layers of history, the empty buildings and the bleached dinosaur bones scattered beneath the prairie around Archer County make a dramatic impression. They leave this author thinking about the characters who walked the streets before me, whose faded photographs found a place on the walls of the historic Spur Hotel and in the minds of countless fans at the picture show.

ERIK CALONIUS is the author of *The Wanderer: The Last American Slave Ship and the Conspiracy That Set Its Sails*. The book inspired the creation of a city museum that attracts visitors from around the world. He is a former reporter, editor, and London-based foreign correspondent for the *Wall Street Journal* and was the Miami bureau chief for *Newsweek*. He also served as an editor and writer for *Fortune*, where he was nominated for the National Magazine Award.

Larry's Oil-Patch Legacy

MY FATHER WAS born and raised in Clay County, Texas, on 160 acres, a working farm with cows, pigs, chickens, a vegetable garden, and a fruit orchard. My grandparents were industrious, unassuming folk with no lofty philosophical notions about their pastoral way of life.

During the 1950s, we visited the farm often. For citybillies like me and little Sis, roaming the countryside around Granddad's farm was always an adventure. Walking the neighbor's fence line through a cluster of scrub oak one summer day in 1954, Sis and I were shocked to see a pump jack on the other side of the barbwire. The trees had been cut down, and the land scoured bare. Creaking and clanging, the eight-foot-tall nodding donkey looked and sounded queer in the quiet countryside surrounding the farm.

That pump jack quickly became a topic of wishful conversation among all the adults associated with the Specht farm. *Sure would be nice*, they'd tell each other, *if some landman showed up one of these days to offer a mineral lease for the farm.*

Alas, my family's dreams of "black gold" flowing out of the Specht farm into their bank accounts never materialized. But ever since I spotted that nodding donkey on the other side of the fence, my fascination with the Texas oil patch has never waned.

In recent years, I have collected more than two hundred commercially recorded petroleum-related songs written and/or performed by songwriters and singers with roots in Texas and the Southwest. While often ignored by folklorists and music historians, this recorded legacy, which spans the period from shellac discs to digital streaming, has yet to be plumbed, an untold story that I'm writing about now.

In gathering these auditory sketches of the oil patch, I discovered that Larry McMurtry left behind a legacy too: an oeuvre of oil-patch narratives that show his astute, incisive, and somewhat wary view of the impact of rampant oil and natural gas development in Texas and across the Southwest.

McMurtry's family were die-hard cattlemen. And as petroleum began to replace cattle as the mainstay of the Texas economy, it caused considerable hand-wringing in the McMurtry household. As Larry put it in the preface to the 1989 paperback reissue of his collection of essays on Texas, *In a Narrow Grave*:

> I recognized . . . that the no longer open but still spacious range on which my ranching family had made its livelihood for two generations would not produce a livelihood for me or for my siblings and their kind. The cattle range had become the oil patch; the dozer cap replaced the Stetson almost overnight. The myth of the cowboy grew purer every year because there were so few actual cowboys left to contradict it.

The tectonic changes that black gold touched off in Texas's way of life consumed pages of McMurtry's literature beginning in 1961 with his debut novel, *Horseman, Pass By*, and continued with McMurtry's series tracing the life of the independent oilman Duane Moore, living in the fictional town of Thalia: *The Last Picture Show* (1966), *Texasville* (1987), *Duane's Depressed* (1999), *When the Light Goes* (2007), and *Rhino Ranch* (2009).

McMurtry's novels and essays demonstrate that he understood the cyclical, boom-and-bust nature of the petroleum industry and kept his eye on constantly changing global developments affecting domestic oil and natural gas drilling. His novels also make clear that while he was sympathetic to the plight of the small rancher and herdsman, he wasn't necessarily nostalgic about the good old days before oil became king.

Small oil and gas operators with roots in their local communities aren't villains in McMurtry's literature. As seen primarily through his portrayal of Thalia's Duane Moore, the owner of Moore Drilling

Company, McMurtry is clear-eyed about the pros and cons of oil and gas drilling in creating both well-paying jobs and ecological damage. In all his novels and essays, McMurtry avoids taking sides in the fossil fuel debate. Instead, he maintains a certain distance that comes across as cool and unsentimental—dishing out a dollop of angst on one page and a pinch of chagrin on another.

In 1935, the year before McMurtry was born, Archer County produced over six million barrels of crude. The county is located in a petroleum-rich region that geologists call the Red River Uplift. Beginning in 1911, significant shallow pools were discovered in Archer County and neighboring Wichita County near Electra and Iowa Park. Small farmers and ranchers reaped the benefits of leasing opportunities. And small, independent oil and gas operators like Duane Moore reaped the benefits of oil and natural gas found at less than two thousand feet, which was cheaper to drill and cheaper to produce.

The spreading prosperity of the oil patch in the 1930s didn't reach Idiot Ridge, the McMurtrys' small ranch about eighteen miles south of Archer City. Unlike my family, however, the McMurtrys weren't disappointed about not getting inducted into the elite class of nouveau riche farmers and ranchers. "My own family had no oil and rather scorned it," Larry wrote in the introduction to *Sacagawea's Nickname*, his collection of essays on the American West. "We belonged, proudly and already a little anachronistically, to the modest small-ranch herding culture."

Still, in *Walter Benjamin at the Dairy Queen: Reflections at Sixty and Beyond*, McMurtry writes that his family became painfully aware that once the oil industry moved in, small-scale ranchers like themselves without oil income were not going to be able to survive for long. "They knew, in short, the odds were heavily stacked against the smallholder in the West who was dependent on cattle alone."

McMurtry lays bare his family's attitude about oil and gas development in *Horseman, Pass By*. The eighty-six-year-old cattle rancher Homer Bannon is still running cattle on his ranch several miles outside of Thalia. His son, Hud, waits impatiently to take over.

Homer keeps two longhorn steers on his ranch to remind him "how times was." Even Homer's teenage grandson, Lonnie, is aware that the oil derricks popping up around their ranch are a threat to his grandpa's way of life. Sitting high on a windmill, Lonnie surveys the landscape and his musings fill the night sky with a sense of melancholy and uneasiness. "Around me, across the dark prairie, the lights were clear," Lonnie reflects. "The oil derricks were lit with strings of yellow bulbs, like Christmas trees."

After learning that his herds are infected with hoof-and-mouth disease, Homer is forced to exterminate the cattle, including his two cherished longhorns. The government agent in charge of purging Homer's herd suggests that the old cattleman lease his land to the oil companies. "A ranch is more than just the cattle that's on it," the agent suggests. But Homer isn't buying the agent's argument. He delivers an impassioned soliloquy expressing the feelings of many small cattlemen of his generation who were faithful to their nineteenth-century way of life:

> Oil. Maybe I could get some, but I don't believe I will. . . . I don't like it an' I don't aim to have it. . . . There'll be no holes punched in this land while I'm here. . . . What good's oil to me. What can I do with it? With a bunch of fuckin' oil wells. I can't ride out every day an' prowl amongst 'em, like I can my cattle. I can't breed 'em or tend 'em or rope 'em or chase 'em or nothin'. . . . Piss on that kinda money. . . . I want mine to come from something that keeps a man doing for himself.

Homer's son witnesses the heated exchange with the government agent but refrains from commenting on his father's refusal to even consider a lease agreement. Instead, he'll lurk on the sidelines until Homer is no longer in charge of the fate of his ranch. Holes will be punched in the land once Homer is gone. For Hud, it's about dollars and cents: What rancher wouldn't covet some combination of income from livestock, crops, and oil and gas royalties to ensure his survival?

In the first Duane novel, *The Last Picture Show*, McMurtry's narrative reveals the extent to which petroleum reigns over the lives of the residents of Thalia. Preparing to graduate from high school, Duane Moore is employed as a roughneck for Gene Farrow, the father of his girlfriend, Jacy. Duane's best friend, Sonny, is driving a butane truck for Fartley Butane and Propane on weekends. Sonny quits his job with Fartley and hires on as a roughneck for better pay with Gene Farrow, then later switches to working as a lease operator, checking and servicing the engines and pumps on various Farrow properties.

Yet in all five of McMurtry's novels in which Duane is associated with the oil industry, McMurtry shows only a passing interest in capturing the rowdy sights, sounds, and smells of an active rig. Roughnecks, drillers, and tool pushers appear, but only as secondary characters, usually without names. In *The Last Picture Show*, McMurtry gives the driller in charge of Duane's crew the name "Abilene," after a town with its own petroleum reputation, and Abilene the driller will return in *Texasville*.

McMurtry, of course, never worked in the oil fields, which may explain why his terminology falters at times. For example, in *The Last Picture Show*, he writes, "One Saturday morning Sonny came in from his tower." The eight-hour shift that a drilling crew works is pronounced "tower" but spelled "tour." In *Texasville*, Duane's tool pusher, Bobby Lee, excitedly informs his boss, "I think we hit that Mississippi," alluding to a formation and geological time period correctly spelled "Mississippian."

Texasville is set in the mid-1980s, when the petroleum industry suffered a massive downturn as worldwide demand for crude oil decreased and prices collapsed, causing an unmanageable glut.

In *Literary Life: A Second Memoir*, McMurtry offers his own historical narrative of how Texas's fortunes became bound up with oil's boom-and-bust cycles. "There had been, in the seventies, a considerable oil boom down in Texas," McMurtry recalled.

> It stirred the community of Archer City; several members of my immediate family became, briefly, much richer than they had been. . . . Everyone knows that booms, by definition, end, just as bubbles always burst. Seasoned oilmen know this, and seasoned bankers should; but, collectively, everyone forgets it until they awaken to the sound of mortgages failing and loans not being repaid.

In *Texasville*, the author illustrates this hard lesson through Duane Moore and the fortunes of Moore Drilling. Duane makes a bundle during the bubble and loses it in the bust. During the flush years of the '70s, his four small drilling rigs operated round the clock, taking advantage of the shallow drilling depths and bringing in as much as 1,600 barrels a day. Duane has also acquired the trappings of wealth: a mansion with pool and hot tub, a fleet of luxury vehicles, and the obligatory club memberships. Against his better judgment, though, he purchases four additional rigs to extract deeper oil. Before long, Duane owes $12 million to creditors, and with the price of a barrel of crude sinking fast, the four new rigs sit idle, "representing doom."

Duane is left to stew over the consequences of his handiwork: "a valley pockmarked with well sites, saltwater pits . . . scrubby oil-stained acres." And as was the practice of most drillers in Texas at the time, Duane has no immediate plans to clean up the well sites:

> Like all such well sites, this place was ugly: the grass had been scraped off, the mesquites bulldozed. The slush pits stank, the soil was rutted, there was not a smidgin of shade, and the trash the roughnecks left had not been hauled away. There was nothing about the site that offered the eye the slightest pleasure. It was just a half acre of ruined earth in the middle of a scrubby pasture. Only the liquid money that the new pump would bring from the ground could redeem the ugliness.

With the glut, rumors of $5 a barrel spread across Texas and become a regular topic of conversation inside Thalia's Dairy Queen.

> During all that time, no one had even seen a Saudi, and the pipes in Arabia had not been thrown open. To most locals OPEC was a shadowy entity, like communism—its threats were met with macho rhetoric, at least at the Dairy Queen. Some doubted that OPEC really had much muscle, but Duane was not among the doubters on that score. If oil went to five dollars a barrel, the costly new pump he was looking at might never be turned on.

Some Can Whistle is not part of McMurtry's Duane Moore chronicles. But this novel has petroleum connections and reintroduces us to Danny Deck, one of the main characters in the novels *Moving On* (1970), *All My Friends Are Going to Be Strangers* (1972), and *Terms of Endearment* (1975)—dubbed the Houston Trilogy. The dust jacket front cover of *Some Can Whistle* is a watercolor by the illustrator Wendell Minor, the artist with credits for seven McMurtry covers. A swimming pool is in the foreground, and drilling rigs and oil storage tanks dot the peachy-brownish-orange horizon.

In *Some Can Whistle*, oil-field storage tanks draw the attention of Muddy Box, T.R.'s boyfriend and the father of her second child. One day Muddy Box decides to wipe the tanks off the map with his AK-47 in an explosive round of target practice. The novel also provides a brief history of the East Texas oil patch. Lloyd Bynum, who lives in Lufkin, has stories to tell Danny about the boomtown days of the 1930s in the oil fields of Gregg and Rusk Counties and about two real-life wildcatting legends, Columbus Marion "Dad" Joiner and Haroldson Lafayette "H.L." Hunt.

When we rejoin the sixty-two-year-old Duane Moore in *Duane's Depressed*, Moore Drilling has survived the turbulence of the previous decade. For Duane, however, "the oil game has lost its thrill, the chase its flavor." To the consternation of his family and residents of Thalia, Duane has opted out of all his high-profile activities in the town. Leaving his pickup truck in the carport, he's taken to walking or bicycling around town and hanging out in his humble cabin a few miles outside of town. His goal is to pass the management of Moore Drilling to his son Dickie:

> It's not Exxon or Texaco, you know. It's just a little family oil business. . . . Now you need to take over and do what I've been doing.
> . . . From now on you make the deals, you hire the crews, you tell who to go where, you check on the rigs, you see that the leases get pumped properly. You see that the trucks are kept in good repair, you go over the contracts, you see that the bookkeeper and the accountant get the information they need. You see that the crews don't go to work drunk and don't go to work stoned.

Yet, even in retirement, Duane remains in tune with the rhythms of the patch. In McMurtry's novel *When the Light Goes*, we find Duane at the cabin. When he has trouble sleeping at night, he sits outside in a lawn chair until he's finally lulled to sleep by the *chug-chugs* of two of his nearby pump jacks.

In the fifth and final Duane novel, *Rhino Ranch*, McMurtry brings the Barnett Shale into play. Covering twenty-one counties in North Texas, including Archer on the northwestern edge, the Barnett Shale became the testing ground and birthplace for a shale boom at the beginning of the twenty-first century, utilizing horizontal drilling and hydraulic fracturing.

Duane's son Dickie devotes his time to staying abreast of potential opportunities for Moore Drilling to cash in on fracking. "I think they've found a way to drill [horizontally] in the Barnett Shale," Dickie tells his father one morning. "It's going to change everything."

His dad isn't convinced. "I've heard about the Barnett Shale all my life," he says. "I've been told many times about techniques that are going to change everything. Of course there are booms and busts. But so far nothing that's come along has really changed everything."

In *In a Narrow Grave*, McMurtry envisioned his then five-year-old Uncle Johnny sitting on top of the McMurtry barn watching the last cattle drives passing by on their way to the railheads in Kansas. Years later, Larry reflected on how oil-field vehicles had replaced the cattle. "I sat on the self-same barn and saw only a few oil-field pickups go by."

Today, if he were sitting atop his barn on Idiot Ridge, McMurtry would see long caravans of tractor-trailers hauling 120-foot-long blades for installation on a gigantic wind farm surrounding Archer City. If he were still sitting atop the barn at night, he would look out on a horizon lined with red pulsating lights flashing in unison, signaling the new age of wind power.

The irony wouldn't have been lost on the author. For the real-life scene would not be so far away from the fictional windmill where Lonnie Bannon perched in *Horseman, Pass By*, observing the strings of yellow bulbs illuminating the oil derricks spreading across the prairie like Christmas trees.

JOE W. SPECHT is emeritus director of Jay-Rollins Library at McMurry University. He is the author of *The Women There Don't Treat You Mean: Abilene in Song* and coeditor of *The Roots of Texas Music* and *Abilene Stories: From Then to Now*. Specht has written on a variety of other Texas music topics, including Blind Lemon Jefferson, Lightnin' Hopkins, Bob Wills, Ernest Tubb, and The Flatlanders. He is currently working on an oil-field song project, *Smell That Sweet Perfume: Oil Patch Songs on Record*, which focuses on commercially recorded petroleum-related songs written and/or waxed by performers with roots in the Gulf-Southwest.

TEACHER &
APPRENTICES

Larry McMurtry teaching creative writing at Rice University.

Leave His Saddle
on the Wall

LARRY WAS MY creative father, a role he neither sought nor acknowledged—except for one time, which I will get to presently—and which he filled largely in absentia. When I took his first creative writing class my senior year at Rice, it changed my life. And when an experience changes your life, that's exactly what it does. Until his death fifty-five years later, there was no one's approval or respect I wanted more, but giving out approval was not a trait Larry suffered in excess.

Like me, Larry had come to Rice University as a teenager from a small town, his a ranching one, mine a refinery one, cowboys and oil, the twin myths that birthed us both. And we had something else very specific in common: freshman-year failure. Larry was so challenged by Math 100, the introductory freshman math course, that he transferred to North Texas. When I came to Rice a few years later, I failed the same math class. And, bad luck, math also happened to be my major.

I was casting about for another major when I wrote an essay in English class about the D. H. Lawrence poem "The Snake," in which the poet observes a snake disappearing into a hole in the garden. I wrote, eloquently I thought, that the poem was about how wild nature intrudes on our civilized life, as it had in the deep woods near my home, where we would sometimes find copperheads on our welcome mat. "NO! NO! NO!" the female English graduate assistant wrote in big letters. "The snake is a PHALLIC SYMBOL!" I had no idea what that was, but when I looked it up, I thought maybe liberal arts was the way to go.

Larry had been similarly inspired by professors in the Rice English Department, one of whom, George Williams, had also taught my mother a decade before. I still have her stories from his creative writing class. She also had a crush on John Graves, who, newly returned from being wounded at Saipan, was working as a graduate assistant. Larry respected Graves's writing, and Graves was another inspiration for me.

I mention this as an example of the many interconnections I shared with Larry, all unknown to him, and also because women played such a large role in Larry's fiction and his life. He once wrote that he started writing because he was trying to imagine what Texas women would say if they would ever talk. My mother, for example, went years being identified as Mrs. W. D. Broyles, my father's name.

By my senior year in 1965, Larry had returned to Rice as a graduate student and then as an instructor. He was just a few years older than me, but I was in awe of him. He had a beautiful proto-hippie wife! He'd published two books! One became a movie starring Paul Newman! Ken Kesey had stopped his *Electric Kool-Aid Acid Test* bus at Larry's house!

For all his country roots, Larry was not absorbed in nature as were earlier Texas writers like J. Frank Dobie and Roy Bedichek. He once said he didn't know enough about nature to throw a picnic. He was more interested in the mysteries of the mating rituals of men and women than in longhorns and horned toads. And he was working on a novel about just that, a novel that D. H. Lawrence—or Flaubert, its more immediate inspiration—could have written had they been from Archer City instead of Sherwood Forest and Rouen. But if they had been, they probably wouldn't have written anything. That's what made Larry so special: he didn't spring from a long European cultural tradition, but was self-created from bookless hardscrabble soil.

I enrolled in his creative writing class, and so did Mike Evans and Greg Curtis, my roommates in a seedy house on Westheimer. We were all aspiring writers. On the first day Larry announced that we'd be writing our own short stories and reading from them in class. He then walked to the board and asked us not to write about several topics. As I recall, he wrote on the board: "How I lost my virginity," "My first LSD trip," etc. For weeks he would begin each class by asking if anyone had a story to read. And for weeks no one did, so Larry read to us from writers he admired.

For me, the most memorable example was the Battle of Waterloo section from *The Charterhouse of Parma*, where the hero, disguised as a binoculars salesman, stumbles across the battlefield from one end to the other without ever realizing it. Larry called it the best writing about war ever done. When I later went to war myself, I saw firsthand how right he was. But the book from which Larry read most memorably was the one he himself was working on—*The Last Picture Show*.

That was when my life began to change forever.

I remember vividly his reading of the hilarious but sad basketball game scene. I *knew* Sonny and Duane, the inept high school basketball players with the shadow of Korea hanging over their heads. I had grown up in Baytown with their counterparts, who were then themselves beginning to go off to Vietnam. I knew Coach Popper, I knew Jacy the unattainable flirt, and oh yes, I knew Abilene, the roustabout whose transgressive sexual energy upends Jacy's family. In the summers I worked around the refinery on a surveying crew headed by John Baggett, my version of Sam the Lion. The head rodman (yes, that is what he was called) was an ex-con who had a glass eye to replace the one he lost fighting in the Pacific. On one memorable water break, while Glass Eye had enthusiastic sex in our pickup with a local wife, John pulled a battered paperback out of the glove box and he and I sat in the shade and discussed the *Dialogues of Plato*. I knew next to nothing about Socrates or philosophy then—it was literally Greek to me—and I knew even less about sex.

My ancestors had come to West Texas in the 1860s and lived in Dripping Springs and Paint Rock and Mingus/Gordon/Thurber. This was south of where Larry's family had come in the 1880s, but sufficiently close to the same frontier that the first of my family members to settle in Texas were driven out by Comanches and left the state. My great-great-grandmother died in childbirth in their wagon as they fled their home; she is buried in Austin with her child. My great-grandfather finally settled in Paint Rock in the 1890s and started the town's newspaper, the *Eden Echo*, which survives to this day.

Recently I have watched with pleasure as writers of color, from cultures all over the world long ignored by the publishing business, have found their voices and made literature from their experiences. For their communities to read about themselves must produce a shock of recognition like the shock I felt when I heard Larry read *The Last Picture Show*.

You mean you could write about *this*?

I'd grown up sneaking out of the picture show to haunt my little local library next door, where I'd learned books were written about England or France or Russia or maybe New England or Mississippi. Not about Larry's Texas or mine, not about the softness of the air, the clouds, the smell of the Gulf, the mosquitoes and the heat, especially the heat before air conditioning made Houston generally habitable. And especially not about characters like me and the people of my town.

After Larry finally tired of us not submitting our own writing, he walked to the front of the room and said, "For the next three hours I want you to write a story on one of the following," and then he proceeded to write on the board "How I lost my virginity," "My first LSD trip," etc. Liberated into the comfort of cliché, we all did as instructed.

To say Larry was not that encouraging about my short stories is hyperbolic understatement, if there is such a thing. I was working in the civil rights movement then, but I decided to go to a KKK rally near my home in Baytown and write about something dark and real. Walking unhooded and unrobed amid the torches and the crosses, I was recognized by a few of my high school friends and their parents. "Broyles, what are you doing here? We thought you were a Commie," was the typical reaction, followed by an invite to have a beer after.

A few winters before, I'd gone snow-goose hunting with one of those friends and his father, but I didn't have the white camouflage coverall we had to wear so the snow geese would think we were fellow geese and land nearby. Generously, the father loaned me his KKK robe, which I remember was covered in ketchup stains. Wearing that robe, I shot the goose that became our Thanksgiving dinner. My sister chipped her tooth on one of the pellets. That was the one and only thing I ever wrote that Larry had something positive to say about; I remember it verbatim to this day, almost sixty years later:

"You'd be a mediocre fiction writer at best, but if you wrote nonfiction you might not starve."

But Larry was writing fiction then, and that was our grail. With nonfiction you walk, he said, but fiction puts you on horseback. Fiction writers were the frontier figures of romance, the cowboys. Nonfiction writers were the sodbusters, the plodders harvesting the beans and corn under their feet and not riding across the mystic plains rounding up cattle. Larry, of course, came to do both. His extensive nonfiction writings include some of his best work. His fiction was not what gained him entry into the salons of New York and put Susan Sontag on his arm. His essays in the *New York Review of Books* made him into the least likely public intellectual since, well, Walter Benjamin. Larry was so well respected among those literati that they made him president of PEN, the writers' organization. During his term, he advocated eloquently for the rights of endangered writers around the world.

That summer, after the class was over and Greg and Mike and I graduated, I had a job reporting for the now-long-defunct *Houston Post*. I was house-sitting two houses down from Larry on Quenby Street. He and his wife Jo were separated, and she lived nearby, but they typically had dinner in his house with their son, Jamie, and watched the late movie on TV. I often joined Larry and Jo, and so did Mike, who lived in Larry's garage apartment. Later in the summer Greg came back to Houston and joined us too.

In those days the late movie, no matter how long it might have run originally, finished at midnight on the dot. The screen then filled with jets flying by, the national anthem played, and the three TV stations went dark till the following morning. Before the movie we would often play pool in the dining room, which was lined with bookcases and movie posters. As Larry walked around the pool table chalking his cue, considering his next shot, I kept imagining that scene in *The Last Picture Show* when Abilene, the lover of Jacy's mother, has sex with Jacy on the pool table.

We watched many movies, but the ones I remember are *The Man Who Shot Liberty Valence*, *The Treasure of the Sierra Madre*, and, most memorably, the gender-bending *Johnny Guitar*, with its fabulous gunfight finale between Joan Crawford and Mercedes McCambridge.

Larry had already seen them all, just as he'd read every book on the shelves. After the movie, Jo would usually walk home, Mike would go out, and Larry and I would be left to end the day. Sometimes we played one last game of pool; other times we talked. I had been out of Texas only a few times, mainly to visit relatives, but Larry had lived in California and was up to date on Ken Kesey and his "Acid Tests," the Beat poets, and City Lights Bookstore, not to mention the New York literary world and the East Village music scene.

Larry told me long, laconic stories about underground groups like the Fugs, who took their name from the euphemism Norman Mailer was forced to use in *The Naked and the Dead*. Larry was admiring of their lead singer, the poet Ed Sanders, who'd also founded *Fuck You: A Magazine for the Arts*, copies of which lay around. To me, the hick from Baytown, Larry was, without seeming to have a cell of coolness in his body, completely cool. During that magic summer when I was lucky to be around him almost daily, he made those unattainable literary worlds seem real.

I spent the first years of my life in my grandparents' house on Hathaway Street in Montrose, which is now the first few blocks of Westheimer Road. Larry opened my eyes to a different Houston. We would drive around book scouting, going to parts of towns where I'd never been. Or he'd take me over to Telephone Road to redneck bars sizzling with violence. Writing about one of them in the *Post*, I was able to use the line I'd always wanted to write: "And then they went for their guns."

Before I went to Oxford in the fall, Larry made sure I was up to date on *The New Statesman*, *Private Eye*, and the postwar British "Angry Young Men." He had me read the usual classics like *Jude the Obscure* and *Brideshead Revisited*, but he also recommended a book I'd never heard of, *Zuleika Dobson* by Max Beerbohm. Beerbohm was an Edwardian dandy, flaneur, and critic. In a surreal, time-bending way,

Zuleika floated through and above Oxford's male students, not unlike Larry's charismatic women in their effortless power over men. Almost fifty years later, when Larry described his last novel, *The Last Kind Words Saloon*, as being "afloat in time," I remembered that he'd used those same words to describe *Zuleika Dobson*. Larry was disappointed that the critics didn't pick up on that sophisticated literary inspiration. Yet again reconciled to being pigeonholed as a writer of Westerns, Larry, as he alone knew, was playing chess while the critics played checkers.

After Oxford, through a series of unintended and unwelcome events too complex to relate here, I ended up in Vietnam. In 1971, recently back from the war and living in Washington, I went to see the movie of *The Last Picture Show*. It was an afternoon screening in an almost empty theater. While the screen was still black, the soundtrack began. It was Hank Williams singing "Honky Tonkin'" and "I'm So Lonesome I Could Cry." I had to choke back tears, it made me so homesick. I hadn't known what I was going to do with my life, but I did know, after watching Larry's movie, that I was going back to Texas.

A year later, recently discharged, I had failed at my first job in Texas and felt unemployable. I sat down and read what Larry had written since I'd been gone—his first two Houston novels, *Moving On* and *All My Friends Are Going to Be Strangers*, and his first book of essays, *In a Narrow Grave*. The Houston novels gave me the same shock of recognition about my city that *The Last Picture Show* had given me about Baytown. You could write about this, here, right in front of my face? About the very streets I was living on, about the heat and the sexiness of humidity and sweat, about creative ambition and sexual betrayal? When Danny Deck at the end of *All My Friends* drowns his frontier novel in the Rio Grande, it was almost as if Larry was sending me a message: write about Texas as it is today, and do it now.

In a Narrow Grave, published with no little courage by Bill and Sally Wittliff and their fledgling Encino Press, made an even bigger impact on me. Among its essays were "Take My Saddle from the Wall," a fond but clear-eyed eulogy for Larry's father and uncles; "Eros in Archer City," on a self-explanatory subject, about which he was nothing less than brilliant; and "A Handful of Roses," about Houston, Dallas, and San Antonio, and how we Texans had moved from frontier to city in a generation and not left the frontier behind but had become, in Larry's words, "symbolic frontiersmen."

Which brings us yet again to Larry changing my life.

I was twenty-seven. My friends from Rice and Oxford all seemed to be doing adult, successful things. They were embarked on careers. They'd gone to graduate school or law school or medical school. I'd been leading a bunch of disposable kids around the jungle trying not to get killed. So when Mike Levy, who was then only twenty-five himself, came to me as one of probably a hundred people he'd interviewed about editing a new magazine about Texas, I thought, *Why not?* And when everyone else basically said no, I found myself in charge of a magazine without a name or a staff. All I knew was that we would be inspired by Larry to take our Texas seriously and that we would write about it with love and honesty and without illusion, as if telling the truth about our eccentric, self-absorbed, but never boring, family.

I wanted the magazine I named *Texas Monthly* to publish literary stories as good as any being published in New York or London, stories that saw into the true heart of Texas like Larry's essays did. In my own mind my model was better versions of that KKK story I'd written for Larry's class, a story no one but he and I ever saw. I suspected the magazine might last six months or even a year while I figured out what to do with my life. The first person I called to work full-time with me was one of my classmates in Larry's class, Greg Curtis. Between the two of us, we edited *Texas Monthly* for its first twenty-eight years, during which it won all the awards there were to win. In 2023 the magazine will celebrate its fiftieth anniversary. Today it's largely edited and written by people who weren't born when we started it. And while I might have gone hungry for a few years between Larry's class and now, he was right: I didn't starve.

The one and only story I got Larry to write for *Texas Monthly* appeared in the May 1977 issue. Larry had already created many of his memorable female characters, so I asked him to write about Texas women. He did not disappoint. His story, with its insight into women recently removed from the frontier, was one that only he could write.

He also touched on some themes he would address twenty years later in *Walter Benjamin at the Dairy Queen*. How could you build a literary and artistic culture in a frontier with a culture based on doing, on surviving each day, on suppressing feelings and looking down on art as useless, to match a culture built on centuries' worth of European art, architecture, museums, literature, and history? How many generations does it take to get from a pioneer family traveling with all their possessions in a wagon (as my family and Larry's had done) to Proust and Virginia Woolf?

"At least until recently," he wrote, "womanhood in Texas involved a great deal more misery than splendor, and held such a quantity of misery largely because Texas women accepted—and in the mass still accept—about as narrowing a definition of woman as the men of the Western world have been able to saddle women with."

Men were judged on what they did, he said, women on if their boys turned out manly and their girls ladylike. For generations their success was measured by birthing more children who survived than who died. Harsh judgments for a harsh world, but his prediction was that, once liberated into a gentler world, Texas women would surpass Texas men, who he rarely bothered to speak to, Larry always said, since they never had anything to say.

He went on to write that of his major female characters up to then, Ruth Popper of *The Last Picture Show* and Emma Horton of the Houston novels were the ones women readers identified with. Both women, he said, "could be described, succinctly, as domestic victims." Men readers, on the other hand, liked Molly of *Leaving Cheyenne*, "the seemingly perfect combination of beauty, sexuality and fidelity," but "women don't believe in her for a minute." Molly is the "least legitimate of my Texas characters. I found her in the rural fiction of Thomas Hardy and George Eliot, not in Archer County."

Patsy Carpenter of *Moving On*—"selfish, snippy, and expectant, a mystery to herself and to her men"—was the most contemporary of those early McMurtry women. Unlike Ruth Popper and Emma Horton, when Patsy discovers her men are incapable of being nudged into larger spiritual spaces, she does in fact move on. Nobody liked Patsy,

Larry wrote (although after the article was published a number of Texas women did write in to say they loved her).

I made two mistakes. I allowed our copy editors to correct a few tiny issues of grammar or punctuation, which Larry was unhappy about. Worse, in the custom of magazines, I put our own title on the story. I called it "Unfinished Women," a play on *Unfinished Woman*, Lillian Hellman's autobiography. That was what really got Larry's dander up. I'd not only usurped what he considered his prerogative to choose his own titles—which he took great pride in—but potentially caused him embarrassment in the New York literary circles that Lillian Hellman herself ran in.

Here is the letter Larry wrote me on his typewriter, a letter now in the Wittliff Collection at Texas State:

> "Unfinished Women" is the worst shock I've had since *New York* changed "It's Always We Rambled" to "Goat-ropers and Groupies." It sounds like I'm so imaginatively impoverished as to have to steal my title from Lillian Hellman, the last person I would want to steal from if I stole.

I called Larry to explain that we wrote all the titles of our stories, to apologize for my bad choice for his story, and to say I thought it was one of the best stories we'd ever printed. Larry allowed as how, other than the aforementioned atrocious title, he thought the magazine was turning out "fine," but he was not mollified.

A year later our book reviewer gave Larry's novel *Somebody's Darling* a harshly negative review. I was put on the spot. I either had to stand by the ideal of free expression for our writers—as the Wittliffs had when they published Larry's demolition of J. Frank Dobie in *In a Narrow Grave*—and publish something critical of my mentor, or kill the review and abandon that ideal. I called to give Larry a heads-up. He asked for details. Before I got far, he said, in that laconic monotone that tilted up into irony and down into anger, that it was all understandable. I was trying to kill my literary father. He'd done it himself, with Dobie, Bedichek, and Webb. Figuratively, he added.

Stunned, I told Larry that I would never want to kill him, figuratively or otherwise, that he was my inspiration, that *Texas Monthly* would not even exist without him, that he was so far above me and the magazine that my minor editing, title atrocities, and negative reviews would have zero effect on his reputation. He dismissed my apology as no more than saying what I thought I should say.

It broke my heart to have Larry angry with me—but it also meant the world to me. Larry said I did something "fine"! He acknowledged he was my creative father! Pathetic, I know, but there you have it.

We didn't speak for years afterwards. Larry didn't write for *Texas Monthly* again until the fortieth anniversary issue in 2013. He revisited his essay on Texas cities from *In a Narrow Grave* and was just as fresh and brilliant in his insights as he'd been back then. I was decades gone from the magazine by then, but I also had a piece in the anniversary issue. It was about the Montrose neighborhood of Houston where I'd grown up and which Larry had written about so beautifully. It was special to be in the same issue as Larry, thirty-five years since the last time.

After I left *Texas Monthly* in 1982, I went on to New York and then to Los Angeles, where I began writing for TV, as did Danny Deck in *Some Can Whistle*, which for Larry was the kind of success that marked you as a failure. But I had failed at editing *Newsweek*, and my prose fiction was going nowhere, so telling the story of the women I'd seen in Vietnam in a TV series called *China Beach* seemed like the one way to keep from starving.

Larry always said that the West had produced no great literature but did produce some great movies. Besides all those novels and all those essays, Larry was quite a screenwriter. As he did writing novels, Larry wrote screenplays with a focus and facility that I, struggling with the fiftieth draft of *Cast Away*, observed with some envy. His first screenplay credit was with the director Peter Bogdanovich for the adaptation of *The Last Picture Show*. In 1971 they cowrote a 286-page treatment about a cattle drive, and then Larry wrote a screenplay based on it. It was intended to be a movie for John Wayne, Henry Fonda, and Jimmy Stewart, a kind of postmodern mockery of the mythic characters they'd played on-screen. The three actors, however, didn't want to play that kind of ending to their own careers, so Larry put the project aside.

Years later he bought the rights back from the movie studio and, with his unerring eye for a good story and his native stubbornness, wrote it as a book. That Western novel Danny Deck drowns in the Rio Grande at the end of *All My Friends*? It came back to life as *Lonesome Dove*. Larry recounted that story in a speech at a packed event after *Lonesome Dove* had won the Pulitzer and become by far Larry's best-known book. Afterwards I asked him how much the novel resembled the screenplay and the treatment. Larry said he had no idea—he never went back and read what he wrote. Then he smiled, as if to say, *you can believe that or not, but that's my story.*

Larry wrote many screenplays, including one cowritten with Cybill Shepherd, who starred in *The Last Picture Show*, and another with the writer and activist Leslie Marmon Silko. Unlike his fiction, which was published with clockwork regularity, the majority of Larry's output, like most screenplays, never got made—a special misery that I know only too well.

Two that did get made became wonderful movies. *The Last Picture Show* was nominated for eight Academy Awards. Larry didn't win Best Adapted Screenplay for that one, but he did for his collaboration with Diana Ossana on *Brokeback Mountain*. When he accepted his Oscar, Larry made a point of saying that the movie was based on a short story by Annie Proulx. Screenwriting was a high-class diversion for Larry, and as a writer of rigid and solitary discipline, he did seem to enjoy the collaborative quality of it.

Larry's work—not just what he did, but how he did it—was at the core of who he was. He wrote about how hard his family worked at hardscrabble ranching. Just getting up every morning and doing the work, seven days a week, answering the call. Throughout his creative life Larry used the same rigid discipline to round up words that his family had used to cut brush, fix fences, and round up cattle. For all that he ran down Texas men for being merely "doers," Larry was a supreme doer himself. You don't write twenty-nine books, endless articles, and dozens of screenplays by lying on the divan with a cocktail. Larry's work discipline left him time to run his bookstores and to carry on as a confidant for many women, who almost invariably found him a sympathetic listener. But after the bypass surgery, he couldn't work, so who was he?

And that brings me to the last time I saw him. We did a panel together at an event in Houston in 2014. Larry arrived with Diana and his new wife Faye, the widow of Ken Kesey, Larry's old friend and fellow Stegner Fellow at Stanford in the 1950s. Back then Kesey was working at the Menlo Park VA hospital and participating in the initial CIA-sponsored MK-ULTRA studies of LSD, which would lead him to write *One Flew over the Cuckoo's Nest*, advocate psychedelics with a passion to rival Timothy Leary's, fake his own death, and spend years doing no writing. He was pretty much the opposite of Larry, who was laser-focused and who I never saw ingest anything much stronger than a Dr Pepper. Faye was gracious but quiet, and I was unable to spend much time talking with her.

At our presentation Larry and Diana shared the stage. They spoke openly about Larry's depression and his mortality fears, which he seemed more interested in discussing than his work. They finished each other's sentences. They were two separate people but as close to one consciousness as I have seen in any two humans who are not identical twins. Not to take anything away from Faye, Jo, Susan Sontag, Cybill Shepherd, or any of the many memorable women who played such large roles in Larry's life, and not to presume to understand from the outside any of those relationships, but it seems to me his relationship with Diana was the most important. For thirty-five years she and Larry were best friends and partners, roommates and collaborators, though never, in their account, lovers.

A man who spent his life writing about women in all their mystery lived the last third of it in a relationship mysterious to everyone, except perhaps to the two people in it (and then three, once he married Faye). If ever there was a relationship that only Larry could write about, that had to be it. But he never did.

The old saw that cowboys get along better with their horses than their women, Larry said, was a tragedy, not a joke. And actually, cowboys treated their horses pretty well. Because horses were loyal, whereas women were incomprehensible. "His loyalty," Diana said, when asked what she most loved about Larry.

At that panel discussion in Houston, I had the chance to turn to Larry onstage and tell him how much he meant to me and how he had changed my life. He nodded an acknowledgment. It was for me a lovely moment.

Afterward I drove Larry and Diana and Faye around Houston, as Larry had driven me a half-century earlier. We barely recognized the place. Our Houston (population 1.3 million) had been buried under the edifices and culture and sheer human weight of the Petroleum Capital of the World (population 5.5 million). The vast meadows that stretched between the few buildings and the stadium when we were at Rice were now covered with new schools and colleges. We decided to see if the houses we'd lived in back then were still there. Larry directed me to Quenby Street without a false turn. And there they were. His old house and, two doors down, mine. Unchanged.

We stopped in front of his old house and sat in the car while Larry reminisced. He even recalled gossip about me having sex with a faculty wife that summer. (I didn't, sadly.) I was stunned that his amazing mind, which could still access so much of the tens of thousands of books he had read, which remembered so much about so many important people he'd known and women he'd loved, still remembered a tiny bit of gossip about me from so long ago. That was the thing about Larry: he missed nothing and remembered everything. Our behavior, our gestures, our speech, our missteps and peccadillos, were his creative library every bit as much as the hundreds of thousands of books that once filled his shelves.

When I dropped Larry and Diana and Faye at their hotel, Larry and I said our goodbyes and I watched him walk away, frail, between two women who spanned his writing life. I remembered the passage in "Take My Saddle from the Wall" where Larry describes the last time he saw his Uncle Johnny.

Uncle Johnny reached for his white Stetson and put it on and all of the brothers and sisters rose to help him down the gentle slope to the

Cadillac. . . . Though he was seventy-five and dying there was something boyish about him as he stood taking leave of the family. He
stood in the frame that had always contained him, the great circular
frame of the plains, with the wind blowing the grey hair at his tem-
ples and the whole of the Llano Estacado at his back. . . . The family
stood awkwardly around the car, looking now at Uncle Johnny, now
at the shadow-flecked plains, and they were as close in that moment
as they would ever be: for to them he had always been the darling,
Young Adonis, and most of them would never see him alive again.

When I got the news Larry had died, I sat on my deck in Santa Fe,
letting all the memories wash over me, all that Larry had meant to me
throughout my life. I remembered the last time I saw him, not in the
great circular frame of the plains that had birthed him but in the valet
parking lot of the Four Seasons in Houston, the city that was his Alex-
andria, his Paris, his Oxford. And mine.

In the foreground was an aspen, its leaves gently quaking in a barely
perceptible breeze. Across the road was a Ponderosa pine, and beyond
it the cloud-shrouded peaks of the Sangre de Cristos. From the Ponderosa a lone raven flew across the road and perched a bare ten feet from
me on a limb of the aspen. No raven had ever come that close before.
It puffed up its feathers and sang to me.

It's Larry, I thought, *making his rounds from the other side.*

And then I laughed, thinking about what Larry would say right
then.

"You did it again, Broyles. First Lillian Hellman with 'Unfinished
Women' and now this. Do you think I'm so imaginatively impover-
ished as to have to steal the bird of my return from Edgar Allan Poe?
At least your taste is improving. Finally."

Thanks, Larry, for everything.

Your saddle will always be on my wall.

WILLIAM BROYLES is the founding editor of *Texas Monthly*. He was also
editor in chief of *Newsweek*. The author of the book *Brothers in Arms*, he also

created the television series *China Beach* and wrote the screenplays for eight movies, among them *Apollo 13*, *Cast Away*, *The Polar Express*, *Unfaithful*, and *Jarhead*. He was born in Baytown, Texas, graduated from Rice and Oxford Universities, served in the Marine Corps in Vietnam, and worked in the civil rights and antiwar movements. He has taught English at the University of Texas at Austin and philosophy at the US Naval Academy.

McMurtry's Mild Discouragement

I REMEMBER SITTING in a classroom at Rice University one evening in the fall of 1966 while Larry McMurtry read in manuscript the final, emotionally charged pages of *The Last Picture Show*, the novel he had just completed. This was a class in creative writing. Every university, college, and junior college has such classes these days, but back then, especially at Rice, a class in creative writing was new, uncharted territory. Who knew what such a class was supposed to be? I think Larry himself wasn't sure.

There were maybe fifteen others in the class, including my friends and roommates Bill Broyles and Mike Evans, and we were all about the same age. But Mr. McMurtry, as we called him—which made both him and us uncomfortable even though there was no clear alternative in the classroom—was only eight years older than we were. He wasn't even thirty, although measured by accomplishments he was light-years beyond us. He had published two novels, one of which had been made into *Hud*, starring Paul Newman, no less. He had just finished a third novel. He had an agent and an editor. He had a young son.

And he just knew things. He knew who were the leading novelists and poets and critics of the era and what publications, well known or obscure, to read to find their works. In one class he casually mentioned reading *bandes dessinées* in French and how important he thought they were. I was hugely impressed and bewildered. How did he know? Where did he find French comic books in Houston? And how did he have time to read them in addition to all the other books and writers and periodicals whose names and titles he handed out to us in class on mimeographed sheets?

We longed desperately to please him. As individuals, we did please him, on the whole. He liked us well enough personally. But as writers, we never pleased him. Never ever. Not once. From the beginning of the class, he adopted a policy of mild discouragement combined with a decision not to lie to us. He would never say that our miserable efforts at fiction were "interesting" or "promising" or "getting better" or any of the other euphemisms for "lousy" that creative writing teachers use, because in fact our work was not interesting or promising or even getting better. He thought that if we really were writers, as we so wanted to be, then nothing he could say would deter us. And if we really were writers, false praise from him, whether extravagant or only faint, would not do us any good.

The only glimmer of approval that I received from him that whole semester was when I turned in a short story I called, for reasons I no longer remember and may not have known then, "Businessmen Are Traditionally Impartial People." When I got the manuscript back from Larry, the only marks were a tiny note on the front page that said, "Title ok."

I don't remember exactly how we made the transition from student and teacher to friends, but it happened very quickly. I think he and I started playing tennis together during the second semester. (Larry was a surprisingly good athlete. He played a more than respectable game of tennis and was a formidable opponent at ping-pong.)

Larry and his young son, James, lived in their house on Quenby Street, along with a hyper little mutt named Suzy. Larry had a pool table and sometimes, when he was lining up a shot, Suzy would burst into an explosion of barking. "What a time for Suzy to become frenzied," Larry would say laconically. But there were undercurrents and difficulties in the household, often invisible to me. One night as we all sat up late watching a movie on television, Larry fixed himself two or three rum and Cokes. That's the only time I remember him drinking any form of alcohol.

Sometimes a few of us would go with Larry as he drove throughout Houston looking for books in Goodwills, junk shops, and secondhand stores of all descriptions. I watched him and listened to him while he was close at hand during these long jaunts all across Houston and deep into neighborhoods I had no idea even existed. With Larry at the wheel and commenting, the drearier quarters of Houston became as exotic and full of hidden riches as Zanzibar. At just the right moment in my life, I had the good fortune to observe Larry McMurtry observing Houston. But Larry wasn't just looking; he was imagining too. "Look at that stairway going up to the roof," he might say. "The roof isn't flat. It's peaked. Why would he want to go up there? Maybe he wants to hide from his wife. Or his wife's lawyer." And so on. With Larry, stories blossomed everywhere.

We remained friends ever after, although it was a rare pleasure when we were able to see each other in person. But there was one more influential moment from the days in the house on Quenby that I should mention. In those days, Larry wrote on a Royal typewriter, and in later years, when they were no longer manufactured, he would buy any used one he found for parts to keep his working typewriters in repair. In that house he worked in a bedroom on the second floor. One afternoon when I was there Larry said he had a deadline to meet and excused himself to go upstairs. As I sat in the living room, I could hear his typewriter. The clicks never stopped. He never hesitated. It sounded as if he were pouring BBs onto a pane of glass. And—stunning revelation—I thought, *Oh, so that's what a writer does. He writes.*

GREGORY CURTIS is the author of *Disarmed: The Story of the Venus de Milo*, *The Cave Painters*, and *Paris without Her: A Memoir*. He started writing for *Texas Monthly* in 1972 as part of the original staff. In 1981 he became editor, a position he held until 2000. That same year he was selected by the *Columbia Journalism Review* as one of the ten best magazine editors in the country. In addition to *Texas Monthly*, he has written for the *New York Times*, the *New York Times Magazine*, *Rolling Stone*, *Fortune*, and *Time*. He lives in Austin.

"Mike, it's Larry.
I'm in Trouble."

ONE NIGHT IN the spring of 1997 I got a phone call. "Mike, it's Larry. I'm in trouble."

The Larry was my old friend Larry McMurtry, and the trouble was that he had bought thousands of books for his vast book emporium in Archer City, Texas, and didn't have time to deal with them. Would I come down during my summer break from teaching high school and organize and price them? I had other plans for that summer, but I didn't hesitate.

"Sure."

This is the story of why he asked me and why I said sure.

I first met Larry in the faculty dining room at Rice University in 1964, when I was a sophomore. The lunch had been arranged by my mentor, the English professor Gerry O'Grady, who thought that as a larval novelist I should get to know the real thing. Larry had joined the Rice faculty after having gone to graduate school there some years before. He had published two novels, and the second, *Leaving Cheyenne*, I liked a lot. He showed up with his beautiful wife, Jo, and his two-year-old son, James, a lively little chap who chased a toy on the floor.

Larry looked far too young to have published two novels. He was skinny—he saw himself as a whippet—wore black-framed glasses, and had a mop of black curls piled on top of his head in a sort of pompadour. He looked more like Buddy Holly than the novelists I was used to seeing on dust jackets. He spoke with a soft Texas twang. Jo says we talked about my upcoming year at Cambridge, where I planned to study philosophy, a field for which I had no gift. Nor did Larry. It must have been the only time we ever discussed philosophy.

Back from Cambridge, I took Larry's creative writing class. Larry made clear that he could not do much for young writers other than provide them with an audience and a reading list. Larry's list ran to four mimeographed pages and included not only fiction and poetry but history, travel, anthropology, film, and whatever else struck his fancy. Classes were supposed to proceed as workshops, on the model of Stanford, where he had been a Stegner Fellow and attended workshops presided over by Frank O'Connor and Malcolm Cowley. He would sometimes pass on to us wisdom from them, always referring to them as Frank O'Connor and Mr. Cowley. The class was not very productive, so he brought in things to read to us. These ranged from the surreal fantasy "The Nose" by Nikolai Gogol to the gritty "The Fishers: 1932" by Hughes Rudd and the hilarious frog chapter from Richard Brautigan's *A Confederate General from Big Sur*. One memorable evening he brought Norman Douglas's classic collection of dirty limericks, which he read to us with Douglas's droll deadpan commentary. Best of all were a couple of chapters from *The Last Picture Show*, which would be published later that year.

Larry also took my housemates and me book scouting a time or two. He was managing a rare-books store called the Bookman, of which more later. When he stepped through the door of our place, he looked around at the piles of books, papers, beer cans, pizza boxes, and a grocery cart full of clothes and said, "I've seen undergraduate squalor in the Haight-Ashbury of San Francisco. I've seen undergraduate squalor in the Lower East Side of New York. But I've never seen undergraduate squalor like this." We were elated. It was good to excel at something in Larry's estimation, even if it was only squalor.

When I graduated in 1966, I did not want to return to my parents' home. I had a temporary job sitting at the front desk in the Rice student center, and I figured something would turn up. What turned up was a request from Larry to house-sit for him while he went with James and Jo to vacation in South Carolina, where Jo's parents lived. He and

Jo were separated by this time, but they remained close, kept together by James and genuine affection.

Quenby Street was a quiet, shady street a few blocks from Rice where Larry rented a two-story brick house whose front porch had a pointed pediment that reached all the way up to the roofline, like an illustration in a fairy tale. The house was sparsely furnished, allowing Larry space for a pool table in the dining room—a classic oak table with leather webbing for pockets, which he had got in a trade for a car. On the walls were posters: *Casablanca*, the Beatles, W. C. Fields squinting down at his card hand in *My Little Chickadee.*

The other great attraction was his library. Larry was at the beginning of the accumulation that would later top twenty-five thousand books. In the living room was a wall of classics: Hardy's works in their modest green cloth Wessex Novels bindings, Oxford editions of Jane Austen and George Eliot, other eighteenth- and nineteenth-century novelists, the Russians, even a number of Gothic novels. Larry believed that a novelist should be familiar with the tradition in which he worked, which meant the whole English realist tradition going back to Chaucer. Those books were still on his shelves fifty years later, some with their receipts still in them (Travis Book Shop, Austin, Texas, $1.50). What weren't there were rare first editions or illustrated books or fine bindings. Those went to the Bookman.

The Bookman, located in River Oaks, the toniest of Houston's neighborhoods, was one of the fanciest and least successful bookstores in North America. In his memoir *Books*, Larry tells the story of the shop, which had been established by the creative and sometimes criminal young Houstonian Dorman David. In that account Larry doesn't do justice to the unique splendor of the shop. The foyer was paneled with brass printing plates for newspaper advertisements; ghostly buildings and implements loomed out of murky texts. The central showroom, which Robert Altman used as a location for a rich man's library in *Brewster McCloud*, rose two stories to a skylight, with shelves all the way up; a catwalk halfway up was accessed by a rolling library staircase. The bathroom was lit by a wall of nineteenth-century glass photographic plates. One room, shelved with cedar, was a tobacco humidor.

It was a beautiful place, but being blocks away from commercial streets where there might be drop-in traffic, it was not a place to sell books. Dorman issued some catalogs, aided by the young Johnny Jenkins of Austin at the beginning of his notorious career, but he went broke. To stave off his bankruptcy Dorman's mother bought the shop and decided to keep it going herself. She began by buying the library of Spindletop, a mansion built on the site of the legendary oil strike. That's where Larry came in.

Grace David was a charming woman from a small town who had great taste in interior decoration and no knowledge of books. She and a friend of hers, a retired librarian, were trying to sort through the Spindletop haul when Larry wandered in. As Grace and her friend held up books and wondered out loud what they were and might be worth, Larry politely told them. This continued for some while, until Dorman entered. "Who is this guy? I wonder if I can get him to work for me," Grace said to him. "That's Larry McMurtry," said Dorman. "He's the best book scout in the Southwest. He'll never work for you."

It didn't take much persuading. Larry had started scouting books during his college days at Rice; in California he became a full-fledged scout, haunting bookstores all down the coast. Back in Fort Worth he and a friend put out a catalog as Dust Bowl Books. The charms of the Bookman were not to be denied. Larry set out to turn it into a good general bookstore with an emphasis on modern first editions. He issued one catalog that did pretty well, and in the spring of 1966 he went off on another buying trip to California.

Texas is not a good place to buy stock for a bookshop. The sultry climate is ruinous, and Texans are not given to reading, anyway. (At that time there were only two new bookstores in Houston, a city of over a million; there was one other secondhand store, in the Village, a little shopping center near Rice.) It was customary for dealers to make buying trips in those days to keep up with trends in the business as much as to buy stock. There was always the chance of finding sleepers on the shelves of careless colleagues; books that appealed in one locality might be discounted in another. And dealers love to talk about books.

Larry was popular with other dealers. He was young and modest, and he liked to trade. ("You speak my language, white man," said Franklin Gilliam of the venerable Brick Row Book Shop when Larry first lugged a box of books through his door and said he wanted credit, not cash.) He was welcomed everywhere, and in Los Angeles he made a great score. The Larry Edmunds Bookshop in Hollywood was the premier cinema bookstore in America. Actors, screenwriters, and everyone connected with films had been selling their books there for a generation. It was now run by Milton Lubovisky, who had bought out Larry Edmunds but kept the name. Milt needed space—always a problem for bookshops. And over the years his customers had brought in a lot of literature, including many signed and inscribed copies. Milt sold it all to Larry—seven thousand volumes.

That's where I came in. Larry needed someone to catalog the Larry Edmunds books. When he got back from his vacation, he offered me the job at $40 a week. Since that was hardly enough to live on, he also offered me his garage apartment. It was a dusty room with a mattress on the floor, a broken table, and some rolled-up movie posters, but it sufficed for me. I was away from home making a living on my own, working with books, and hanging out with a real writer. I could not have been happier.

Our days settled into a quiet routine. In the mornings I would head into the shop and type up a half-sheet of paper on each book, listing the publication information and condition. Larry provided me with copies of John Carter's *ABC for Book Collectors*, McKerrow's *An Introduction to Bibliography for Literary Students*, and a shelf of catalogs from other dealers. Then he turned me loose. He would show up for an hour or so, read the mail, price some books, and check on what I was doing. We put out two catalogs at the end of the summer and two more in the fall. They sold well enough for Grace to want to keep us going. I wound up doing fifteen catalogs for the Bookman over the next three years. Although I've had other careers, I was hooked and have always been involved in bookselling.

In the evenings I would return to the house, where Larry would be with James, a beautiful child with enormous dark eyes. At four, he was in a day school, which gave Larry time for writing and book work, and a series of women came in to run the vacuum cleaner, fix lunch, see that a nap was taken; James's favorite was named Erleen. There were pets: a sweet but neurotic Sheltie, a turtle, and a rabbit that lived in a cage in James's room but sometimes escaped and was apt to be found in the kitchen. Larry loved to play with James, to listen to him, to roughhouse with him on the lawn. In the evenings we might take James for a walk to the little park a few blocks away, where he hauled his basketball with him and tried to get it up to the hoop.

Jo was almost always with us. She was in graduate school in English at Rice, and she had an apartment a few blocks away. She would zip over in her little Sunbeam Alpine, play with James, and have dinner with us. Larry, James, and I might go for a hamburger at a drive-in. When Jo was there we ate better: we'd go to the Stables, a steak house run by former waitresses; Gaido's, a seafood restaurant out on South Main; a pancake house that served good omelets; and a hamburger joint at Westbury Square that introduced an amazing innovation, the bacon cheeseburger.

What we didn't do was cook. I recall Larry once preparing a roast beef with a few potatoes and carrots in watery gravy. He tried to roast a Smithfield ham that Jo had brought, but he didn't soak it, so it was all but inedible. When I experimented with some recipes from a gourmet cookbook, he was bemused. "What are we having tonight—braised hummingbird tongues?" But in general Larry was indifferent to food; what later attracted him to places like Chasen's was the atmosphere, not the grub, and he was happy to patronize the Dairy Queen in Archer City.

Nights we might watch an old movie on TV. I don't recall ever watching network shows, except later when James and Larry became fans of *Get Smart*. I remember *Red River*, *The Maltese Falcon*, and *The Treasure of the Sierra Madre*, which led to naming James's pet turtle Fred C. Dobbs. There were also long pool games with friends.

Sometimes after everyone left Larry and I would sit in the kitchen, he with a Dr Pepper and I with a beer, and he would tell stories—startling stories to a middle-class lad like me—about Stanford, the denizens of Perry Lane, and Ken Kesey and the Merry Pranksters. And about Billy Lee Brammer, with whom he had lived for a while in Austin when Brammer, trying to keep awake at all-night parties, afraid he would miss something, was just beginning to get addicted to the pills that would kill him. When his first wife was trying to serve divorce papers on him, Billy Lee had hidden out in the garage apartment where I was living. The sheriff would come around and chat with Larry, while out back Billy Lee huddled under a tent he had made around the air conditioner and cooked in a bean pot.

Larry also liked to reminisce about his years in graduate school at Rice in the late '50s. He claimed to have written his master's thesis on Ben Jonson in a month before his official studies began, so that he had time for his classes and the writing of *Horseman, Pass By* and a draft of *Leaving Cheyenne*. In those days graduate students were given keys to the library, which Larry loved, and the department sported colorful figures like Jackson Cope, a demonic professor who made his graduate students run with him, and the future novelist and screenwriter John William Corrington, who proposed to knock out his PhD dissertation by throwing a party at which he would pass around copies of the varying texts of a Renaissance play and they would read it aloud and edit it. (Cope heard about this plan and scotched it.) Larry particularly admired the aging legend Alan Dugald McKillop, who was the kind of humane and catholic reader he aspired to be.

Larry taught a section of freshman English, and one of his students has told me they loved him: to the assigned curriculum, which he told them they would still read, he added *On the Road* and *Howl*. Later he decided that the Beats were third-rate except for *On the Road*, but they were the new thing, and Larry's antennae were always perfectly tuned to the new. The classics were his foundation, but he liked to discover books left out of the canon—lost novels, as he called them, like Julian Claman's *The Aging Boy* and *Weeds* by Edith Summers Kelley. He was fascinated by psychology and anthropology, reading Freud, Erik Erikson, Claude Lévi-Strauss, Robert Ardrey. Man as a killer ape was easy to accept in Texas.

The Houston summer nights were soft and warm, dense with swampy smells. The only sounds in our neighborhood were the singing of cicadas and maybe the far-off wail of an ambulance heading for the medical center. Larry's voice was soft too, and though he often spoke with amusement, especially when it came to the sexual peccadillos of his friends, there was an edge of sadness in his talk, an undertone of melancholy, as if the people he was remembering were from a world lost to him. Larry was the most affable of men and could be a merry companion, but I think in his mind he was always alone, like his alter ego Danny Deck in *Some Can Whistle*: a nomad, on a plain with no landmarks and few boundaries.

Larry's tinge of melancholy may have helped make him attractive to women. He was not a womanizer, though, but a serial romancer. He could not fall in with Ken Kesey's notion in the Stanford days that everyone ought to sleep with everyone else. Larry stuck to one woman at a time, and the woman then was the lovely Marcia Carter, whom I think he met at James's day school. She had a daughter James's age named Ceci. Larry had a theory that the way to approach a woman with a daughter was to make up to the daughter, which would awaken feelings of jealousy in the mother or at least get her attention.

I don't know if that's what worked with Marcia, but something did. Marcia may simply have been attracted to Larry as a talented novelist and a charming conversationalist, not to mention as the father of an adorable boy. An English major who had written a thesis on Muriel Spark, she had come to Houston with her journalist husband, Philip Carter, who was the Houston bureau chief for *Newsweek* (and who later became well known as Hodding Carter III, when he was an assistant State Department secretary during the Carter administration). The space program was in full swing then, and there was always news out of Houston. Marcia and Phil's marriage was ending, Larry and Jo's divorce was coming through, and Larry and Marcia began meeting in the afternoons.

Larry had spare time that summer because he was between novels. *The Last Picture Show* was at the publishers—it came out that fall—and he hadn't started another book. He still put in hours writing every morning, having long ago established the daily habit he likened to having a regular bowel movement. The rattle of his massive Underwood typewriter could be like the sound of a machine gun; later came

Royals, an Adler, and finally the Hermes 3000, to which he dedicated his Golden Globe. When he had no access to a typewriter, he would write in longhand—I once found a manuscript scrawled in felt-tip pen on a ream of paper that he may have gotten in a hotel. In the summer of '66 he was mostly pounding out reviews, film scripts that did not get produced, and his correspondence with other writers. He kept their letters in shoeboxes in a closet. I hope those letters and carbons of his are in an archive somewhere; they would make a valuable and entertaining addition to Larry's oeuvre. Larry was fascinated by literary circles, and he missed having one.

Our main literary pal was Max Crawford, who had completed a novel he had titled *The Penis of Jesus*. It was later published after much revision as *The Backslider*, his best book by far. Max was a great companion—ebullient, funny, profane. We often took him book scouting. Grover Lewis came and stayed at the house for a few weeks and even worked for a while at the bookshop. His ties to both Jo and Larry went back years, to North Texas State—he claimed to have introduced them—but Grover managed to break all ties. He was bitter, frustrated by a literary career that wasn't going anywhere, and a difficult drunk. He had not yet hit on the style of semifictional reporting that took him to *Rolling Stone* and a degree of celebrity. A shy, infrequent visitor was Glenn Lord, the collector and editor who resurrected the works of Robert E. Howard and launched Conan the Barbarian into the world beyond *Weird Tales*. At the end of that summer James Baker Hall came from Kentucky and took some brilliant photographs of Larry for an essay that never got published.

The most famous of Larry's literary friends was Ken Kesey, the would-be stud duck, in Larry's words, from the Stegner writing program. In *The Electric Kool-Aid Acid Test*, Tom Wolfe describes the first visit to Larry of Kesey and the Merry Pranksters in 1964, when the girl known as Stark Naked jumped out of the bus and ran off up the street with little James, Larry trotting alongside saying, "Ma'am! Ma'am! Just a minute, ma'am!" Wolfe does not mention that after the bus left, Larry visited the girl in the psychiatric ward, contacted her boyfriend in California, flew him to Houston, and sent them both home.

In 1967 Kesey and the Pranksters came through again for what was billed as the "Acid Test Graduation" at Rice, but it was a dud. I felt Ken's charisma but didn't think much of his entourage; only his wife, Faye, taking care of the kids, seemed like a grown-up. Larry's affection and respect for Ken never flagged, though, nor did Ken's for him. Larry was well liked by people like Kesey and Brammer, in part because he had no interest in taking drugs, drank very little, and didn't like parties; in the parlance of the time, he was square. As Jo said, Larry was the one who drove everyone home.

In the winter of 1966–1967, Larry invited me to move into the house—the garage apartment had become drafty. My bed was in a small room upstairs that also housed Larry's runs of pulp magazines and his extensive pornography collection. The pulps were mainly jungle comics; science fiction and mysteries didn't interest him much. But pornography did. He had hundreds of books, magazines, and pieces of ephemera. His collection was no secret—male visitors to the house usually spent a little time there, and he would be called upon to testify as an expert witness in trials of local magazine dealers. Larry argued that pornography serves to educate the young and stimulate the old and shouldn't be criminalized. His interest in it was almost clinical. For a while he was cataloging paperbacks from Nightstand Books, soberly analyzing the symbolism of their cover art. Before James got to the age when he might be educated, the pornography collection disappeared.

That fall *The Last Picture Show* was published, and Larry spent a lot of time on the phone trying to calm his mother. Like everyone in Archer City she was horrified by the novel's portrait of the town, to which he had conspicuously dedicated it. The townspeople took out their rage on her and the family. This led to an angry letter from him in the local paper telling folks to abuse him all they wanted but to leave his family alone.

Most dismaying was their identification of Ruth Popper in the book with his high school English teacher, who had naturally considered him her favorite student; their relationship never went beyond mentoring, but the town suspected she had had an affair with a high school student and made her life miserable. The town's opinion began to change, however, when the movie people moved in to film the novel, and it warmed up even more after *Texasville*. In 2000 the old movie theater was renovated as a music venue. But in 1966 there had been threats of violence.

In the summer of 1967, Larry took Max and me on a buying trip to California, not only to acquire stock but to introduce me to the California dealers, because Larry was quitting the Bookman. He was still available for consultation, but he didn't have time for it anymore. He was writing a novel again and he had classes to teach. We hit the bookshops, visited the poet and sometime book scout David Meltzer and his beautiful wife in North Beach, and spent a hilarious evening with Gus Guthrie, the daughter of the great Montana novelist A. B. Guthrie Jr.

Gus was working in the music business in Memphis and was in California to promote a little-known guitar player named Glen Campbell, who was coming out with a great song; she recited its opening lines to us in the car: "It's knowing that your door is always open and your path is free to walk / That makes me tend to leave my sleeping bag rolled up and stashed behind your couch." We thought it sounded pretty good. I'm dragging Gus into this—she died not long ago and she's on my mind—because it's typical of Larry to be friends with someone like Gus. He had a wider range of friends than anyone I know.

The key to Larry's range of friendships was that he liked to be entertained and he was nonjudgmental. He did not forgive cruelty, and he would cut the cruel or the exploitative right out of his life. Toward the rest he was forbearing, perhaps seeing us the way he saw the characters in his novels. He did not like stupidity or craziness, but he took them in stride—we are all stupid or crazy sometimes. He began a recommendation to a court to get me off a charge of attempted burglary by saying, "Mr. Evans is a young man, and like most young men he drinks too much from time to time." He rarely argued, except on issues about which he had strong opinions, like selling pirated editions of the works of living authors. If you said something with which he disagreed, he would tuck that away as just another thing about you, like your taste in ice cream. In Washington he found the kind of literary circle he had longed for, and his frequent dinner partners were Joe Alsop and Leon

Wieseltier. You could hardly find people more politically opposed than those two. But to Larry what was important was that they read widely and could talk well.

Larry was also breathtakingly generous. He supported Jo all through her years of graduate school, even after their divorce, without complaint. When she got her PhD, he gave her a complete twelve-volume set of the *Oxford English Dictionary*, a princely gift; at the time he was hardly making any money and was so strapped that he was reduced to collecting paperbacks. I had started collecting detective fiction, and he gave me a run of Mickey Spillane first editions in flawless dust jackets. (I gave them back because I didn't like Spillane; they would now be worth thousands.) When I wrecked his elegant Mercedes, he shrugged and did not even suggest that I pay for repairs. I gave him $100 toward his deductible out of funds I won in a poker game, and he told me that the next time I played he would like to stake me. In later years he paid for many a relative to go through rehab.

In the spring of 1968, Max and I started a little magazine, the *Redneck Review*. For our first issue Larry gave us a chapter from *Moving On*, which would become his love letter to Rice graduate school. One night he got a phone call from Michael Korda, the newly appointed editor-in-chief at Simon & Schuster. Korda had picked up a copy of the *Redneck* at the Gotham Book Mart, where I had sent a dozen copies, and he had read Larry's chapter and wanted to publish the novel. Happy to leave Dial, which had done nothing to promote *Picture Show*, Larry went to work.

Within weeks he read to us the hilarious chapter in which a little man shoots up a beer joint because there aren't enough beans in his chili. The chapter was inspired by a newspaper story Larry had clipped and pasted to his refrigerator door about two guys who had shot each other at the Red Lily Café. They got into a quarrel, said onlookers, "and both men went for their guns." Texas seemed funny to us then, not scary. Whoever thought that one day the gun-toters would be in charge?

Although the '60s are remembered as a time of violent protest and countercultural revolution, life on Quenby Street was serene. There was little protesting in Houston, aside from a police riot at Texas Southern University. Max and I joined an antiwar march in LA, but Larry preferred to spend the day reading. The music touched us a little. Larry had a couple of Johnny Cash and Bob Dylan albums, Jo played folk songs on her guitar, and she and James were Beatles fans. I went to see Ray Charles at the Sam Houston Coliseum. When the Rolling Stones rolled into town, though, we passed. Larry was an early subscriber to the magazine *Rolling Stone*, but mainly for cultural criticism. I can't remember Larry ever discussing politics. The revolutionary '60s seemed a country away.

The year 1969 marked the end of our easy life in Houston. Getting her PhD meant that Jo would be moving to an academic appointment somewhere, which was worrisome for her relationship with James. She had gotten fourteen interviews at MLA the previous winter, and one of them led to a job offer from Westhampton College at the University of Richmond, which she immediately accepted. She had been born in Virginia, and some of her happiest early years had been spent on a family farm in the mountains there. By a lucky chance Marcia Carter decided she wanted to move to Washington, DC, near her family home in the horse country of northern Virginia. So we all headed north at the end of the summer of 1969—Jo and I to Richmond, Larry and James to Georgetown. A pattern of frequent weekend visits began that would continue all through James's childhood.

In Richmond, Jo and I married, and Larry seemed fine with that. He picked up James after the ceremony and in our apartment found my collection of his books, which he proceeded to inscribe, one of them "whimsically while on his way to hear James Dickey play the guitar" (i.e., at a writers' conference organized at Hollins College by George Garrett, a boondoggle that merits a wry chapter in *Literary Life*).

Through the next few years James would spend weekends and vacations with us, and I would take him camping and fishing—two activities that had no appeal for Larry; we would chat when picking James up or dropping him off, sometimes staying over at one of a series of houses Larry rented in and around Waterford, a village fifty miles west of Washington. There James acquired a best friend in a boy named

Clayton Adams, whose father, Sam Adams, was the top CIA analyst for Vietnam. Sam and his wife, Eleanor, had a Black Angus farm where James spent many happy days. They became close friends of Larry's, and Clayton joined our camping trips and vacations.

Waterford would have been ideal except for the commute to Washington. Larry acquired so many speeding tickets that his license was suspended. He explained to the judge that he was writing in his mind and sometimes just got excited. What Larry was speeding to, of course, was the bookstore in Georgetown he and Marcia Carter had started, Booked Up.

The first Booked Up was a tiny room on Thirty-First Street in Georgetown; it later moved to larger quarters across the street. As a novelist, Larry did not make much of an impact on Washington's literary elite. He liked to wear a sweatshirt Marcia gave him emblazoned with the words MINOR REGIONAL NOVELIST. But after he got an Academy Award nomination for the screenplay of *The Last Picture Show*, he was welcomed into the Washington dinner circuit and eventually was invited by the Reagans to the White House to have dinner with Prince Charles and Princess Diana.

Larry enjoyed Reagan, who told good stories and was a reader—he liked one of Max Crawford's novels, a Western called *Lords of the Plain*. Larry became pals with Diane Keaton, with whom he wrote an unproduced screenplay and went to swap meets. He was dining regularly in good restaurants and gaining weight, developing a plump belly and cheeks. Back in Houston, Larry seldom wore blue jeans or boots. But outside Texas it was jeans and boots everywhere, even at the Oscars.

The novels got darker. When I mentioned to him that *Somebody's Darling* seemed depressing, he said he didn't much care for it himself, but that was the book he wrote that year. He did cheer up when he experienced what he called the miracle of *The Desert Rose*, with its optimistic heroine Harmony, who taught him that optimism is a form of courage.

Larry's characters existed as real people in his mind—a feeling for them that he shared with William Faulkner. For years his favorite of his novels was *Terms of Endearment* because of his love for Emma

Horton. He wrote the novels *Duane's Depressed* and *Rhino Ranch* just to follow the life of Duane Moore, who had first stepped into the pages of *The Last Picture Show*. *Desert Rose* came during a break he took from working on what he referred to as his "cattle drive" novel, still lacking what he always needed to get going on a project—a title. Then, driving around North Texas, he spotted the derelict bus from the Lonesome Dove Baptist Church. Title in hand, he never paused again.

When James reached high school age, he went off to an elite boarding school, Woodberry Forest, in central Virginia. This wouldn't seem to have been a good fit for the future writer of "We Can't Make It Here" and "Choctaw Bingo," but he chose to go there to reunite with old friends from Loudoun County. Jo and I got divorced, and I moved to the small city of Charlottesville, near enough to Woodberry Forest to visit and for James and his friends to visit me, but the weekends and camping trips ended, and I saw Larry rarely over the next few years.

For a while Larry moved into an apartment over the shop, where he had a bed surrounded by piles of books on the floor and bookshelves that reached the ceiling; it looked as if he had burrowed into a mound of books. Booked Up expanded into Houston, Tucson, and even Archer City, where Larry's sister Sue Deen ran a branch. Eventually he moved back to the family ranch house outside Archer City, filling every wall with books, including the hallways and the kitchen. Larry also hid a collection of guns behind the books on the theory that thieves never touched books. They did, though, and the guns—mostly James's guns—were stolen. Larry wasn't happy about the stolen guns, but he purchased more because he liked to go hunting with James, who claimed Larry was particularly good at finding downed birds—"the best human bird dog I ever knew."

At the end of the '80s, he and Marcia decided to move Booked Up entirely to Archer City. Buying failing commercial buildings until he had five, he housed half a million books in them. He hoped to turn Archer City into a book town like Hay-on-Wye in Wales. He also talked the town fathers into selling him their golf course clubhouse, which had once been a rich man's mansion. Larry's "big house," with shelves again in every room—including a bathroom—was filled with his library. He started buying up bookshops that were closing because their owners were dying or retiring and their heirs didn't want the business. That's what led to the phone call that brought me back into his orbit.

Larry had a river of books flowing into Archer City, especially a large collection he had just bought, and he didn't have time to deal with them. He was no longer living there. After the triple bypass surgery that he endured after his heart attack in 1991, he lived in Tucson, close to his screenwriting partner, Diana Ossana. He had several people working at Booked Up, but they weren't experienced—they lacked what he called book savvy. I had owned a bookstore in Richmond for a while in the '70s and in the '80s had worked for the widely respected dealer Paul Collinge at Heartwood Books in Charlottesville. Would I be willing to bring my book savvy to his rescue? He would make it worth my while.

Sure. The prospect of sorting through all those books was appealing, if a little daunting. But what made me answer without hesitation was the prospect of hanging out again with Larry. In June I drove down with my dogs and moved into the ranch house. There was no television or radio. I ran with my dogs in the dawn and read in the evenings. A few days each month he would come and stay in the big house and attend to shop business. He discovered to his fury that his trusted manager had been using the shop's funds to buy packaged toys, which filled an entire storeroom, and had installed a hidden camera in a bathroom to spy on the girls who worked for the shop. Larry spent days at an adding machine on his dining room table, cranking through records and receipts, untangling his errant employee's depredations. His fury at the wretch did not diminish, but he stopped short of having him imprisoned.

Nights we would go into Wichita Falls for dinner and talk, and then both of us would go back to our books. It was much like the old days in Houston, without the pool table. And the stories now were about Leslie Silko, whom he regarded as the most creative person he knew; Susan Sontag, a reader after his own heart; Norman Mailer and other New York writers he had met during his stint as president of PEN; and Peter Bogdanovich, Irving "Swifty" Lazar, and Hollywood.

Larry once asked me if I knew of any books that might make good films. I told him about David Wagoner's *The Road to Many a Wonder*, a delightful novel set in the Pike's Peak gold rush and published in 1974. He read the book and liked it, and he and Diana wrote a treatment that they pitched to several potential backers. But there were no takers. I still think it would make a good movie.

The fame that had come to Larry after *Lonesome Dove* did not always sit well with him. He could be downright rude to fans who came up to him in the shop, and his signature in their books became a single line. But when a young friend and former student of mine who loved his books visited from Charlottesville, he took her to dinner at the town café and charmed her. What made him unfriendly in the shop, I think, was that he was there to work, pricing and sorting books with intensity and dispatch. And sometimes with his shirt off in the heat.

What Larry didn't realize—and neither did I—was that the arrival of the internet would upend the book business. The bookstore was no longer a necessary or even important part of it. You could get any book you wanted without even leaving home. And the internet drove prices down. Books that had been scarce were coming out of basements and attics, and anyone could set up shop on eBay, Amazon, AbeBooks, or Biblio. Only the cheapest copy or the best copy would sell; mammoth dealers had programs that automatically lowered their prices to undersell the competition. Traveling by booksellers dwindled; that had been a main source of income for Booked Up. Visits from collectors tapered off. Larry's longtime manager, Khristal Collins, started listing books on AbeBooks, but there were always cheaper or better copies out there.

In 2012 Larry sold off most of the stock at an auction that brought me back to town, along with dealers from all over the country. We had a good time together, and it was nice to get to know his second wife, Faye Kesey, whom he had recently married, a decade after Ken died. But it was sad too.

Larry later became afflicted with Parkinson's syndrome. He was taking eighteen pills a day, he said. I suspected that this might be the last time I would see him, and one night I told him that he had always stood in my mind as my model, in my work and in my life. He frowned and waved a hand at me, embarrassed, but I'm glad I said it. I wasn't there when the depression that had always stalked him returned with a vengeance; there were hospital stays and electroshock therapy. James made frequent trips from Austin to Tucson, and Diana stepped up to care for him. But the days were darker and the writing stopped for a while.

Larry kept the shop going with the help of the loyal Khristal, at considerable expense. He still came from Tucson to work in it, buying and pricing. After his death, I went back to help James and a team appraise the stock—over two hundred thousand books—and we discovered that for some time he had worked to no good end. The prices often didn't make sense, the condition was ignored, and editions were wrongly identified. He had lost touch with reality. There were many good books, but they were in a mess.

Now Larry's personal library will probably be disbursed too; no college or university today wants the burden of maintaining a collection of twenty-five thousand books. So much for a lifetime of building a book collection.

Larry built his career as a novelist around the theme of the death of the old agrarian West and its replacement by a new urban West with fundamentally different values. Larry himself called this his "Exodus" theme. A parallel Exodus was taking place during Larry's lifetime in the two great professions to which he was dedicated. Today the novel, with its complexity and profundity and beauty of language, has been shouldered aside by film and video. And the book trade, which once depended upon memory and knowledge and taste, has been largely supplanted by a digitized world cruised by amateurs and hucksters on machines. People still read fiction and will continue to buy books. There are still fine novelists and great bookstores. But the traditions that sustained them are vanishing, like so much that has sustained the land. None of this was apparent, though, back in the summer of 1966, when we were young and the country was hopeful, and the world of books spread out before us like a prairie that had no end.

MIKE EVANS grew up in houses full of books. He went to Rice University, where he took Larry McMurtry's writing class. He worked for Larry in an antiquarian bookshop and fell in love with the trade. For four years, he worked as a machine operator in a book bindery. Evans picked up a master's degree at the University of Virginia and taught high school English until 2013. He also spent several summers organizing and pricing books at Booked Up in Archer City. He is still close friends with his first wife, Jo McMurtry, and his stepson, the singer-songwriter James McMurtry.

MYTH BUSTER &
MYTH MAKER

Larry's workhorse: his Hermes 3000 portable typewriter.

Ranging across Texas

EARLIER THIS YEAR I had one of the most remarkable reading experiences of my life—so intense that it's taken a while to recover from it or at least to process what happened. First, though, I should explain *how* it happened.

In 2014 and 2015 I spent a couple of semesters in Austin, Texas. I liked Texas, becoming interested in it in a passive sort of way, but not so interested that I felt like committing to read Stephen Harrigan's nine-hundred-page history *Big Wonderful Thing*. I heard Harrigan give a talk at the 2019 Texas Book Festival, where he said that at an early stage in the book's composition he realized that the myth of Texas was an inextricable part of its real history, that the latter could not be told without taking a full account of the former, even when—especially when—the two were most at variance. I picked up a copy of his monstrously big book after the talk, mainly as a souvenir. On the plane home I glanced at the prologue and—to cut this part of a long story short—made as few stops as possible until I got to the far side of the epilogue.

In that epilogue, Harrigan recalls a visit in about 2010 to Archer City, where he was treated to the kind of vision literary pilgrims dream of. "It was in August, a West Texas afternoon at its worst—probably 110 degrees in the full glare of sun. Nobody was out in the street except for one person. Larry McMurtry, Texas's greatest living author, dressed in a T-shirt and shorts, seventy-something years old, was pushing a wheelbarrow full of books." Born where spotted, in 1936, McMurtry has written about Texas relentlessly over the course of six decades in essay collections, memoirs, and god knows how many novels. Even when subdivided by series, the McMurtry oeuvre, with its proliferation of sequels and prequels, can be tricky to navigate. First published in 1966, *The Last Picture Show* is available as the final part of an omnibus edition of the so-called Thalia trilogy (Thalia being his fictional version of Archer City), but—the last shall be first!—it is also the opening volume of a five-novel series tracing the life of Duane Moore, one of the secondary characters from *The Last Picture Show*.

And then there's *Lonesome Dove*, published first (in 1985) but coming third, if what eventually emerged as a four-volume sequence is arranged in chronological order of events depicted. It is probably the single most successful book in a career so marked by success that even McMurtry's first novel, *Horseman, Pass By*—destined, it seemed, to be passed over by the reading public—was turned into a film with the radically abbreviated title *Hud*, starring Paul Newman in the title role. *Lonesome Dove* was itself made into a highly acclaimed miniseries (featuring the youngish Harrigan in a cameo role as an undertaker), the popularity of which accounts for the way that the book has been partially eaten by its own adaptation. (Something similar has happened with James Dickey's *Deliverance*.) So, despite *Lonesome Dove* having received the imprimatur of a Pulitzer Prize, it is also regarded as an extended piece of superior entertainment.

Regarded by whom? By that sector of the reading population that plays a far greater role in the perception of an author's work than is sometimes adequately acknowledged: those who haven't read it. It's not simply a question of where a writer stands in the league table of literary reputations, but—another way in which myth and reality interact—of the perceived shape or suggested contours of that reputation. "A writer is in the end not his books, but his myth," writes V. S. Naipaul in an essay on John Steinbeck. "And that myth is in the keeping of others." "Others" whose direct experience of the books might be nonexistent.

Lest this sound condescending, I was, for a long time, one of these others. In 1990 I'd read Cormac McCarthy's *Blood Meridian* and had then reviewed *All the Pretty Horses* and its follow-ups in a state of sustained critical rapture. While I was in the midst of this phase of intoxication a friend asked, in the politely curious tones of concerned intervention, if I happened to have read *Lonesome Dove*. I hadn't and had no intention of doing so, because I knew—on the basis of zero knowledge of anything except the cover of the British paperback—that it was not of the same literary quality as McCarthy's Border trilogy.

The book's cover wasn't the only problem. There was also its off-putting length, which in 2020 came to seem like a solution to a different problem: how to spend the endless and bar-less evenings in lockdown. As many of us have discovered—and as my experience with the Harrigan made clear—once you get into a huge book, it seems to take no more time to read than does a volume half its length. Anyway, this is all preamble to saying that I embarked on reading *Lonesome Dove* shortly *before*—a source of considerable regret—we were all confined to quarters.

The book deals with one of the most myth-drenched parts of American history: the cattle drives that occupied only a tiny increment of actual time but which have had an effect so profound and far-reaching as to have defined our image of the West for all time. *The Oxford History of the American West* is a rather daunting academic reference book, but the gorgeous painting on the cover of cowboy, horses, cattle, and sky—*Open Range* by Maynard Dixon—makes it looks as alluring as *Riders of the Purple Sage*, or even an album by New Riders of the Purple Sage. In *Dreams of El Dorado*, his altogether more reader-friendly history of the American West, H. W. Brands notes that, after starting in 1866, the cattle drives from Texas to Kansas—where the cattle were loaded onto trains taking them to the stockyards of Chicago—lasted less than a decade. Once the railroads reached Texas, it took just days rather than months to herd cattle to the railheads. "The exception was a particular kind of drive, of cattle meant not for market but for stocking new ranges," Brands wrote. That's what is attempted in *Lonesome Dove*, and while the exact date of the undertaking is left deliberately vague—notwithstanding Robert Warshaw's claim that in Westerns "it is always about 1870"—the destination is fixed: Montana.

As soon as you have an actual journey—in films (up the Nung River in *Apocalypse Now*, into the Zone in *Stalker*) or in books (*On the Road* by Jack Kerouac, *Voss* by Patrick White)—you have automatic narrative momentum. This is particularly appealing if the reader is physically confined in some way. So it's something of a surprise that for the lengthy opening stretch of *Lonesome Dove* the action hardly shifts beyond the sparse settlement that gives the book its name. Among others, we meet characters such as Augustus McCrae and Woodrow Call, aging Texan Rangers, veterans of the wars against the Comanche, who now run what they rather grandly call a "cattle company and livery emporium." When not working, they sit around talking, drinking whiskey, and occasionally visiting Lorena, the whore whom several of them are—or will be—in love with. An air of resignation has settled on the place that no one has the initiative or energy to dispel until another ex-Ranger, Jake Spoon, turns up after a ten-year absence, full of stories about the wonders of Montana. The torpor does not lift exactly, but a stir of dissatisfaction makes itself felt, just a breeze of possibility in the still and motionless heat. As a little taste of what's to come, they cross over into Mexico to steal horses and cattle—encountering on the way back Mexicans who've been over to their side of the border, stealing American horses—but it's more than 220 pages before sufficient hands and cattle have been assembled to set out on the drive itself. This would seem a strategic mistake on McMurtry's part, but something held me, nevertheless, and kept my impatience in check during the novel-length preamble.

What? It's easier to say what it was not. It was not an immediate manifestation of literary intent such as we get in the opening sentence of *All the Pretty Horses*: "The candleflame and the image of the candleflame caught in the pierglass twisted and righted when he entered the hall and again when he shut the door." *Lonesome Dove* starts: "When Augustus came out on the porch the blue pigs were eating a rattlesnake—not a very big one." McCarthy invites us to linger on his prose, to bask in it. McMurtry delivers a statement of fictive fact—an offputting one for anyone with a deep-seated fear of snakes. The writing is not seeking to raise the question of or draw attention to its own merit, but this does not mean that we are obliged to accept a *lower* standard. McMurtry's prose establishes itself as the medium in which the story will unfold, and I tacitly agreed to the contract or covenant by simply continuing to read. The writing would be functional, but in the way that requires a discerning reader to make allowances for it (such as what has to happen to make Len Deighton's *Bomber* unputdownable). There seemed something appropriate about it.

No sooner have Call, Gus, and their crew set out at the end of part 1 than part 2 begins with a shift—more delay!—to another bunch of characters in Fort Smith, Arkansas. The sheriff, July Johnson, reluctantly agrees to look for Jake Spoon, who accidentally killed the town's dentist. In July's absence, his wife leaves town to seek a former lover, and so July's deputy sets off, still more grudgingly, to alert the sheriff to this development. Now everyone's on the move, with lots of people hunting for each other, but there's no need to get hung up on the details of a plot in which the permutations of searches and searchers will change multiple times in the course of the ride. All that matters is that, across vast and slow distances, there is the possibility, however geographically remote, of destinies converging.

When we rejoin the cowboys, still at the preliminary stage of their great trek north, something happens—something so awful that this snake-phobic reader might have been expected to throw the book aside as if it had bit him, but which instead left him gripping it in white-knuckled dread. I was reading in bed, about to sleep, and kept on reading to put as many pages as possible between this episode and the nightmares it seemed likely to provoke. The incident occurs as the crew cross a river, and at this point (I don't remember exactly where it is in the book and can't bring myself to check) I had crossed some kind of Rubicon. From here on we were entering the unknown. Anything could happen. Now this, in a Western, is not just highly unusual, it is anathema. Although set in a time and place of lawlessness—that shifting geographical and historical entity known as "the frontier"—the Western has been governed by conventions not only rigidly enforced and accepted but so ardently desired by audiences and readers that it resembles the consensual ideal of a law-abiding social democracy. A side effect of this is that the Western is characterized by a *form* of existential boredom so potent as to make itself felt even in quotation or parody (those interminable scenes starring Rick Dalton in *Once Upon a Time in Hollywood*!). But here we were, in *Lonesome Dove*, simultaneously in

the midst of the generic herd—a cattle drive—*and* entering the narrative unknown. For characters and reader there is no turning back. All
I could do was keep turning the pages.

What follows in those pages is an epic, an odyssey of plain and
prairie. McMurtry "thought of *Lonesome Dove* as demythicizing, but
instead it became a kind of American Arthuriad, overflowing the
bounds of genre in many curious ways." The myth, in other words, is
so entrenched that Brands's descriptions of the historic cattle drives of
the 1860s and '70s initiated by Charles Goodnight, Oliver Loving, and
Joseph McCoy read like summaries of scenes from the novel by Mc-
Murtry—who, in the 1980s, had used the cattlemen's original memoirs
and recollections to ground his fiction. Harrigan, in the section of his
book devoted to Goodnight and Loving, pauses to observe that "if all
this is starting to sound familiar, it's probably because you either read
Larry McMurtry's *Lonesome Dove* or watched the miniseries that was
made from it."

The men and women riding through the fiction are firmly painted
and properly fleshed out. If it's hard not to cheer inwardly at the hard-
ships endured and surmounted by the characters—*The Oxford History*
dutifully acknowledges "stoic indifference to pain" as a characteristic
of the original cowboys—it is all but impossible not to be moved to
tears by the things that befall them. (Every reader will remember the
words carved on the makeshift memorial: "CHERFUL IN ALL WEATH-
ERS, NEVER SHERKED A TASK. SPLENDID BEHAVIOUR.") This, the human
drama, is engrossing, but as with Willa Cather's *My Antonia*, it is always and necessarily tied to the larger nonhuman drama of the landscape. We don't get the kind of vista paragraphs favored by McCarthy,
but the land is insistently there, as a determining part of the characters'
collective consciousness, even when it's not mentioned. After seeing
the film of his first novel McMurtry was struck by the way the camera had captured "a land so powerful that it is all but impossible to
live on it pleasantly." From the film's screenwriters he also learned an
invaluable lesson about "how careful one must be of the lyric impulse
when writing about the Southwest." Prose, he came to believe, "must
accord with the land." Some writers "can occasionally get away with

the Faulknerian density. For the West, it doesn't work." That's from the 1968 collection, *In a Narrow Grave*, but he returns to the same point more than thirty years later in the essay-memoir *Walter Benjamin at the Dairy Queen*. (Even his essays generate sequels!) "In time I came to feel that there ought to be some congruity between prose and landscape. You wouldn't adopt a Faulknerian baroque if your story was to be set on the flat unbaroque plains of west Texas." By this austere and purposeful logic James Wood seems justified in heralding McCarthy as "one of the great hams of American prose."

Lonesome Dove moves through a range of landscapes, from the sun-scorched desolation of Texas to the vastness of plains and prairie. Halfway through the immense journey of the book, Gus encounters "an old man with a dirty white beard, pushing a wheelbarrow across the plains. The wheelbarrow contained buffalo bones." (Although impossible within the novels' fictive timelines, I like to think that this old man is somehow an avatar of Miller, leader of the doomed buffalo hunt recounted in John Williams's *Butcher's Crossing*, published twenty-five years earlier, in 1960.) This sight gives way to a vision of emptiness that is at once spatial and temporal. The buffalo have been wiped out and the Indians are mostly gone, so "the great plains were truly empty, unpeopled and ungrazed. Soon the whites would come, of course, but what he was seeing was a moment between, not the plains as they had been, or as they would be, but a moment of true emptiness, with thousands of miles of grass resting unused, occupied only by remnants."

So there is a lyricism, yes, but moments such as these are both few and far between and, as it were, *all around*. The cowboy's life is one of unremitting hardship. Land and animals are there to be worked. They are observed with a view to function (of expression in McMurtry's hands) rather than beauty (ditto), but this involves the kind of "deep response to nature" that was a foundation of the Romantics' poetic faith.

McMurtry grew up with ample evidence of the toll exacted on the bodies of his cowboy ancestors and relatives: "I have known cowboys broken in body and twisted in spirit, bruised by debt, failure, loneliness, disease, and most of the other afflictions of man, but I have seldom met one who did not consider himself phenomenally blessed to have been a cowboy." Again, this observation from lived experience has deep historic roots. "The life of the cowboy," McCoy noted in the 1870s, "is hard and full of exposure, but it is wild and free, and the young man who has long been a cowboy has but little taste for any other occupation." The principal narrator in Philipp Meyer's epic Texas novel *The Son* (2013) challenges this claim by simply reversing its order: "The life of the cowboy has been written about as if it were the pinnacle of freedom in the West but in fact it was a sleepless drudgery almost beyond imagination—five months of slavery to a pack of dumb brutes." McMurtry—the *father?*—had, as it were, precountered this counterclaim by enlarging the frame of reference beyond the American West. The cowboys' redeeming grace came down, McMurtry insisted, to one thing: "that they had gone a-horseback." As such, they shared the same birthright as the Bedouin, who enjoyed "the freedom of the skies." So much had changed—the technology, the economy—between the vanished era of the cattle drives and McMurtry's own childhood in the 1940s, but the sky, not at all. Yesterday was in this sense the same as today. To the cowboy out on a horse there is no history, only weather (amazing quantities of it in *Lonesome Dove*) and geography.

This was McMurtry's direct inheritance, as valuable as the bequest from Kingsley Amis to his son Martin, but different in two important ways. If Martin "felt no particular sense of achievement in becoming a writer," that was because "nothing is more ordinary to you than what your dad does all day." Sitting in a room writing was second nature—"business as usual"—to him. McMurtry was conscious of his legacy in part because he knew from an early age that what his dad and uncles did all day was not for him, that the clothes he had inherited would never quite fit. At first this manifested itself as a feeling of awkwardness, the equivalent, let's say, of the teenager who, though he may not know there is such a thing as being gay, is conscious of a slight unease as he joins in the banter about faggots or communal lusting after girls (a big part of *The Last Picture Show*). Or, to adopt that phrase of McCoy's, McMurtry *did* have a taste for another occupation—he just didn't know, back then, that such an occupation even existed. Then, in 1942, chance intervened in the form of a box of books given to him by his cousin Bob, who had enlisted in the armed forces. From that point on McMurtry became a reader (to put it mildly), which led, in turn, to his becoming a writer. Literature was to Martin Amis what cowboying was to McMurtry. It was in his blood, but he *could* have discovered it elsewhere later, as McMurtry did, at school or in a library. But there was no other way McMurtry could have been the beneficiary of his primary or inherited source material. On the one hand, he became conscious of a slight tension between the beckoning world of reading and the "frontier utilitarianism" he was born into (and which later plays its part in giving the prose of *Lonesome Dove* its vital sturdiness). On the other, he saw literature as an extension of the life his family had known, "a vast open range, my equivalent of the cowboy's dream."

The work that resulted—not just as writer and critic but also as book dealer—demonstrates an important point that has a relevance beyond McMurtry's own example: the person who eventually discovers books, having grown up in a house without them, has the most privileged relation to literature imaginable. And few people have absorbed more literature—or acquired more books—than McMurtry (who ended up filling not just his home with books but his hometown, Archer City, with book*shops*). McMurtry would never go as far as George Steiner in announcing "Our Homeland, the Text" as the title of an essay, but he does admit that "I can never be quite sure whether home is a place or a form: the novel, or Texas." Writing, as he saw it, became a form of herding words down the page and the reader from page to page; searching out rare books became a form of tracking and scouting (skills possessed, in almost preternatural abundance, by Deets in *Lonesome Dove*).

These elisions of page and land were emphasized by McMurtry's reputation as "the Flaubert of the plains." It's an honorific that captures nicely the world of *The Last Picture Show*—torpor, adultery, and betrayal in a small town—but is misleading if Flaubert's name is intended as a synonym for meticulous or obsessive attention to the construction of sentences. Near the end of *Walter Benjamin at the Dairy*

Queen McMurtry writes, "I would have liked my fiction to have a little more poise, a little more tact," but this formulation is itself so casual as to suggest that the regret is fleeting rather than deep-seated. It's not just that he had neither the desire nor the patience to be a stylist. *Lonesome Dove* might well have been hobbled by such an ambition. One could go through it, tinkering with sentences here and trimming paragraphs there, but the effect of such editorial exertions on the reader's experience would be minuscule. The writing is never an obstacle in the trail it creates for the reader. I said at the outset that it does not draw attention to itself in either a good or bad way, but it does more—and less—than that.

By the halfway point in my journey through *Lonesome Dove* two things started happening. As I began communicating my Keats-on-Chapman's-Homer "discovery" to friends, it became clear that the book inspired something more akin to faith than admiration or love. People hadn't just read the book; they had converted or pledged allegiance to it. When a friend came to dinner and saw my copy on the table she explained that she had been given the middle name MacRae (with slightly amended spelling), in honor of the Texas Ranger. I fell prey to a kind of jihadist fanaticism myself, emailing an unsuspecting Zadie Smith to ask why anyone would bother with even a page of Saul Bellow when they could be immersed in *Lonesome Dove*. When she wrote back that she couldn't bear Bellow or Westerns, I was tempted to respond, insanely, that it wasn't a Western. And yet—to deploy a favorite hesitation of Steiner's—perhaps an underlying sanity or logic was at work.

One of the questions McMurtry gnaws away at in *Walter Benjamin at the Dairy Queen* is the relation between the culture-crammed life of European cities—"London, Paris, Prague, Petersburg, Vienna"—that formed the mental horizons of someone like Steiner and the empty plains that constituted his own. Almost as soon as McMurtry discovered Europe (in books) he began to "read my way toward it." This left him wondering, characteristically, not about the ability to absorb culture across an ocean (easy enough), but how it might be homegrown: "How many centuries does it take to get from a pioneer family with all their possessions in a wagon to Proust and Virginia Woolf?" Or, he might have added, to a Henry James or a Roberto Calasso.

In *The Celestial Hunter*, Calasso ponders the way that life since prehistory has become "immensely lighter." By the late nineteenth century—at roughly the same time as the huge elemental labor of herding animals north from Texas—it had become so light, for the propertied upper classes of London and New York, "that the world can no longer exert pressure on those who observe it." This, Calasso goes on, was the favorite human material of Henry James, who "reconstructed a web of intrigues that, by then, had nothing to do with the world outside. Nature was an occasional backdrop. Everything happened inside, or sometimes in the street or in comfortable surroundings." As an extreme example Calasso considers one of the many story ideas that James jotted down but never got around to properly composing. Recalling something that a certain Mrs. Procter said to him, James had an inkling of "the tiny little germ of a tiny little tale." Having had a long life of many troubles, Mrs. Procter's deepest luxury was "to be able to sit and read a book: the mere sense of the security of it, the sense that, with all she had outlived, *nothing could now happen*." What fascinates Calasso about this sketched outline of a tale is that it contains nothing less than "the boundless story of *Homo sapiens*, who tried, for several tens of thousands of years, through trial and error, and proceeding in numerous directions, to lighten himself of the world. Distancing himself first from animals. And protecting himself from nature in general." After all of this, humanity—or at least those parts of it freed from the harsh necessities of survival—came to resemble Mrs. Procter in that the state aspired to was a scene of "perfect peace," as embodied by sitting in an armchair reading, "comforted by the thought that *'nothing could now happen.'*" James's genius, for Calasso, was that he conceived how this longed-for peace might be "shattered," how it would generate its own dissolution "*from within*."

We don't need to go that far. Reading, for McMurtry, had no element of luxurious retirement—remember Harrigan's Sisyphean vision of him in his seventies, trundling that wheelbarrow of books like a literate version of the old man with his wheelbarrow of buffalo bones?

It remained an active happening (the word is doubly appropriate if we recall the scene in *The Electric Kool-Aid Acid Test* when Ken Kesey and the Merry Pranksters turn up at McMurtry's house in Houston)—part of the lifework trajectory he had glimpsed in a university library, aged eighteen, when "the whole of the world's literature lay before me un-read, a country as vast, as promising, and, so far as I knew, as trackless as the West must have seemed to the first white men who looked upon it." There are echoes here of Milton, Matthew Arnold, and Fitzgerald, and of course there are pre-echoes of the written landscape that will unfold in *Lonesome Dove* and its horrible river crossing—after which anything could happen except the possibility of stopping reading. The difference, the course correction that McMurtry will make, is that lit-erature is not trackless at all. In this respect the canon resembles the trails habitually used by the cattle drives. From *The Oxford History of the American West*: "Travelling ten to fifteen miles a day in herds num-bering two to three thousand head, the cattle wore troughs as deep as shallow canals, which remained visible for years." (Rather conveniently for our purposes, the same volume offers this summing up of Mc-Murtry: "Prolific and immensely popular, he has proved difficult to assess or even categorize.")

In the midst of the cattle drive plotted by McMurtry—an account of men, women, and their animals, all exposed to everything nature can throw at them—I realized something unprecedented was happen-ing, or at least something so unusual that to recall a precedent I had to go back fifty years, to when I gulped down Alistair MacLean's thrillers as a twelve-year-old. Since then the words on the page had steadily increased their grip on my readerly consciousness, often to the point of stifling the pleasure they have been designed to induce. On those occasions—while sinking into the slow quicksands of *The Ambassa-dors* or *The Wings of the Dove*, ironically enough—I had fallen prey to something even more insidiously corrosive than that conceived by James in his "tiny little tale." But now, with *Lonesome Dove*, the words first faded and then disappeared. It was like the spell famously evoked by Wallace Stevens as "The reader became the book"—an experience I'd had multiple times—but stronger and stranger. I was not reading a book. There was no book and no reader. There was just this world, this huge landscape and its magnificently peopled emptiness.

As mentioned at the beginning, I'd bought Harrigan's history of Texas as a souvenir of a talk he gave. For those of us who never borrow, who read only books we own, our volumes are themselves souvenirs of the experiences they contain. *Lonesome Dove*, though, reactivated a dormant craving for something else. Even before I spent those two semesters in Austin, I had loved cowboy boots but had never owned a pair because I am too tall. In Santa Fe, hoping to vicariously assuage that longing, I bought a fantastic pair for my wife. In Texas, where they breed 'em big, I had come close to taking the plunge myself, only to feel relieved, on returning to the shorter worlds of California and London, that I had avoided a costly and lanky mistake. But then, the day after reading the last page of *Lonesome Dove*, we rode—I mean *drove*—over to Boot Star on Sunset Boulevard. I explained to the dudely sales assistant that I was after something at "the rock 'n' roll rather than the functional end of the boot spectrum"—another example, perhaps, of the lightening described by Calasso. When I mentioned my fear of height, he gazed up with a look of astonishment that seemed genuinely untainted by the prospect of an imminent sale. "You can't be too tall," he said. Twenty minutes later I came looming out in the Hollywood sun, wearing the first pair I'd squeezed into. I've been swaggering around in them ever since, not at home on the range but on the range at home. They are the most extravagant, least functional slippers I have ever owned.

GEOFF DYER's many books include the essay collection *Otherwise Known as the Human Condition* (winner of a National Book Critics Circle Award for criticism) and *The Street Philosophy of Garry Winogrand*. A recipient of a 2015 Windham Campbell Prize for nonfiction, he is an Honorary Fellow of Corpus Christi College, Oxford, a Fellow of the Royal Society of Literature, and a member of the American Academy of Arts and Sciences. He spent two semesters as a Visiting Fellow at the Michener Center in Austin and now lives in Los Angeles, where he is writer-in-residence at the University of Southern California.

Gus, Call, Danny, and the Rangers

I TALKED TO Larry McMurtry only once, long ago, for about half a minute. Sometime in 1972 he gave a lecture at a community college I was attending in a bleak suburb of Dallas. McMurtry had recently published his fifth novel, *All My Friends Are Going to Be Strangers*. In one scene from that book the protagonist, Danny Deck, is driving through the Texas outback when two Texas Rangers confront him. One of the Rangers is named Luther; the other goes by E. Paul. Offended by Deck's long hair—he looks like "a little old fairy," one of them says—Luther and E. Paul slap him around and toss him into a cactus patch.

McMurtry delivered his talk, then agreed to answer a few questions. Hoping for a lesson in how a writer spins painful memories into novelistic gold, I asked if he had drawn the Ranger incident from personal experience. He shook his head and said, "I don't think I've ever even *met* a Texas Ranger."

Neither had I, but I certainly had a mental image of the Rangers. Like many others, I had formed mine in my early youth through a Walt Disney television series, *Tales of Texas John Slaughter*. Disney's noble Rangers didn't harass longhairs, so Danny Deck's unfortunate fate was an eye-opener.

The episode in *All My Friends* was not McMurtry's only literary brush with the fabled lawmen. Not long after our brief encounter I read *In a Narrow Grave*, his 1968 collection of essays on Texas. McMurtry spent a few pages therein assessing Walter Prescott Webb, the University of Texas history professor whose 1935 hagiographic tome,

The Texas Rangers, was for many years considered the first and last word on the topic. When Webb described the Rangers and their storied feats, seldom was heard a discouraging word. "As a consequence," McMurtry wrote, "the book mixes homage with history in a manner one can only think sloppy."

McMurtry complained that Webb ignored or soft-pedaled the scandalous behavior of several Rangers, including Leander McNelly and Captain Bill McDonald. "The difficulty was that he simply could not bear to think badly of the Rangers," McMurtry wrote. "Even when he is forced to discuss the career of a Ranger who was an out-and-out bastard the worst he will say is that the man was not suited to Rangering and should not have been hired."

Webb's Rangers behaved as righteous knights in cowboy hats, while the Mexicans they fought—and often murdered in cold blood—were generally depicted as devious miscreants. "In a book of almost six hundred pages," McMurtry wrote, "[Webb] records virtually no instance in which a Ranger treats either a Mexican or a Negro as anything but a recognized inferior, and he seems to accept the still-common assumption that a Ranger can tell whether a Mexican is honest or dishonest simply by looking at him."

The drubbing of Danny Deck and the savaging of Professor Webb planted a seed within me, though it took a while to sprout. Some forty-eight years later I published my own history of the Rangers. In it I wrote about their nearly two hundred years of valorous frontier taming. Texas, I acknowledged, would not be Texas without the Rangers. I also documented their two centuries of bloody atrocities, international war crimes, racial injustice, arrant incompetence, and widespread corruption, much of which had been thoroughly whitewashed by the Rangers and their supporters.

After publication I did dozens of interviews to promote the book. Time and again interviewers posed a version of this query: *Okay, so maybe the Rangers did some bad things. But what about Augustus McCrae and Woodrow Call? They were Rangers, weren't they? And they were good guys.* It was clear that Gus and Call had captured readers' hearts in ways that Luther and E. Paul could only imagine.

Yes, I would say to these questions, the dual heroes of McMurtry's masterpiece *Lonesome Dove* were brave, strong, honest, and just. But, I would add, by the time they mounted their famous cattle drive they had retired from the Ranger force. More important, *Lonesome Dove* was a novel. However appealing they might have been, ex-Ranger captains Gus and Call were fictional characters.

This response seemed to satisfy most of the interviewers. But the line of inquiry had arisen so often that I decided to take a second dive—many decades after my first—into *Lonesome Dove*. As before, I was captivated by the novel's sweep, its narrative force, and its vivid evocation of time and place. Once again I stood in awe of McMurtry's ability to create indelible characters. (Looking at you, Blue Duck.) This time, though, I paid more attention to Gus's and Call's erstwhile careers as Rangers.

Their Rangering exploits are recounted almost wholly in recall. They remember fighting Comanches and patrolling the border, and they regard themselves as lawmen who had discharged their duty as they saw it, in a hard country and a tough era. Yet some of these recollections do not canonize Gus and Call as sagebrush saints. At one point Gus even refers to the Rangers as a "bunch of half-outlaws."

One former Ranger from Gus and Call's company, Jake Spoon, reminisces: "We hung plenty of Mexicans when we were Rangers. Call never wasted no time when it came to hangings." And when Call, consumed by rage, nearly beats a man to death, his partner recounts a similar incident from their Ranger days. "He killed a Mexican bandit that way before I could stop it," Gus says. "The Mexican had cut up three white people but that wasn't what prompted it. The man scorned Call."

Nor is Gus immune to scorn. "Gus was touchy about such things," McMurtry writes. "He enjoyed being a famous Texas Ranger and was often put out if he didn't receive all the praise he thought he had coming." When a callow bartender doesn't treat him with sufficient deference, Gus smashes the man's face into the bar and points a Colt revolver at his head. "I'm Captain McCrae," he explains.

Perhaps McMurtry's sharpest take on the Rangers in *Lonesome Dove* comes via the feckless Jake Spoon. Jake had been a member of Gus and

Call's Ranger company, though he was far from one of the best. His claim to fame derived from his dispatch of a galloping Mexican bandit. "One lucky shot," McMurtry writes. "Jake shot blind from the hip, with the sun in his eyes to boot, and hit the bandit right in the Adam's apple, a thing not likely to occur more than once in a lifetime, if that often." The incident had nevertheless hardened into myth: "There was hardly a man from the Mexican border to Canada who hadn't heard what a dead pistol shot Jake Spoon was, though any man who had fought with him through the years would know he was no shot at all."

Beyond that, his moral compass didn't work—a conspicuous failure in the realm of Ranger romance. "When [Jake] left the Rangers Augustus said more than once that he would probably end up hung," McMurtry writes. This prophecy comes to pass after Jake accidentally kills a dentist, shoots an unarmed settler, and falls in with a murderous gang of horse thieves. Gus and Call track the gang down before they can kill again and place nooses around their necks. Jake's last acts are gallant ones; he gives away his horse and his gambling winnings and tells his old compadres to feel no remorse over their grim task. "Hell, don't worry about it," he says. "I'd damn sight rather be hung by my friends than by a bunch of strangers." Then, with an "*adios*, boys," he spurs the horse on which he sits—in essence hanging himself. "He died fine," Gus says. "Go dig him a grave."

It's a brilliant scene: two ex-Rangers executing a figure of manufactured reputation who ends a cowardly killing spree with one last bit of courage and dignity. Here, encapsulated, rest many of the Rangers' manifold contradictions—the glory, the brutality, the bravado, the swashbuckling application of justice, the crafting of false legends, the saving of lives, and the spread of unnecessary death.

I don't know if he ever managed to meet one. But in *Lonesome Dove* and elsewhere, McMurtry gave us the Rangers—as he did with so many other Lone Star totems—exactly as they were.

DOUG J. SWANSON is the author of five novels and two nonfiction books. His most recent book is *Cult of Glory: The Bold and Brutal History of the*

Texas Rangers. A member of the Texas Institute of Letters, he was for thirty-three years a reporter and editor at the *Dallas Morning News.* He has been a finalist for the Pulitzer Prize for Feature Writing and was a Knight Fellow in Journalism at Stanford University. Swanson teaches fiction and nonfiction writing at the University of Pittsburgh and is working on a biography of the Gilded Age industrialist Henry Clay Frick, to be published by W. W. Norton.

Snakes in a River

I USED TO HAVE a brother-in-law who was Texan in all the ways that people who have never been to Texas imagine men who live in Texas must be like. The word "strapping," which I don't normally use to describe men, whether related to me or not, comes to mind. He dressed Texan, he talked Texan, he walked Texan. For the eight years he was married to my sister they lived west of Houston in a rural subdivision that backed up to a creek, which led to them occasionally finding rattlesnakes or cottonmouths near the house, something my brother-in-law hated with a passion. He once told me that he would drive halfway across the state to kill himself a snake, which I took to be an exaggeration, but only slightly. I'm not a big fan of snakes either, but in my case, I would drive halfway across the state just to avoid seeing one.

Other than glancing at them coiled behind the thick glass in the herpetarium at the zoo or squashed in the middle of the highway, I can't remember ever seeing a snake in nature. Which means my one and only encounter must have been reading that scene in *Lonesome Dove*. If you've read the novel, you know what I'm talking about. It happens a few days after the start of the epic cattle drive from Texas to Montana, when the outfit of cowboys is crossing the Nueces River.

Then his eyes found Sean, who was screaming again and again, in a way that made Newt want to cover his ears. He saw that Sean was barely clinging to his horse, and that a lot of brown things were wiggling around him and over him. At first, with the screaming going on, Newt couldn't figure out what the brown things were—they seemed like giant worms. His mind took a moment to work out what his eyes were seeing. The giant worms were snakes—water moccasins.

Holy shit, I say now, just as I probably did twenty years ago when I first read that passage. "Brown things" in the river and lots of them, swarming. So many of them that Newt, the cowboy closest to poor Sean, couldn't even make them out in the water, which meant that the rest of us couldn't either and had to hear the "screaming again and again," to the point of wanting to cover our own ears, if only because we just knew this wasn't going to turn out well. Then whatever the hell Sean was screaming about was now "wiggling around him and over him." Wiggling, I think most of us would agree, is different from slithering. With slithering you can easily imagine what might be coming next. Wiggling is generally reserved for worms and toes and maybe toddlers sneaking into their mommy and daddy's bed on a Sunday morning. But it was exactly that juxtaposition of "wiggling" and "screaming again and again" and the dissonance it created that made the whole episode so damn terrifying and nightmarish.

> Then the screams stopped abruptly as Sean slipped under the water—his voice was replaced almost at once by the frenzied neighing of the horse, which began to thrash in the water and soon turned back toward the far bank. As he gained a footing and rose out of the water he shook three snakes from his body, one slithering off his neck.

This was early 2002, when I first read *Lonesome Dove*. I know this because I had recently sold my first book, a collection of short stories, and was now struggling to write my first novel. I had the sense that studying how Larry McMurtry had structured his classic Western novel, including when certain characters and plot points were introduced, might help me figure out how to navigate the formidable distance between short fiction and a novel. For instance, the deadly encounter with the water moccasins happens on page 231, but Sean and his brother, Allen, are first introduced around page 89, which gives

readers ample time to get to know something about the two Irishmen
before all that screaming and wiggling catches their attention.

It was around this time that I also received a voicemail notifying me
that I had been awarded a Dobie Paisano Fellowship, which amounted
to a six-month residency at J. Frank Dobie's ranch house in the Texas
Hill Country, just outside of Austin. Established in honor of the legendary writer and folklorist, the fellowship program has been hosting
writers since the late 1960s. The property sits on 258 acres of gorgeous
Hill Country and includes part of Barton Creek, one of the more sce-
nic tributaries that feed into the Colorado River. The fellowship director gave me the option of picking the time of year when I wanted to
be on the ranch, either March through August or September through
February. Most people would look at these options as a choice between
the warmer months and the cooler months in Texas. But to me it was
a choice between the "snake months" and the "fewer-snake months."

I grew up on the border, in Brownsville, and spent a fair amount of
time in the country with my father, who was a livestock inspector for
the US Department of Agriculture and would bring me along on the
weekends when he visited ranches and farms in the area. And because
he always had a horse for those days when he patrolled the Rio Grande
looking for stray cattle, I learned to ride horses before I learned to ride a
bike. So it wasn't like I hadn't been outdoors, and it wasn't like I spooked
so easily, though everything I've said up to this point might have already
convinced you otherwise. No matter these earlier experiences, there was
something about snakes that triggered a primal reaction in me, just as
it seemed to do with almost every cowhand who witnessed what happened to Sean when he and his horse entered the Nueces River.

> Jasper and Bert had seen the snakes, and Jasper was so terrified that
> he couldn't look at the water. Soupy Jones was almost as scared. The
> Rainey boys looked as if they might fall off their horses.

The weather was still warm when my wife and I arrived at the Paisano Ranch in early September. The house has two bedrooms, two
baths, a small kitchen, a good-sized living room, and a study that faces

the front yard, the cattle guard, and the caliche road that leads down to the creek. In the living room there was a bookcase containing a few of Dobie's books and those written by earlier guests: fiction and nonfiction writers, poets and journalists. In the kitchen I found a thick binder filled with short narratives of how several of the fellows had spent their time on the ranch. Most of these accounts told of one hardship or another. One fellow's car had been swept away in a flood after they'd parked it too close to the creek. Others had gotten stranded for days when it rained a bit too much and the low-water crossing became hazardous. I popped open a beer and read a few of these, wondering what sort of mishap awaited me over the next six months.

As it turned out, the mishap occurred only four days later—on a Sunday afternoon, as I remember it—when my wife told me she thought we needed to separate and she had already put down a security deposit on an apartment in San Antonio. That evening she left the ranch and, by extension, me. At this point, we had been married barely two years, though it hadn't taken us half that amount of time to realize we had made a terrible mistake. She had just been braver than me in admitting this out loud and then doing something as definitive as finding herself another place to live. The divorce papers would be prepared and signed within the next six months, only a few days before I left the ranch and my first book was launched.

After sulking for a couple of weeks, I told myself that I still had a novel to write, which was true but not as true as my need to distract myself with something. I had brought a milk crate full of books with me to the ranch, but it was *Lonesome Dove* that I kept returning to. Reading the novel more than once led me to more closely notice certain imperfections. It meanders in places, but name another 843-page book that doesn't wander. I had reservations about the two main protagonists and their glory days as Texas Rangers, though I understood they belonged to an earlier battalion of the Rangers, long before their notorious history of murdering Mexicans and Mexican Americans along the border. Still, it was hard for me to not be taken by the interiority of McMurtry's characters, particularly as they struggled privately and oftentimes inconsolably with their yearnings and losses.

If I timed it right and finished my writing by noon, the creek was just perfect in the early to midafternoon, when the sun was its strongest. The water was refreshing and calm in a way that took my mind off my next book, which still wasn't clear to me and wouldn't be for a couple more years. Sometimes I would see how long I could float on my back before drifting too close to either bank or the live oaks that hung over the water. It would've been easy to drift the afternoons away and forget all my worries if not for the snakes. Not the real ones, but the ones I could've sworn were wiggling right beneath the surface of the water, waiting for me to turn my back and be caught unawares. Sure, it was always a twig or a branch or a reed, anyone could see that up close, but up close isn't where you want to figure that out.

Sometimes as I floated I wondered if a snake bite was really the worst way to die, though it seemed pretty horrible from how it happened in the Nueces.

> His eyes were closed, his body jerking slightly. Augustus cut the boy's shirt off—there were eight sets of fang marks, including one on his neck.

But at least Sean had been pulled out of the water almost immediately. To me, what seemed worse than being stung multiple times was for it to happen and for there not to be any witnesses, and no one to pull me from the creek, for my waterlogged body to be found tangled in some branches or lodged in the culvert four or five days after the fact.

I never did see a real snake in the creek or anywhere on the ranch. I slipped once on a patch of ice near the low-water crossing and sprained my wrist, and another time I went for a hike and ended up with chigger bites up to my knees, but otherwise I made it through my fellowship without another major mishap.

It was my last night on the ranch, after I had packed my books and clothes, when I happened to take one last look at the bookshelf. I had glanced at the spines on the first day and even read a couple of the novels but somehow missed one book tucked away at the far end of the bottom shelf. But there it was all this time, waiting for me. *A Field Guide to Texas Snakes* by Alan Tennant. I turned to the section on water moccasins and the Western cottonmouth (*Agkistrodon piscivorus leucostoma*) and then, under the heading of "Behavior," I found this:

> The most widespread story about cottonmouths concerns the water-skier purportedly killed by a flurry of bites after tumbling into a "nest" of these reptiles. For years various retellings of this fictious event have circulated in boating circles, and a river-crossing version involving a cowboy on horseback appeared in the television special *Lonesome Dove*. All such episodes are untrue: No water-skier or river-fording horseman has ever suffered A. piscivorus envenomation.

Tennant went on to explain that cottonmouths do not "nest," as the cowboys in the novel and miniseries kept saying when referring to how the water moccasins were gathered when Sean came upon them. One reason for this is that among cottonmouths the larger snakes attack the smaller ones. Also, cottonmouths only bite fish underwater and generally swim away when approached by humans. Other articles that I've found since then back up these findings and even point out that water moccasins aren't found as far south as the Nueces River. So who am I supposed to believe, several herpetologists or one fiction writer?

It'd be easy to say that the scene in question was all made up, imagined by McMurtry, just like every other scene in his novel. It'd be even easier to say that I was duped, but that would presume my fear could have been remedied with logic, that reading about the cottonmouth's "Behavior" at the beginning of my stay at the ranch instead of at the end would've changed my behavior when I was in the creek. And that if today I were to take the thirty-minute drive from my home in Austin to my former home just outside of Austin and get in the water, I wouldn't be looking back over my shoulder for what I rationally knew wasn't there, but could be.

As the author of two noted books, **OSCAR CÁSARES** earned fellowships from the National Endowment for the Arts, the Copernicus Society of America, and the Texas Institute of Letters. His collection of stories, *Brownsville*, was selected by the American Library Association as a Notable Book of 2004 and is now included in the curriculum at several US universities. His first novel, *Amigoland*, received a "starred review" from *Publisher's Weekly*, which called it "a winning novel." A graduate of the Iowa Writers' Workshop, Cásares teaches creative writing at the University of Texas at Austin.

Finding Home

LARRY MCMURTRY CHANGED my life by changing who I thought I was. It was November 1971, another gray, drizzly day in Leeds, England, where I, a particularly oblivious twenty-one-year-old backpacking and Eurailing her way around Europe, was visiting a fine fellow I'd met the summer before on Spain's Costa Brava. We'd struck up a very sweet romance and planned to move to Hong Kong together and live the life that I, as a military kid, believed I'd been bred for: that of a rootless nomad. On that day, however, when the drizzle metastasized into a downpour heavy enough to force me into the first movie theater I passed, that illusion dissolved forever.

As I was finding my seat, a shot of a gloriously horizontal, impossibly vast landscape scrolled across the wide, wide screen and a wave of homesickness so intense walloped me that I had to read the title through a scrim of tears: *The Last Picture Show.*

Homesick? I'd certainly missed my family before, but a place? A specific landscape? Especially a Texas landscape? My conceit was that I could live anywhere; I was at home in the world. But those tears, and ultimately McMurtry himself, told another story. Whether it was labeled "Texas" or "New Mexico" or simply, most accurately, "the American West," I was homesick for a world and a people of broad vistas and long views, and the only remedy was a one-way ticket out of a land and a future that I now saw was claustrophobically wrong.

Back at my family's home in Albuquerque, McMurtry cured me with *The Last Picture Show; Horseman, Pass By; Leaving Cheyenne; Moving On; All My Friends Are Going to Be Strangers;* and *In a Narrow Grave: Essays On Texas.* In those pages, I discovered not John Wayne's uninviting West of blazing masculinity, but a West of grandeur and gaucherie peopled by misfits and irregulars. In McMurtry's Texas the men were diffident, the women determined, and they were all forever setting off for a new frontier, even as they mourned the one that had just vanished. Or accepted that it had never existed to begin with.

In 1973, I moved to Texas. Eventually, I married one native Texan, gave birth to another, and had the happily rooted life I believe I was meant to live. Do I owe it all to Larry McMurtry? Who knows? But I will be forever grateful to him for introducing me to a West that was as messy as it was mythical. A West that he made feel like home.

SARAH BIRD is an award-winning novelist, screenwriter, essayist, and journalist. She was recently honored with the University of New Mexico's 2020 Paul Ré Award for Cultural Advocacy. Bird is a Dobie Paisano Fellowship honoree; she has also been voted into the Texas Literary Hall of Fame and named the Texas Writer of the Year by the Texas Book Festival. She is a two-time winner of the Texas Institute of Letters' Best Fiction Award and has received the TIL Lifetime Achievement Award. Bird has written for numerous magazines, including six years as a columnist for *Texas Monthly*.

READER & BOOKMAN

The Bookman, the first bookstore Larry managed in Houston.

Larry McMurtry, Reader

BEFORE HE WAS anything else—cowboy, author, celebrity—Larry McMurtry was a man of books, a reader. He frequently confessed that he started buying and selling books in order to *read* them. Asked what advice he would give to an aspiring author, "Read," he said. "Read, read, read."

That's the Larry McMurtry I knew, the reading Larry. His work habits were disciplined. He began every day, seven a week, seated at the big mahogany table in the dining room of his Archer City home, a stack of fresh paper stacked next to his ancient Hermes typewriter. There for a few hours he would attend to the business of writing.

But Larry's true love wasn't writing. "I spin out my daily pages as rapidly as possible," he said, "in order to get back to whatever I'm reading." The reading fed the writing. "If you're going to write fiction," he once told a group of young writers seated around the table at Booked Up One, the flagship of his fleet of Archer City bookshops, "you should read Tolstoy and the Russians. Flaubert and the French. Dickens, George Eliot, Dresser, Twain, and on and on."

On and on was almost anything he encountered. Of the 450,000 volumes that eventually crossed the loading dock into his Archer City book empire, he claimed to have sampled at least a page or two of each.

Long before the books came to Larry, Larry went looking for the books. As a boy, he plundered the Archer City school library before going on to the town library and the paperback rack at the drugstore. "I had found my thing—reading—and never abandoned it," he recalled years later. His first serious read, he records in his memoir *Walter Benjamin at the Dairy Queen*, was *Don Quixote*, devoured in the loft of the barn at Idiot Ridge whenever he could escape chores. *Madame Bovary* followed, acquired from the lone bookstore in Wichita Falls. Then came *War and Peace,* the Modern Library edition. The University of North Texas expanded his reading horizons, as did a year teaching at Texas Christian University. But those horizons exploded at Rice University, where he lectured in the English Department when he wasn't reading in the university's library.

By then, to support his reading habit, he was buying and selling books, "herding them into larger and larger ranches." One of those was the family homestead on Idiot Ridge, an otherwise barren hill southwest of Archer City. In the coming decades he would stock the old frame ranch house where he had grown up wall to wall with his books. Many years later, the intellectual and essayist Susan Sontag, whose own reading habits were possibly a match for Larry's, visited Idiot Ridge and stared in bemusement and wonder. "She remarked that I seemed to be living in my own theme park," Larry recalled.

It was a theme park where Larry had ridden all the rides. In *Walter Benjamin,* which is partly an extended meditation on reading, he discusses the French intellectual and poet Paul Valéry on one page before turning to the Texas novelist Dorothy Scarborough (*The Wind*) on the next. He was comfortable comparing and contrasting Marcel Proust and Virginia Woolf because he knew their work almost as intimates. He was as much at home in James Joyce's Dublin as in the mean streets of Mickey Spillane.

Larry had a thing for off-trail exploration. His collection of nineteenth-century female travel writers contained some two thousand titles. He had read them all. He was fond of obscure English mystery novels. He had a personal collection of comic books and porn.

His reading flowed in patterns. Until the age of thirty, he recalled, "I was an avid reader of fiction," not just any fiction but the work of the Greats: Balzac, George Eliot, Dickens, Hardy, Thackeray, Gogol, Dostoyevsky, Flaubert, Tolstoy. Then he switched to historians, biographers, anthropologists, and memoirists.

What lay behind this restless exploration and acquisition? Larry claimed that his father, a lifelong rancher, "studied cattle with the same fascination with which I study books." There's no doubt that, as a reader, Larry had the discerning and critical eye that his father brought to evaluating beeves. No mere gourmand, no mindless devourer of books, Larry was a gourmet. He thought deeply about what he read, weighed it, savored it.

One he weighed carefully, for example, was Cormac McCarthy, a blue-ribbon champion whose reputation perhaps stood toe to toe with his own: "I think his early books are not very good," Larry told a group of aspiring writers one afternoon while holding court in Booked Up One. "His great book, if he has a great book, is *Blood Meridian*. I'm not sure it alone lifts him out of the category of being a minor regional writer."

No disgrace, he added. He himself would probably be remembered as a minor regional writer. "It's okay to be minor. I think when you boil down the Mailer-Roth-Bellow generation, there's not much really that I wouldn't call minor." He did single out one perhaps unlikely candidate to separate from the herd of minor writers—a woman, a Southerner, a Catholic: "I think Flannery O'Connor has the clearest claim to be more than minor. She was a great writer."

I happened to be among those seated at the table in Booked Up One that sullen, sultry afternoon. Rain clouds were massing over Archer County, and Larry was clearly in a hurry to finish with us and leave, to get back to whatever he was reading.

As we broke up, I mentioned a book I had encountered many years before across the street in Booked Up Two. *Unknown Mexico* was my kind of book, an account of travel and exploration in nineteenth-century Mexico by the Norwegian anthropologist Carl Lumholtz. My wife and I had been headed to Santa Fe and the book would be perfect vacation reading. I took the book down from the shelf and opened the cover. There, Larry had neatly penciled a price. It was far more than I could afford at the time and would have depleted our vacation budget. Many years later I acquired the inexpensive two-volume Dover paperback edition.

But that very morning, before our meeting with Larry, I had encountered the Lumholtz again, shelved amid the private stock in his home. As the rain closed in, I mentioned the book to Larry, half hoping he might at last offer it at a price I could afford.

"Yes, the Lumholtz," he murmured almost inaudibly. He had read it. "Wonderful book."

I didn't offer to buy, and he didn't offer to sell. A bookman to the end.

BILL MARVEL worked as art critic and senior arts editor at the *National Observer* and as senior staff writer at the *Dallas Morning News*. His collaboration with R. V. Burgin, *Islands of the Damned*, was released in 2010 and coincided with the premiere of the HBO series *The Pacific*, which was produced by Steven Spielberg and Tom Hanks, and portrays in part Burgin's experiences as a Marine in World War II. *The Rock Island Line*, Marvel's history of the famous railroad, was published in 2013. "The Miner and the Millionaire," about the bloodiest labor war in US history, is awaiting publication.

An Afternoon with Larry

DURING MY FIRST season of playing professional basketball overseas in 1988, I spent nearly all my time off the court reading. But not the sort of books you'd expect would appeal to a fanatical hoops player like me—sports classics such as Bill Bradley's *Life on the Run*, for example, or *Pistol: The Life of Pete Maravich.*

Instead, I was swept up in the spellbinding Western sagas of Larry McMurtry: *Horseman, Pass By*; *Leaving Cheyenne*; *The Last Picture Show*; *Lonesome Dove*; *Cadillac Jack*; *Anything for Billy*; and all his other novels. I read and reread Larry's work not only because his stories were riveting and his characters captivating, but also because I connected to them on a deep personal level.

After all, Larry and I both grew up in Archer County and shared a common bond: our ranching heritage. Our fathers were respected ranchers who taught us how to ride, rope, castrate, and brand cattle. Though neither of us made cowboying our career, our roots in rural Archer County ran deep. We had walked the same halls, driven the same dirt roads, seen many of the same sights.

During a cattle roundup one year, I spotted Larry's father on horseback. But I had never seen, or met, Larry. I finally got my chance in 1988 when I returned home during the off-season of playing international basketball at the same time that Larry was relocating his antiquarian book business from Washington, DC, to Archer City. I walked through the door of one of Larry's bookshops, the Blue Pig, named after the smart and adorable pigs dining on a rattlesnake in the opening scene of *Lonesome Dove*. Larry's loquacious sister, Sue Deen, who managed the shop and liked to share town gossip, soon had me wrapped up in a witty story about her brother, whom she assumed I knew.

"Well, you know how Larry is," she said.

"No, I don't. I've never met the man."

"Oh my gosh. Next time he's in here, I will call you so you two can get together."

A few days later, Sue called. Larry was in the store and wanted to meet me. Hoping to get Larry's autograph, I scooped up my McMurtry collection and raced to the Blue Pig. Our greeting was perfunctory, but the hour-and-a-half meeting that followed profoundly changed the trajectory of my life.

Sitting at a scuffed-up table, Larry began inscribing my books as I peppered him with questions. At the time I didn't realize how fortunate I was that he agreed to sign my collection. I learned later that Larry considered it burdensome to sign books, and that readers who managed to convince Larry to just sign his initials considered themselves lucky.

But with my collection, Larry was extremely gracious. In *Horseman, Pass By*, Larry wrote: "My first little effort—I can only dimly remember it now." In *Leaving Cheyenne*, Larry inscribed, "Romantics usually like this Best of my Books." In signing *In a Narrow Grave: Essays on Texas*, Larry was also upbeat about his fandom's reception: "Many readers think is my Best Book." Though I thoroughly enjoyed *All My Friends Are Going to Be Strangers*, I was surprised to learn how Larry felt about it. "My own favorite of my early Books," he wrote.

As I handed Larry my copy of *The Last Picture Show*, I mentioned that his novel's first sentence mirrored my own feelings growing up in Archer County: "Sometimes Sonny felt like he was the only human creature in town." Larry opened my copy and wrote on the flyleaf: "I agree this first sentence sets a very bleak mood." In *Texasville*, Larry's inscription, describing what's inside, is also bleak: "A grim vision of the oil-patch in decline."

In signing *Lonesome Dove*, a trail-drive novel that earned him a Pulitzer Prize and transformed our hometown author into an international celebrity, Larry didn't disclose his own sentiments about the book other than that it was long. "A long trail requires a long book."

One of the books I asked Larry to sign made his eyes sparkle: a paperback copy of *The Desert Rose*. He wrote the novel about a bewitching Las Vegas showgirl while wrestling with the research and writing of *Lonesome Dove*. *The Desert Rose* was dear to Larry. Writing *Desert Rose*, in just three weeks, rejuvenated him. "I had hardly written a sentence I liked in eight years," he wrote in his memoir, *Literary Life*. "To actually enjoy my own prose again was a big, big deal."

Because *The Desert Rose* meant so much to Larry, his inscription in my copy of his book calling attention to our close connections, having both grown up in Archer City, means much to me. "For Greg a fellow graduate of ACHS with good wishes."

As Larry signed my books, I mentioned my fondness for Tom Robbins, author of *Even Cowgirls Get the Blues* and eight other bestsellers. I told Larry I considered Robbins a big-league writer, as good as or better than Thomas Pynchon, author of *Gravity's Rainbow*, which won the National Book Award for fiction. Larry politely dismissed my claim without insulting my judgment. Instead, he penned a witty inscription inside my copy of his novel *Anything for Billy*: "Read Pynchon. A page of Pynchon is worth a volume of Robbins."

Many years later, with Larry's inscription tossing around in my head, I decided to revisit the literary pleasures of my youth by rereading *Jitterbug Perfume*, Robbins's fourth novel. I didn't hate the book, but the excitement I once felt was gone. I had to admit to myself that Larry was right. A page of Pynchon *is* worth a volume of Robbins.

The last question I posed to Larry on that memorable afternoon at the Blue Pig produced a reading list, handwritten by Larry, that's now framed in glass. I asked, "What books should everyone read?"

Larry grabbed a pad of Blue Pig shop stationery that the staff used to record purchases. Tearing off a sheet, Larry turned it over and began writing. He topped the list with "Flannery O'Connor, Short Stories" (various titles) followed by Thomas Wolfe's *Look Homeward, Angel*. Four Faulkner novels were next: *Sartoris, Light in August, The Sound and the Fury*, and *As I Lay Dying*.

Under Faulkner, Larry wrote "Hemingway Short Stories" and *The Sun Also Rises*. Then he began to write *"On the Road* by Jack Kerouac."

But Larry scratched Kerouac off his list after I told him I had already read *On the Road*. Twisting Blue Pig's stationery sideways, Larry jotted down J. D. Salinger's *The Catcher in the Rye*.

Ceremony by Leslie Marmon Silko also made Larry's reading list. So did three titles by British authors: D. H. Lawrence's *Sons and Lovers*; Joyce Cary's *The Horse's Mouth*; and E. M. Forster's *Howard's End*.

When Larry completed his recommended reading list and handed it to me, I immediately thought of it as a cool souvenir to show off to my basketball teammates and friends who read Larry's books or at least had heard about the celebrity author. But in the years to come Larry's reading list became much more than that. It set in motion a tectonic shift in my career plans—from athlete to academic, to a life devoted to and transformed by books.

GREG GIDDINGS, an Archer County native, played pro basketball internationally, then returned to Wichita Falls, where he has taught American literature at Midwestern State University for the past twenty-five years. Giddings has published scholarly articles on *The Last Picture Show*; *Horseman, Pass By*; and works by Pat Conroy and Bruce Springsteen, among others.

On Book Scouting and Ghostwritten Erotica

EVERYONE STARTS OUT in the basement—metaphorically or even physically. Experience gets you out eventually, pulling you up from the underworld into the light of commerce. Everything that is not on the selling floor is down there. Deadstock, overstock, out-of-print, forgotten authors, vapid bestsellers, misplaced consignments; evidence of bugs, rodents, dust, dampness, mildew, questionable or hasty storage decisions, and shelving mistakes.

You can—and will—hit your head on something down there, usually plumbing. It can be hot and damp, or cold and damp, and always dirty. Being dirty is part of the book world, lurking in the stacks, rubbing edges, touching spines, opening covers to peer within.

Near a corner of this particular basement—that of Gotham Book Mart, New York, circa 2004—at the top of an unsteady island of dented boxes was one marked "McMurtry." A recent transplant from the Lone Star State, I felt duty bound to peek inside, where I discovered, not a rarity, but copies of a decades-old novel not much in demand. On the cover, oil derricks and storage tanks punctuated a vast West Texas sky, an expanse of plains stretched beyond manicured lawn and azure pool, and over all hovered the title: *Some Can Whistle*. I folded the flaps back together and closed the box.

In his 2008 memoir, *Books*, McMurtry recalls a similar disappointment in his early days while scouting Brock's, a San Antonio bookseller.

One day, as I was descending to the basement, which Norman eventually filled to the very brim, I saw what looked to be a perfect copy of Nathanael West's *A Cool Million*, a few steps down under a few novels. I had never seen the book before, and was very excited, only to discover, when I pulled it out, that rats had chewed off the back cover. I remember the shock of disappointment to this day.

In my three years at what was then New York's oldest literary bookstore (founded 1920), I rose from the basement to the first floor, to the second floor, and eventually to the collectible/research position I held until the store's 2007 demise. I followed my curiosity into unknown territories, temporarily paralyzed my finances, and often had my faith in the shifting desires of the market undermined. Such is the bookman's journey, at least mine.

About the time McMurtry consolidated his stores into Booked Up in Archer City, I was leaving the University of North Texas for New Haven and a master's degree in sculpture. But during my first semester, in a used bookstore on a cold, rainy evening, I purchased a fine first edition of Salinger's *Franny and Zooey*. Years later it would become the first collectible book I sold, kick-starting my scouting and selling career.

In the early 2000s, I moved to New York. My first jobless weeks there I spent scouting used and collectible bookstores, checking out the "new" stock, conversing with booksellers, learning what to look for, and why.

I kept want lists in my wallet for quick reference. In one downtown behemoth, I came across a first American edition of Albert Camus's *The Myth of Sisyphus* in a bright dust jacket. I didn't have $25 at the time, so I moved it to the highest shelf I could reach, telling myself it was mis-shelved anyhow. I came back a few times to move it, until it eventually vanished. Years later, I saw a copy on the shelves of McMurtry's Booked Up in Archer City. The asking price was three times what I had first encountered. It too found another buyer.

In a recent phone call with a former Gotham Book Mart colleague and NYC book scout, he and I recalled the day he was digging through boxes of collectibles at the instruction of the shop's proprietor, Andreas

Brown. My friend had been culling prizes from the stock to sell when he encountered an inscribed copy of McMurtry's ode to scouting, *Cadillac Jack* (1982). Inside was a laid-in, typed presentation letter to the person who had introduced Larry to the art of book scouting in 1960. McMurtry recalled that moment in *Books*: "I don't think I had ever heard the term 'book scout' until, one night, I wandered into the Discovery Bookstore [next door to the fabled City Lights], in North Beach [San Francisco], and met the poet David Meltzer, who sometimes ran the shop at night."

This crossroads moment between the two authors deeply intrigued us. The book, priced at $800, promptly sold to a Northwest Coast bookseller. But before the sale, my friend and I made photocopies of the letter. In it, McMurtry recalled a large rat that lived in his DC bookstore and had a thing for his stash of Nestlé Quik. In the letter, McMurtry also anointed *Cadillac Jack* as a "curious fruit of those scouting arts you taught me so longago [*sic*]." He closes with a wish to see Meltzer again, as he was "much in LA"—his screenwriting was in full bloom—"but never seem to get north."

Half a decade later, I returned to Texas, making two or three trips a year to Archer City to explore the vast canyons of books McMurtry had assembled in his hometown. I struck up a few conversations with him, but I generally steered clear when he was at the large sorting table in the rear of Building No. 1.

Earlier, I had come across a curious piece of McMurtry ephemera: a pamphlet titled *Splendors & Miseries of Being an Author-Bookseller*, the transcription of an address given in 1995 at the Antiquarian Booksellers' Association of America annual meeting in Chicago. On the first page, McMurtry recalls San Francisco scouting with Meltzer and others the year before he published his first novel, *Horseman, Pass By*. The closing paragraph of the pamphlet's second page transported me to the discovery, five years earlier at Gotham, of the inscribed presentation copy of *Cadillac Jack* with the letter to Meltzer tucked inside. Larry wrote:

The first inkling I had that I might be a collected author, and that this might create a certain fission in my relations with the book

trade, and even with my bookscout friends, occurred when David
Meltzer, who I liked very much and whom I still like very much,
sold 120 of my letters to the Gotham Bookmart [*sic*]. I understand
that David is a starving poet with a family, who frequently needs to
sell everything he owns because, on occasion, I've bought everything
he owns; but it didn't occur to him to sell me my own letters—I've
never quite forgotten the shock of realizing that I was an author who
could be sold. And, not just sold by strangers—sold by friends.

Clearly the sale to Gotham of McMurtry's Meltzer letters and the
book were separate transactions maybe a decade apart, and McMurtry's awareness of the two sales would be awkward for Gotham's Andy
Brown, especially after Larry's complaint in *Splendors & Miseries of Being an Author-Bookseller*. When I spoke with Larry in 2011, there was no
love lost between the two men. He told me that when he visited Gotham
early on, Brown would still "overwhelm him with material to sign."

I never told Larry about coming across his presentation copy of *Cadillac Jack*, nor was I ever able to question Brown regarding the trove
of McMurtry letters he had originally purchased from Meltzer and
presumably sold. But with all three characters in this bookish dustup
now gone, I decided to search for the correspondence that had changed
Larry's mind about being a collectible author and bookseller.

After getting off the phone that day with my friend from the Gotham Book Mart, I found myself in my storage space clambering over
boxes and combing through books, looking for my remaindered copy
of *Cadillac Jack* with the copied Meltzer letter inside. Over several decades, I have honed a sixth sense regarding the books in my own library—even those in deep storage—and I was in and out within ten
minutes, book in hand. ("The ability to remember *exactly* where books
are," Larry observes in *Walter Benjamin at the Dairy Queen*, "is a skill
vital to the serious book scout—but it is such a peculiar skill that one
suspects it must be genetically determined.")

Four days later I left Dallas for Austin, on the trail of a collection of
letters from McMurtry to Meltzer spanning most of the 1960s. During
a pit stop, I peeked at my emails and was happy to see my suspicions

confirmed by the library assistant at the Briscoe Center for American History: "I checked the holding record and with our archival team, and I can confirm that the University of Texas Library purchased the letters from Gotham Book Mart on June 18, 1971. Hope this helps, and we'll see you this afternoon."

I was buoyed by my amateur internet sleuthing, and my next thought was that if the 1961–1969 letters were sold a second time (after Meltzer's undated sale to Gotham), by Andy Brown in 1971, why would McMurtry still be perturbed speaking to a room full of people twenty-four years later? These documents were preserved for future scholars. I had a feeling the reason was about to slip out of the two file folders resting at the front of an archival document box.

Gotham's Andy Brown must have sold the letters to the Harry Ransom Center's director, Warren Roberts. Brown had worked with Roberts from 1963 to 1965 while scholar-in-residence at the Humanities Research Center. During my time at Gotham, Brown had told me stories of meeting McMurtry while they were both in Austin in the early '60s, when they spent time at the fabled Brick Row Bookshop and scouted the city together.

I settled in the back corner of the reading room, laptop open, pencil and paper within reach. I unfastened the box and pulled out the first file of letters between the two scouts, dated 1961–1962.

After a few exchanges, Larry makes a series of requests of Meltzer of a bluish hue, a stack of newly published erotica: *Amour Erotisme, 120 Days of Sodom, Technique de l'Erotisme, Métaphysique du Striptease,* and a work on eroticism in the *1,001 Nights.* He notes that "in Texas one requires expensive sexbooks."

They discuss supply and demand, the desires of their clientele, and the excitement this stirs in a twenty-five-year-old book scout. Customers, he says,

> are now dickering for one [pornography book] worth $5000—they are rich & quite serious about their dirty books—one individual among them employs a private buyer who scouts England and the Continent the year round buying nothing but pornography. They're

real badasses and I would probably risk a felony charge in the hopes of being able to stick it to them good and deep.

The noted folklorist and critic Gershon Legman enthralls McMurtry with his publications, his quotes, and his overall command of erotica, eventually convincing the young author to issue a "mammoth desiderata. . . . A good weird book about screwing that has got an automatic head start on books about the dryer [sic] activities."

McMurtry closes out the letter of April 6, 1962, by informing Meltzer that he "decided to make sadistica and the gothic my collecting bit for a while, so quote anything on punishments, tortures, gothicism or other horrors . . . flagellation material acceptable."

Through almost eight years and hundreds of pages of correspondence, McMurtry tracks the lure of book scouting and the torments of love and desire. Gershon Legman clearly had a profound influence on McMurtry's scouting, selling, and soliciting of books of a certain sophistication.

Near the end of the "Book Scouting" section in *Walter Benjamin at the Dairy Queen*, McMurtry recalls the time Meltzer passed on a book he describes as of "talismanic significance," "Gershon Legman's brilliant *Love and Death*," and remembers reading "his fascinating work in folklore and erotic bibliography."

McMurtry further chronicles his fascination with Legman in chapter 72 of his memoir, *Books*, covering their overheated correspondence; his pilgrimage to Legman's home and library in a Knights Templar monastery in the South of France; his attempt at buying erotica at estate auctions to appease Legman; and his subsequent funding of Legman's memoirs, "called *Peregrine Penis*, in which he becomes his own Casanova . . . very long and very thorough."

At McMurtry's "Last Book Sale" in August 2012, I spotted, lying open on a table, an ordinary-looking ledger bound in dusty green cloth. It was somewhat soiled, with crimson leather corners, and every page was locked firmly in place by a metal rod—an industrial-strength mechanism that reminded one of the storied chastity belts of the Dark Ages. A double-hole punch penetrated this union of "nearly 1,200 typescript pages of erotica, containing 82 original and classic stories, poems, songs, and jokes assembled by the legendary collector and Oklahoma oil man, Roy Melisander Johnson."

I had noticed only one bookseller of note standing in the room; the East Coast bookseller was keeping close to the prized lot of erotica as I lurked in the opposite corner. When the lot came up, I raised my hand a few times. But bidding soon galloped into the low thousands, well beyond my budget. The hammer came down at $2,750, the victor the East Coast bookseller.

I had no previous knowledge of the ledger. But McMurtry deemed it the star lot of the "McMurtry 100"—individual hand-selected lots plucked from three buildings of stock. I left Archer City that sizzling hot August afternoon empty-handed, not knowing exactly what I had missed out on as an underbidder.

Four years later, that ledger of erotica, fully collated and cataloged, was being offered for sale for $9,500 by Between the Covers Rare Books, a quality shop just outside of Philadelphia. Now long sold, the collection was apparently only one of many binders assembled for Johnson, the wealthy and influential Ardmore oilman, deacon, and conservative newspaperman. They were filed away, according to *Fine Books and Collections,* "in olive-drab steel filing cabinets in his business office because his wife refused to allow them in their house."

From the 1930s into the early 1940s, Johnson built what is understood to be the largest collection of "profane literature" in the world. To feed his fantasies, he enlisted agents in major cities to assemble these salacious texts and commissioned authors to write new material, according to *Fine Books and Collections.*

One of those engaged was Legman, who procured several authors—some notable, though uncredited—to indulge Johnson's appetite. Legman had arranged an appointment with Henry Miller at Gotham Book Mart in Manhattan to discuss the commission. Instead, Miller sent his lover and friend, Anaïs Nin, to work out the details. Legman also recruited her for the task.

As McMurtry recounts in *Books*: "The millionaire [Johnson] died [in 1960] and somebody got the contents of that filing cabinet—Legman would probably have known who." Legman died in 1999, and *Books* was published in 2008, four years before "The Last Book Sale." Was Larry being coy about his acquisition of the erotica ledger, or was he still on the hunt? Or was he merely holding his cards close to his vest until he was ready to reveal the ledger's whereabouts at the sale? My hunch is that the wily bookman had owned it for a while and was looking to make a show of selling it at his long-awaited and highly publicized book auction.

A few years after the sale, I was perusing the unsold lots of a rare-books auction and my memory was instantly transported back to Gotham's basement and staring into that open box filled with an un-popular McMurtry title. Moved by an unconscious book scout's urge, I let my trigger finger click on "Buy Now" and purchased the original cover art for *Some Can Whistle* for what would've been the opening bid. By then I had learned that *Some Can Whistle* was the sequel to one of my favorite early McMurtry novels, *All My Friends Are Going to Be Strangers*. The cover earned a place on my wall. One day, I figured, I might even give the book itself a read.

BRANDON KENNEDY is an artist, book collector, curator, and writer. He is a regular contributor to *Patron* magazine and an occasional essayist for *Fine Books & Collections*. Kennedy lives in Dallas, Texas.

Runaways

I EXCHANGED BUT two sentences with Larry McMurtry. No doubt, there should have been more. I was in the man's mansion, after all, with only a couple dozen other writers vying for his attention. Assertiveness is generally not a problem for me. I once chased a Stalinist for nine blocks in Moscow, pleading for an interview. McMurtry was just a couch away. But something held me back.

It was July 2009, and my life had reached a crossroads. Since graduating from college twelve years earlier, I had spent every waking moment trying to turn travel writing into a sustainable career. Exploring forty countries had yielded three books and scores of essays but not enough paychecks to cover the rent, so as I followed stories from town to town the anxieties of nomadism were overshadowing the joys. When I arrived on McMurtry's doorstep, I was weeks away from matriculating at the University of Iowa and feeling sad about it. Though I knew, at an intellectual level, that the publishing industry was capricious, I had built my entire identity around being a travel writer. It was hard not to view resorting to academia as a personal failure.

Fortunately, these insecurities didn't keep me from joining a caravan to Archer City along with other guests of the Mayborn Literary Nonfiction Conference. Susan Sontag once joked that McMurtry was living in his "own theme park," but that description belies the sanctity of entering a house of twenty-eight thousand books. For me, it was like lighting a match in a dark cave and discovering paintings on the walls. In room after room, first editions ascended from the wooden floor to the faraway ceiling, gilt lettering emblazoning their spines. Some were bound in vellum; others wore dust jackets. Slender volumes of poetry stood beside fat French novels. Biographies. Works of history, criticism, geography, and psychology. I absorbed as many as I could as we filed past case after case. Dickens. Hardy. Shelley. Thomas de Quincey. George Eliot. H. G. Wells. An entire shelf of Nabokov followed by half a shelf of Solzhenitsyn followed by two shelves devoted to Stravinsky. After touring the carriage house out back, where McMurtry kept his comics and skulls, we returned to one of his many sitting rooms. He plopped down on the couch, wearing blue jeans and a polo. Everyone gathered around him.

Here was my chance to chat up the star scribe of my home state. But the truth was, I had neither read McMurtry's work nor seen any of the films it inspired. I had witnessed firsthand his motivating subject—the passing of the cowboy—and didn't care to revisit it. My great-great-great-grandfather Juan de Dios Silva migrated from the foothills of Tamaulipas, Mexico, to the King Ranch of South Texas around 1879, and his progeny wrangled its cattle for a century. My mother spent every summer of her childhood on that ranch, while I whacked piñatas there every Easter. Then, in the 1980s, the King Ranch modernized and corporatized. My *tios* lost everything in the process: their jobs and their benefits, the horses they rode, the long row of cottages housing everyone they loved. We couldn't so much as visit our family graveyard without a permit anymore.

So no, I didn't need to read about the sorrows of cowboys. I had inherited their ache. It's one reason why I fled Texas long ago. Rather than try to talk to McMurtry, then, I wandered off to study his collection. Earlier, I had noticed a sunlit nook that struck me as the finest in his mansion. Which books warranted such prime real estate? One title immediately popped out: *The Englishwoman in America*.

What? No, it couldn't be.

But there it gleamed, between *Six Months in the Sandwich Islands* and *The Yangtze Valley and Beyond*. It was the first-edition debut of one of the most celebrated female travel writers of all time: Isabella Bird. Sick from a spinal tumor, she was prescribed travel as a cure, and she didn't stop roaming—from Canada to Hawaii to Japan to Korea to Persia to Kurdistan—until her death in 1904, at the age of seventy-three.

The Royal Geographical Society tapped her as its first female member. Here was her life's work, eight volumes in all, lined up in a row.

As I raised a reverent hand to touch one, I saw something equally exceptional: half a shelf of Alexandra David-Néel. The first Western woman to visit Lhasa, she purportedly mastered *thumo reskiang*, the meditative practice that enables Tibetan monks to survive the cold by raising their own body temperature. I backed away in disbelief, for not far from David-Néel's collected works were antiquarian editions of Amelia Edwards's *Pharaohs, Fellahs, and Explorers* and *A Thousand Miles Up the Nile*, and just beyond those rarities stood Anna Leonowens's *The English Governess at the Siamese Court* beside Mrs. Archibald Little's *The Land of the Blue Gown* next to Lady Lawrence's *Indian Embers*.

While writing my first book, I had read every woman-authored travelogue that Half Price Books had in stock. Mary Morris's *Nothing to Declare* was my most vintage find: 1988. McMurtry's travelogues were centuries old. I'd heard whisper of these antiquities, but never thought I'd see one. Here, they filled a whole wall. Taking one down, I marveled at its heft, at its vaguely vanilla smell. The endpapers were ornamented, the frontispiece lavish. Turning the pages, I found a wood-engraved plate of a camel strutting across the desert. A multi-paneled map of Arabia so delicate, I could hardly breathe. And a prose style so immediate, so familiar, that I had the same realization as the cave explorers of long ago. *Those paintings etched high upon those walls? My ancestors put them there.* For that's what these writers were to me. My *madrinas*.

Someone called my name. Our shuttle was departing. McMurtry stood at the door, bidding each writer goodbye. Fumbling for my camera, I snapped a photograph before jostling into line. When my eyes met McMurtry's, I blurted out, "Oh-my-fucking-God-your-women's-travelogues!"

He grinned. "Those are my runaways."

His *what*?

No time to clarify. The writer behind me was already extending a hand. I boarded the shuttle with a dizzied mind. Runaways? The term seemed dismissive—if not patronizing—yet he said it with such fondness, I gave him the benefit of the doubt. He'd clearly read more travelogues than me. Maybe he'd gleaned something I hadn't. But what?

———————

Two months later, FedEx dropped a parcel on my newly leased doorstep in Iowa City. Inside were more than three hundred submissions to an anthology I had agreed to edit called *Best Women's Travel Writing*. Not an advisable way to spend the first semester of grad school, but since my nomadism had ended, it was either vicarious adventuring or no adventuring at all. For weeks I dipped into that box wondering: *Is she a runaway? What about her?* Meanwhile, I scoured the library stacks for the books I had ogled at McMurtry's. I thought I had solved the mystery when I found this passage in Maud Parrish's *Nine Pounds of Luggage*, published in 1939:

> So I ran away. I hurried more than if lions had chased me. Without telling him. Without telling my mother or father. There wasn't any liberty in San Francisco for ordinary women. But I found some. . . . You got married, were an old maid, or went to hell. Take your pick.

This must have been what McMurtry meant: that, for my *madrinas* on his shelf, escape was the only freedom. Even the mighty Bird declined a trip to New Guinea when her new husband protested. (Fortunately, he expired five years later, and she hit the road again.) The McMurtry mystery solved, I moved on. Halfway through that first Iowan winter, I started pining for the landscape that raised me. Instead of snowy cornfields, I longed to look out the window and see nopales blooming in a desert. I began flying home to my parents on weekends and spending every summer there. South Texas turned out to be just as interesting as the other countries I'd written about once I poked around and listened. For every Stalinist aspiring to be a Soviet again, there was a Tejano grieving that he was no longer a vaquero. My notebooks of writings slowly accumulated.

This was when I should have read McMurtry. His work would have affirmed that my own corner of Texas was equally worthy of witness. Alas, I didn't tackle his oeuvre until he had died and that book had long been published. By then, I was living in North Carolina and growing succulents in all my windows. I had just declined a lucrative job that would have returned me home to Texas and needed someone to explain me to myself. *Was I a runaway too?*

McMurtry is best loved for his novels, but I sampled his nonfiction instead: two essay collections, two memoirs, two travelogues, and dozens of short pieces written by and about him over half a century. Nowhere did he explain why he had spent tens of thousands of dollars collecting vintage women's travelogues, but I decided the skunk woman had something to do with it. In *Walter Benjamin at the Dairy Queen*, McMurtry relates how, as a child, he was told that the old woman he often saw hitchhiking along a dirt road had been traded for a pile of skunk hides when she was thirteen. His dad always offered her a ride. She never said a word. "There was a judgment in her silence that I could not fathom," McMurtry wrote.

His mother likely influenced his reading too. "In her mind's eye, swimming led inevitably to drowning, flying to falling, driving to car wrecks, walking to snakebite, the highways to murder and rape, and visits to big cities to even more certain murder and rape," he summarized in his 2001 travelogue *Paradise*.

These two women—one silent, one fearful—loomed large in his boyhood, so it made sense that McMurtry would later be fascinated by gutsy female travelers, especially since he harbored so many phobias himself (of owls, roosters, hens, peacocks, turkeys, swine, shrubbery, water gaps, and taut cables, to name a few). But while the *New York Times* praised McMurtry in his obituary for creating "memorable and credible" female characters in his novels, the women who animated his nonfiction were mostly objectified. In his 1968 essay collection *In a Narrow Grave*, McMurtry bemoaned the "short straggle-haired farm women with dumpy breasts, thin legs, and fat behinds" of East Texas; of a sex worker in Matamoros he remarked that "only love or the omnivorous horniness of adolescence could have transformed her into a palatable sexual object." He also deprecated the "lowbred sluts" of rodeos in his 1999 book-length essay *Walter Benjamin at the Dairy Queen*. Chronicling his tour of the islands of the South Pacific in *Paradise*, McMurtry eroticized virtually every indigenous female he saw, including a group of high school girls with "hip movements that would have earned them immediate employment at any lap-dancing establishment in Las Vegas."

Such degradations put a new spin on the term "runaway." If any of those Victorian travelers on his shelves had ever met him, that is likely what they'd have done.

What nearly provoked my own departure was *In a Narrow Grave*. For two hundred pages, I had been wondering where all the Mexicans were in his work—a conspicuous omission, considering we constitute more than a third of our state. Here finally came our mention, six pages from the end:

> I had always supposed [Uncle Johnny] a truly gentle man and was
> very shocked, one night, to hear him say that the way to handle
> Mexicans was to kick loose a few of their ribs every now and then.
> . . . The cowboy's working life is spent in one sort of violent activity
> or other; an ability to absorb violence and hardship is part of the
> proving of any cowboy, and it is only to be expected that the violence
> will extend itself occasionally from animals to humans, and partic-
> ularly to those humans that class would have one regard as animals.

Although McMurtry expressed sympathy for undocumented Mexicans in other books, I found no instance where he unpacked his uncle's racist comment—or his own swift rationalization of it—any further than that. This is not just an essayistic failure. It is a moral one as well. The dehumanization of Mexicans that occurred after Texas achieved statehood incited hundreds of lynchings and extrajudicial killings. Neglecting to condemn such brutality in a book reissued in 2018 as a "Pulitzer-Prize winning author's homage to the past and present of the Lone Star State" is unconscionable.

As much as these portrayals aggrieved me, I nevertheless found myself returning to McMurtry. His cowboy grandfather had settled in the plains of West Texas right around the time my vaquero *bisabuelo* arrived in South Texas. We had both absconded from those regions the minute we graduated from high school, but McMurtry had, in middle age, returned. Having just declined, at the age of forty-seven, what might have been my best opportunity to do so, I worried I never would. That is why I kept reading McMurtry—to process what I had lost, and what I had gained. An illuminating passage arose in *Walter Benjamin at the Dairy Queen*, in which McMurtry grapples with why his father died so unhappy:

> I suspect it was because he saw too clearly the crack, the split, the gully that lay between the possible and the actual. He had attached his heart to a hopeless ideal, a nineteenth-century vision of cowboying and family pastoralism; such an ideal was not totally false, but it had been only briefly realizable.

None of my *tios* who retreated from the King Ranch in the 1980s regained their former glory either. One *tio*—a handsome vaquero with an easy laugh and a handlebar mustache—grew so depressed that he shot himself in the head. It astonished me to see his story on the page I was reading. And then came a passage I felt in my bones:

> The sense of that crack in reality between what is and what might be, my father passed on to me; I, in turn, may well have passed it on to [my son] James. It may be the crack where books and songs are born.

Surely travel writing rivals cowboying in the annals of romantic vocations. I still mourned the fact that I hadn't made it sustainable. And yet the publishing industry had modernized and corporatized just as the King Ranch had before it. I needed to unhitch my heart from this unobtainable ideal before it broke like McMurtry's dad's . . . or like my *tios'*.

I exchanged but two sentences with Larry McMurtry. No doubt, there could have been more. Another passage in *Walter Benjamin at the Dairy Queen* relieves me of regret, though. In it, McMurtry recalls being a graduate student at Rice and walking past a classroom where Walter Prescott Webb was lecturing. Though he knew Webb was a key figure in Texas letters, he didn't try to meet him, for he never imagined that he'd be interested in Webb's motivating subject himself.

> I have at last grasped that the task of understanding where one came from and how one came from it are not as simple as I would have supposed it to be when I was younger. Then, of course, I was involved in an act of escape: the escape from the cowboy life, the life of men and horses, into the culture of books. In fact, I read my way out of that culture, and now, in my seventh decade, have been catching up on a few of the writers who read their way out before me.

I hadn't just met my literary *madrinas* that day at McMurtry's mansion. I had also met my *padrino*. Every last one was a runaway. Now, in my fifth decade, it is time to read them.

STEPHANIE ELIZONDO GRIEST is the author of three travel memoirs: *Around the Bloc: My Life in Moscow, Beijing, and Havana*; *Mexican Enough*; and *All the Agents and Saints: Dispatches from the US Borderlands*. Widely anthologized, she has also written for the *New York Times*, the *Washington Post*, *The Believer*, *BBC Travel*, and *Oxford American*. She is Associate Professor of Creative Nonfiction at the University of North Carolina at Chapel Hill. The Corpus Christi native has performed on five continents in capacities ranging from that of a *Moth* storyteller to that of a literary ambassador for the US State Department.

Bonding over Books

UNLESS YOU'RE AN artist or an art book collector, you probably never heard of the book *British Water-Colour Art*. But that book, dedicated by the Royal Society of Painters to King Edward VII at his coronation, turned a potentially disastrous encounter with Larry McMurtry into a memorable, even pleasant experience that changed the course of my writing career.

The first time I saw McMurtry in person, he was standing on a ladder in the back room of his antiquarian bookstore, Booked Up, in downtown Archer City. He glowered down at me with owlish eyes behind round, black-rimmed glasses as if I had horribly inconvenienced him. I introduced myself and reminded him that I was there to do a story about his book business for *Texas Monthly*. Former editor Evan Smith ran into McMurtry at the Texas Book Festival in the late 1990s and mentioned that the magazine was interested in running a piece about the "book town" he had created in Archer City. McMurtry seemed agreeable, so Smith assigned me the story. I was thrilled; I'd been working as a freelancer for the magazine and knew this could be a big story. I didn't realize how big.

When I called McMurtry to schedule the interview, however, he sounded curt and didn't recall the conversation with Smith. "You're welcome to come up," he said in a brusque tone. We agreed on a day and time. Then he added: "I may or may not be here."

My upbeat mood vanished. With a deadline looming, I decided to drive from my home in Fort Worth to Archer City the next day. I grew more depressed with every mile. Here was my chance to interview a

Texas literary legend. I feared I was going to blow my opportunity if I couldn't get McMurtry to talk.

When I arrived at the main Booked Up store, a young staffer pointed me to the back and said McMurtry was "in the stacks." The cavernous room—the former garage of a Ford dealership—held rows and rows of towering white bookshelves with thousands of volumes. McMurtry perched on the ladder flipping open books and marking the price inside the cover with a pencil. He knew books so well he didn't need to consult a price guide.

I knew I was going to have to do something to get him to come down and talk to me. I also knew from interviewing difficult people that the way to get a conversation going was to find something in common, something that the other person was passionate about. As I browsed the shelves, I spotted *British Water-Colour Art* by Marcus Huish. The volume stood out, ornately bound in royal blue cloth with gold and red embossed letters and stylized flowers, leaves, and other decorations on the cover. I had bought the same title several months earlier, because I painted watercolors; it was a first edition, dated 1904.

"Oh, I have this book," I announced. That got McMurtry's attention. The rare-book scout in him was curious. I noticed he hadn't priced the book yet.

He climbed down the ladder. "Where did you buy it?" he wanted to know. At a rare-books store in Champaign-Urbana, Illinois, near the University of Illinois campus. He knew the store. "How much did you pay for it?" he wanted to know. Fifteen dollars. "What condition?" My copy had some worn areas on each end of the binding but otherwise was in fine condition. We discussed the book for several minutes.

Sensing his interest, I mentioned that my husband and I collected books and sometimes sold them. Like what? he wanted to know. The best buy I ever made was at an estate sale, when I shelled out $20 for a signed, limited-edition, mint-condition copy of *Chick Evans' Golf Book*. I sold it on a bookseller's site for $400. He agreed I made a good buy.

The main Booked Up building held rare books, biographies, belles lettres, and Western Americana. I recognized a book of floral designs in the store, and we discussed *William Morris: Arts and Crafts Designs, A Book of Postcards*. McMurtry certainly didn't project warmth, but the cool indifference seemed to fade.

McMurtry informed me that he needed to go over to the building that housed Booked Up's poetry collection and asked if I wanted to join him. Of course I did. The wind coming off the plains whipped up dust around the courthouse square. McMurtry wore blue jeans and a black shirt and had wrapped an enormous cape around his shoulders that swirled in the wind, making him look like a scruffy Heathcliff, the protagonist of Emily Brontë's novel *Wuthering Heights*.

We walked across the street, and McMurtry took out a ring of clinking keys to unlock the door. This building held poetry as well as history and twentieth-century English and American fiction. McMurtry had recently bought up all the poetry books at a store in New York that was closing. I had loved poetry since childhood. As an English major at Trinity University, I studied T. S. Eliot and Ezra Pound. I mentioned to McMurtry that I had worked for a professor who was a scholar of Elizabeth Barrett Browning and Robert Browning and had helped her transcribe a collection of letters between the Brownings and their contemporaries. I also worked for a professor who wrote "concrete" poetry, sometimes called visual poetry, which emphasizes shape and typography. He didn't say much, but his nods seemed to communicate interest.

I'm a published poet now, but when I walked into McMurtry's poetry building, I was just beginning to think about writing verse and felt unsure of myself. Seeing so many volumes of poetry in one place—from Dylan Thomas to Charles Bukowski—stirred something deep within me. Although McMurtry focused his own work on fiction, nonfiction, and screenplays, he had a passion for poetry. He even wrote some poems during a creative writing class at North Texas State University (now the University of North Texas), but noted in his memoir about books that he "couldn't write anything short. I was neither a poet nor a short story writer." His reviews of verse collections for the *New York Times Book Review* reflected his knowledge of and appreciation for poetry, and his first novel, *Horseman, Pass By*, takes its title from a poem by W. B. Yeats.

Next McMurtry took me to the other buildings, which housed books on art, nineteenth-century books, translations, and books about books, acquired from the last of the stock at Battery Park Books in New York. Another small building contained books about drama, music, dance, and film. At the end of the street stood the crumbling ruins of the Royal Theater, made famous in the 1971 film adaptation of *The Last Picture Show.* The town that McMurtry had lamented was utterly bookless when he was growing up was now full of books—more than one hundred thousand volumes in 1997, and half a million by the time McMurtry in 2012 held a giant sale and sold three hundred thousand of them. The book town drew patrons from all over Texas and the United States and from abroad.

I was surprised when McMurtry invited me to his house, the Prairie-style mansion he used to admire as a youngster. We went out to the carriage house where McMurtry kept his personal library. Like Booked Up, it held white floor-to-ceiling shelves. This was where McMurtry kept his Western book collection. My earlier misgivings began to ease. Now we were just two people who loved books.

When I asked what kind of writing projects he was working on at the time, he said he had one more novel he'd like to write. That would be the final volume of the Archer City trilogy, *Duane's Depressed.* Then he added: "I've written enough fiction."

It took a few moments for that statement to sink in. "But you're Texas's most famous novelist. You can't say that!" I wanted to shout. Instead, I nodded and asked why. He said that he was more interested in stories about real people and was working on a biography of the Sioux warrior Crazy Horse.

Of course, I had to ask his advice about writing. He said he wrote five pages every day—no less, no more. It didn't matter if it was a holiday or a weekend. Writing only five pages, he explained, kept him engaged and didn't use up all the good material, leaving him ready to write the next day. Even more helpful was his explanation of the concept of "herding"—that he herded words into sentences, sentences into paragraphs, paragraphs into chapters. That metaphor, which enabled me to visualize writing, was especially helpful with longer magazine pieces and, later, books.

I stayed in Archer City long into the afternoon. We didn't eat lunch—McMurtry said the only decent place back then was El Chico in Wichita Falls and I should go there if I was hungry. But I was too excited to eat. After I said goodbye, I drove back to Fort Worth, exhilarated.

When *Texas Monthly* ran the article in December 1997, the editors chose McMurtry's quote as the headline: "I've Written Enough Fiction." I recall reading a book reviewer's comment that McMurtry's powers as a novelist were fading and it probably was a good idea to shift to nonfiction, but many of his devoted readers expressed shock and disappointment. McMurtry's pronouncement proved premature, of course, and he went on to write more novels, nonfiction books, essays, and screenplays.

In August 2000, I encountered McMurtry in Archer City again when the magazine assigned me to cover the reopening of the Royal Theater. He was cordial, answered my questions, and didn't mention the *Texas Monthly* piece. When I asked him if he saw it, he said he hadn't read it. "I've been busy," he explained. We mainly talked about the Royal. McMurtry said he was pleased that the Royal had been reborn as a multipurpose entertainment venue rather than a movie theater. Why try to re-create something you can't? he reasoned. *The Last Picture Show* theater belonged in the past.

But it belonged in my future. Years later I landed a contract to write a biography of Ben Johnson, the world champion cowboy and character actor who won a Best Supporting Actor Academy Award for his portrayal of Sam the Lion in the film adaptation of *The Last Picture Show*. (The book is scheduled for publication in 2023.)

Director Peter Bogdanovich recounted the story behind the scene in which Sam the Lion and Sonny Crawford, played by Timothy Bottoms, sit by the water tank and Sam reminisces about "old times." The scene arguably won Johnson the Oscar, but it wasn't the scene McMurtry originally wrote. "In the book, it's a totally different story about getting up on the dam and pissing off into the water," Bogdanovich explained. "And I said, 'Larry, this just isn't going to work.' He said, 'Why not?' I said, 'Well, it's not a romantic scene, it's not a romantic image, somebody pissing off a dam. It just doesn't work. You better write something else, something about horses or something.' So then he wrote that other speech, and that's what we used."

During our conversation McMurtry and I discovered that we had something else in common. My in-laws had bought a ranch south of Glen Rose (where I now live), and he had bought the library of Miles Hart, a lawyer in Glen Rose who often corresponded with writers whose work he collected and who he asked to sign his bookplates. That's how McMurtry acquired some letters from the poet Robert Graves—a "little surprise," he said.

I had found a little surprise from the Hart library at Booked Up too—a first edition of *America and Alfred Stieglitz: A Collective Portrait*, a collection of essays about the photographer and pioneering champion of modern art who promoted Georgia O'Keeffe's work and later married the artist. I wanted the book because of O'Keeffe's curious handwritten note on Hart's bookplate: "I have not read this book." McMurtry priced it at $125, which was a lot for me to spend back then. But ten years ago I sold the book to a foreign collector for $250.

McMurtry the savvy bookman likely would have viewed that as a nice return on my investment. He might even have advised me to sell the British watercolor book, currently listed for $250 on antiquarian book sites, and make a handsome profit. But I'm keeping it. The book holds sentimental value, especially since McMurtry's death. It reminds me of that windy day in Archer City when I saw him in his element, herding books instead of cattle and showing a young writer the ropes to lasso her own words.

KATHRYN JONES is a journalist, author, and poet who has written for the *New York Times*, *Texas Monthly*, *Texas Highways*, the *Dallas Morning News*, and the *Dallas Times Herald*. She is the author of a soon-to-be-published biography of actor and world champion rodeo cowboy Ben Johnson, who won an Academy Award for his supporting role as Sam the Lion in *The Last Picture Show*. She is a member of the Texas Institute of Letters.

COLLABORATORS
& CONFIDANTS

Larry McMurtry and Diana Ossana on the set of the *Dead Man's Walk*
miniseries, filmed in 1996 in the Big Bend area of West Texas.

Stirring the Memories

His memories were too sad, his hopes too thin. To have to say things on paper seemed a terrible task, for it stirred the memories.
—Larry McMurtry, *Lonesome Dove*

Larry McMurtry and I shared a love of the humble fried catfish, which may explain how and why we met in 1985 at Mr. Catfish, an all-you-can-eat restaurant in Tucson, Arizona. I had just read *Lonesome Dove* several weeks before and found this occasion serendipitous and intimidating. I managed a five-attorney litigation law firm and had gone out to dinner with two lawyers. Larry was with friends; I was with friends; our friends knew one another. So we joined our two groups and totaled twelve for dinner at a long Last Supper–style table.

I was shy and leery of sitting too close to Larry and the notably brilliant Native American novelist Leslie Marmon Silko, who were holding court in the center, so I huddled down at the very end. They spoke nonstop throughout the meal, sharing stories that grabbed the attention of us all. After dinner, I was introduced to them while everyone headed out to the parking lot. Larry and Leslie were charming and confident; I was introverted and quiet. Although assured in the professional world, I've never felt secure in social situations, and wanted to get out of there with as little interaction as possible with these two strangers, as charming as they were.

Larry and I continued to encounter each other at various social functions involving our shared acquaintances, and we soon became friends. He was polite and erudite and made a point of putting me at ease during our visits. Before long, Larry began arriving at my home for the occasional meal and became acquainted with my young daughter, Sara. When Larry told Sara how the caws of Leslie's beloved parrots and cockatoos, who had come to number in the double digits, drowned out the evening desert sounds, Sara suggested staying with us whenever he came to Tucson.

So began our lives with Larry.

He parked one of several manual Hermes 3000 typewriters, his writing model of choice most of his career, on a desk in the guest room to write his five pages a day every morning. He kept a thick supply of blank paper on the left side of the Hermes while a pile of written pages grew exponentially on the right side. Resting in front of the typewriter was a plain manila folder with his stirrup letterhead, the stationery he used to write letters, special notes, manifestos on the contents of our refrigerator, or an ode in defense of butter and bacon. Extra typewriter ribbons and Pilot's extra-fine-point rolling ball pens lived in a cigar box on the table to the right of his written pages.

A supply of plain Hershey bars and a glass of Dr Pepper on ice rested above the blank pages on the left. Ever the epicurean, Larry would sometimes have a glass of Dr Pepper *and* a glass of milk on the table. We kept five or six retired Hermes from which to cabbage parts. We got used to the sound of the typewriter each day, and it became reassuring to hear the clickety-clack of those keys on the mornings he was with us. It's a ghost sound I sometimes hear even now during those early morning moments crossing between dreaming and waking.

The next several years were spent getting to know one another's histories and families. We took an abundance of road trips, since Larry enjoyed driving, and so did I. We attended the wedding of Larry's son, James—a gifted songwriter and a storyteller in his own right—to the lively, lovely, and creative Elena Eidelberg in 1989 in Austin. The uniquely inspired McMurtry-Eidelberg genes continue in Larry's talented and bright light of a grandson, Curtis, also a songsmith, who was born in October 1990 and shares his birth date with my father.

Some of Larry's happiest moments were those we spent at his Prairie-style mansion with Curtis and my grandson Anthony. When Larry was a boy, his folks moved into a modest home in Archer City from the family ranch house outside of Windthorst. At night Larry would gaze out his window at a big house down the street and imagine living there when he grew up. When the opportunity presented itself, he purchased it and had it restored. It's one of the largest homes in Archer City, the small Texas town where *The Last Picture Show* and *Texasville* were filmed. Five minutes down the road is the DQ where Larry wrote much of his book *Walter Benjamin at the Dairy Queen*. We could walk to the DQ and pick up lime Dr Peppers for the family, a twist on his beverage of choice. A modest Larry McMurtry shrine occupies a wall there.

I always preferred the unassuming comfort and character of Larry's family ranch house outside of Windthorst, which is where Larry and I got to know one another during the first years we spent together. We'd sit outside in the evenings on a decrepit sofa situated on the covered side porch, telling stories or enjoying the silence, the stars, and sometimes an evening rain shower.

Larry, Sara, and I flew to Italy together, where we met my Italian family and saw where my father had grown up. It was Larry's idea for Sara and me to accompany my father to our family's village. Larry had met him and was taken with his European charm and humor. Although I was reluctant—my father and I had had a historically contentious relationship—it turned out to be one of the highlights of our lives, and in fact one of the most intense experiences of my life. Larry believed it was important for my father and me to connect with each other before it was too late. He also said that understanding where we came from, our ancestry, would be valuable for Sara and me.

My father had come to America alone on a ship from Venice when he was fourteen years old, and our relatives are still there, living high up in the Dolomite Alps. We flew into Rome, and my father flew into Milan. My father and my cousin Romano drove down to pick us up and take us north to our family village. Larry was with us in Rome for three days, just long enough to assure him that my father had connected with Sara and me and we weren't left alone in a foreign country. Then he returned to America. His intuition about all of this was spot on.

By 1990, Larry was a fixture in our family and lives. I continued working at the law firm, which had become so successful that a few of our attorneys were inducted into the Best Lawyers of America, a network of nationally acclaimed barristers. Larry began spending longer and longer stretches of time with us and would drive Sara to school in the mornings and pick her up after basketball practice in the evenings. Sara had started playing basketball when she was nine years old and continued to play through high school and into college. Larry eagerly joined me at her games, where he made it clear to us that she was an exceptional athlete. Hauling ourselves to these games in his giant white Cadillac, we drove to venues dotting the Arizona desert and beyond. He would invite a few parents and team members to dinner after a match and regale us with anecdotes about his modest high school basketball career, entertaining us with his singular, self-deprecating humor.

In the second half of the 1980s, at the height of excellent health, I suddenly became gravely ill. I was bedridden for several months. Sara was worried about whether I would recover. Unbeknownst to me, she and Larry had a few conversations about what would happen to her should I not survive.

She asked me one morning what it meant to have godparents. I explained that godparents were close friends of parents who agreed to take care of a child should their parents be unable to do so. I found out after I recovered that Sara had written Larry a letter asking him to be her godfather if I could no longer care for her. He agreed, and by the time she entered high school Larry had taken on that role.

In August 1990, Larry began his novel *The Evening Star*, a sequel to *Terms of Endearment*. He had moved his typewriter and writing layout to my kitchen counter and wrote while Sara and I were getting ready for the day—hers starting with early basketball practice before school, while I was off to work.

One summer morning in 1990, Larry was in Archer City working in his bookstore, unpacking, pricing, and shelving a library he had recently purchased from an estate in South Texas. We would trade phone calls throughout the day, sometimes up to five or six times before a final good-night conversation around nine. The phone rang as I walked out the door to take Sara to school.

"I'm in the hospital," Larry said.

"What?!? What happened?" I said.

"I hit a cow last evening driving the rental Cadillac on the dirt road near the ranch house. The airbag light came on and stayed on," he said.

"Were you hurt?" I said.

"The cow was, sadly, but I wasn't. I was having trouble breathing this morning, but I think it's mainly book dust. I went to the doctor, who said I was having a heart attack, and he ordered an ambulance. The doctors here are trying to convince me it's a heart attack."

"Have they done bloodwork? What do the tests show?" I said.

"They tell me the tests show it *is* a heart attack," he said. He was getting annoyed.

"Then they're probably right, Larry," I said.

"I don't think so. They said I need open-heart surgery, but I don't believe it. They want to do it here in Wichita Falls. I want a second opinion," he complained, ever the skeptic.

"Do you want me to come there?" I said.

"No, I'm getting out of here," he said.

I knew better than to argue with him over the phone, since I carried a lot more weight in these discussions when we were together.

He told me he had been having a hard time taking it all seriously since the EMTs who picked him up from the doctor's office to take him to the hospital insisted that he be placed on a stretcher and carried to the ambulance. Once they discovered he was the author of *Lonesome Dove*, one of the stunned EMTs clumsily dropped his end of the stretcher and nearly rolled him off into the dirt, which Larry found amusing.

Larry washed up on my doorstep a few days later, eager to resume pecking away at *The Evening Star*. That night he told me his friend Nina Matheson in Baltimore had recommended a superb heart surgeon at Johns Hopkins. His surgery was scheduled for early December, nearly four months ahead. The surgeon wanted him to have the operation immediately, but Larry insisted on finishing his novel first.

Larry completed *The Evening Star* on December 1, 1990. On December 2, he flew to Baltimore for his December 3 open-heart surgery. I assumed I would be going with him, but he blew up when I suggested making the reservations for both of us.

"This is an intellectual decision, not an emotional one. I don't need you there," he said.

It was the first time since I'd known him that he'd spoken to me so harshly. I knew not to argue.

The surgeon did a quadruple bypass and, utilizing a new procedure, pulled a mammary artery to pump blood to and through the heart. Physically, Larry's open-heart surgery was a great success. He returned to Tucson in January 1991 and checked into the Arizona Inn to begin his own version of physical therapy, swimming laps in the inn's luxuriously heated pool. Sara and I visited him every day. After several weeks of swim therapy, he was making obvious progress with his bodily recovery, and he resumed his nomadic travels to his bookstores and apartments from Tucson to Los Angeles to Georgetown to Houston to Archer City.

When Larry arrived in Archer City, he called me from the bookstore. I had spoken to him several times a day during his travels, but his voice was barely recognizable that day. He sounded faint and shaky. He told me that he began to feel weak and frightened when he drove up to the bookstore. Larry couldn't tell me why he was so terrified, but he said he needed to get back to Tucson as soon as possible.

I picked up a wan and wobbly Larry from the airport the next day and took him straight home. Thus began his rapid decline into a deep depression and the beginnings of an alarming emotional breakdown.

We sat down to dinner that first evening, and he described to me how he felt like an outline of his former self, as if he were a cardboard cutout, without dimension or depth.

Larry began writing *Streets of Laredo* at my kitchen counter the day after his return. He would get up at dawn, take his bath, put on his blue Oxford button-down shirt, Levi's, black belt, and black Stewart boots, and eat a bacon-and-egg breakfast washed down with a cup of Earl Grey tea. Open-heart surgery hadn't beaten him back from his time-honored eating habits, including Dr Pepper and Hershey bars when at his typewriter.

He'd herd Sara into his rental car and drive her to school, then return home to write during the early morning hours. I'd pop home midday to find him sitting on the living room couch reading one of his five daily newspapers (the *New York Times*, the *Wall Street Journal*, the *Washington Post*, the *Financial Times*, and *USA Today*) or one of his many magazines (the *New Yorker*, the *Spectator*, *Newsweek*, the *New York Review of Books*, *National Enquirer*, and more) or devouring one of his weekly six or seven books.

Larry's editor at Simon & Schuster, Michael Korda (soon to be my editor too), asked whether I might agree to type Larry's draft into my computer so that he would have floppy discs to work from rather than Larry's challenging-to-decipher typewritten manuscript. Michael explained that it would speed up the transcription and copyediting process if I could, for example, correct typos as I went along, and so I agreed. Deciphering the chicken scratch—strikeovers and handwritten notes—on many of Larry's pages was like trying to translate Mandarin. Larry's handwriting was at times illegible even to him. He'd bring his handwritten notes to me to interpret when he couldn't decipher them himself.

As the novel progressed I often found myself near tears while I transcribed Larry's words into my computer. I came into the kitchen one morning and Larry was already at work, tears streaming down his face as he typed. I'd never seen him cry, and it was profoundly unsettling. One set of his five pages was so despairing that I felt compelled to rewrite them, trying to pull the story away from what I felt were irretrievable depths.

I printed them in the morning before Larry began his day's set of pages and sat down at the counter next to him. I explained why I believed he was taking the story down an irredeemable path from which neither the reader nor the character would recover. He frowned and appeared puzzled. I handed him the five pages I had rewritten and asked him to read what I felt would give his Maria the strength she needed to carry on for her two damaged children. Dubious, he took the pages and agreed to read them. I left to take Sara to school and headed to my office.

I didn't return home until late in the day. Larry handed me his work, as he did every evening. I was surprised to discover that the pages he gave me were nearly identical to those I had handed him that morning. The only changes were in the first sentence; everything else was exactly as I had written it. We didn't discuss this at the time, but he brought it up some years later in interviews.

As the novel progressed I made minor changes here and there, but rarely did anything that materially altered the story line. Whenever it did, I'd show those changes to Larry, who never questioned them or asked that I change them back to his original wording. I believe this is in large part why, over time, he came to trust me as a cowriter.

When Larry finished *Streets*, his mood continued to deteriorate. His melancholy deepened, and he stopped writing. I came home midday to find his newspapers and magazines stacked and unread. I bought books I thought he might like, but he never opened them. After some weeks had passed, Larry began to reread books he'd read years before: Marcel Proust's *Remembrance of Things Past* and James Lees-Milne's *Diaries* were two sets he began to read repeatedly, attempting to retrieve and hang on to the self he felt slipping away.

"I feel like *Streets* was faxed to me from my former self," he said during an especially low evening. "I feel like I'm disappearing."

Larry no longer left Tucson for other parts of the country. He hunkered down in my house and sat on the living room couch staring out the picture window at the Catalina Mountains. Sara and I found him like this every day for months and months.

What meager enjoyment Larry seemed to experience was attending Sara's basketball games. It got to the point where he wouldn't leave the house alone.

I was able to coax him out to dinner occasionally or to take walks in the neighborhood most days, but that was the extent of his travels. He insisted on traipsing the roads in his Stewart boots for a year, even after he complained of occasional heel pain. He refused to consider sneakers. I finally purchased a pair of New Balance 990s and tucked his boots away in my closet. He wasn't at all pleased with the prospect of a wardrobe change, but it was the only way I could get him to try on the sneakers.

Larry continued to receive proposals for screenwriting jobs through Irving "Swifty" Lazar, his agent. Offers came in from several directors, including the likes of Steven Spielberg and John McTiernan, but Larry batted away every offer without considering it. I did my best to explain to Irving that Larry wasn't up to the task, but Irving continued sending him proposals.

I sat on the couch next to Larry most evenings. His aura of aloneness was heartbreaking. He occasionally asked about my day and sometimes found the stories of my difficulties and frustrations working with lawyers amusing. But we mostly sat in silence. I'd read or talk on the phone with my boss, who'd call to pick my brain after work about pending trials and concerns about our cases.

Prior to Larry's heart surgery, he awoke every morning with a migraine headache. He would leave the window shades open in his bedroom because he said the sunlight quelled the pain. His morning headaches stopped after his heart surgery, but what took their place was far worse. He'd awaken before it was light, terrified that he was dying. I started getting up before dawn and heading into his room to convince him he wasn't. His terrors happened early every day for almost a year. Tending to Larry and his health and safety became a full-time job. In 1991, I quit working at the law firm to stay home and take care of him.

Before his open-heart surgery, Larry did most of the talking during our conversations on the phone or in person. Every evening after dinner, whether we were in Georgetown, Arizona, Texas, or a hotel, he'd man the phone and talk to four or five different gals, one after the other. During those calls, I noticed that he didn't talk much but mostly listened, commenting now and then as the conversation progressed. I called these sessions their "Therapy with Larry." After he finished these nightly phone visits and before bed, Larry would recount parts of his calls to me, primarily for his own amusement. When I asked him who these women were, he referred to them as "my girlfriends." I asked him if any of these women knew about the others, and he looked horrified at the thought. I laughed, and he glared at me.

After his surgery, when Larry's melancholia intensified, he stopped answering or initiating any calls. He would respond to messages now and then from his bookstore, but he eventually stopped responding to those too. Larry's sadness had begun to bleed into my daughter's life. When I arrived home from errands one evening, Sara cornered me.

"Mama, Larry is so sad it hurts me to look at him. I don't even want to go into the living room anymore. I'm afraid he's going to die."

I hugged her and reassured her that I would figure out what to do, that Larry wouldn't die, and not to worry. She wasn't convinced. She retired to her bedroom and shut the door.

I went outside to the backyard and began to weep uncontrollably. I realized that this couldn't go on, that if it did, the Larry his family and Sara and I knew and loved, the Larry the rest of the world admired and respected, would soon disappear. The stoic, unsentimental son and grandson of Texas pioneers and ranchers was fading away.

Near the end of 1992, almost two years into Larry's hopelessness, Irving called with a job offer for Larry from the producer Jerry Weintraub and Warner Bros.: to write a screenplay about the Depression-era outlaw Pretty Boy Floyd.

I decided then that enough was enough: Larry would take this job, or at least I would do everything possible to convince him to take it. I headed to the main library in downtown Tucson to research Charles Arthur Floyd, aka Pretty Boy.

By the next day I had cobbled together more than twenty yellow legal-pad pages of facts, myths, and conjecture about Charley Floyd. That afternoon I sat Larry down and told him he was going to hear all the reasons he should take the screenwriting job from Weintraub. He rolled his eyes and sighed heavily. But he listened.

I emphasized the truth-versus-myth elements of Charley's story, knowing that Larry's own writing often focused on the opposition between fact and fiction, as in *Anything for Billy*, or in the mythology of "the good old days" against the brutal realities of the history of the West in *Lonesome Dove*. I saw Larry's eyes begin to light up after I'd made it through the first ten pages. By the time I finished he was looking more awake and aware than he had in months and months. I asked him if he'd commit to write the script.

"I'll write the screenplay. But only if you agree to write it with me," he said.

My hope had been that he would be inspired to write again, but I never expected that he would want me to collaborate with him. And I was concerned about whether the studio would agree.

"We'll have to convince Jerry Weintraub and Warner's if you're serious about this," I said.

He got up and called Irving. He explained his conditions for taking this job and told Irving to set up a meeting for us at the studio in Los Angeles. I hadn't seen Larry this animated since before his open-heart surgery in late 1990. If writing the screenplay with him could jump-start Larry back into life and writing, I wanted to do all I could to make this happen.

We traveled to LA and met with Jerry Weintraub, the producer, to convince him that we were the right duo to tackle Charley Floyd's life story. I brought along my vast pages of notes and answered the few questions Jerry had about our take on the script. Larry appreciated that Jerry was one of the last big studio moguls. The producer was a character straight out of central casting: tall, tan, glib, a sharp dresser with a pinky ring, full of self-aggrandizing stories in which he took full credit for the success of the films *The Karate Kid* and *Nashville*. Most of our meeting was taken up with Jerry's swaggering charm rather than talk about the script.

"I just don't want Floyd to come off like a hick," Jerry said.

"Charley was a country boy with few prospects, but we'll see where the story takes us. I can assure you that we'll create characters whom actors will want to play," Larry said.

On the way home, I asked Larry if everything Weintraub told us about himself was true.

"I doubt it, but then he's an example of when sometimes the truth is overrated," he said. "Jerry is sort of the P. T. Barnum of Hollywood."

Our first substantive disagreement working together had nothing to do with writing. When I insisted we hire an attorney to represent us, Larry balked.

"I've gotten this far in life just fine without an attorney," he said.

I felt differently. Larry and Irving had focused on getting as much money as possible upfront on Larry's previous deals; consideration of any back-end or ancillary monies was an afterthought. I'd worked in law for over twenty years and understood how a faulty contract could come back to haunt both parties years later. I didn't back down. I told Larry our partnership wouldn't be possible unless we hired an attorney.

In the end, Larry relented. We were fortunate to have the same excellent legal representation for nearly thirty years. And after Irving became too ill to represent us any longer, we were beyond fortunate to have Andrew Wylie, the distinguished head of the Wylie Agency, take us on as his literary clients.

We discussed how to begin Charley's journey. We agreed that Larry would start first with his five pages a day. I would enter those pages into my computer, adding, subtracting, altering until I was satisfied, then print them out that same day for Larry to move forward from the following morning. Once we began writing, Larry's night terrors began to diminish.

Our writing process was collaborative and without argument. We talked about the story as ideas came to us throughout the days we spent on the project, but our momentum didn't vary. While writing *Pretty Boy Floyd*, the most valuable lesson I learned from Larry concerned momentum. Write every day. Weekends, holidays, no exceptions. Writing with Larry did not allow for laggards. Our main goal was to complete a first draft. I learned early on to minimize the rewriting on my first-draft work and stay focused on my primary goal of finishing my pages for each day. We had a completed draft within weeks. I spent the following month refining, tightening, and restructuring the second draft of the script. Larry left the issues of story structure to me. He no longer had the head for thinking in those terms, he said, and considered it one of the adverse side effects of his surgery. He instructed Irving to accept only screenwriting offers that included me as his collaborator.

When we handed in our completed draft of *Pretty Boy Floyd* to Weintraub and Warner's, we realized that our collective imagination was still brimming with Charley Floyd and his world. We promptly launched into writing a historical novel based upon Charley's fabled and tragic journey. Our process remained the same: Larry handed me his five pages each day, and I entered them into my computer and reduced, edited, increased, and expanded until I felt satisfied with the day's work. Then I would print the pages for Larry to read before moving ahead. Our continuing collaboration on *Pretty Boy* was gratifying, from beginning to nearly the end.

I say "nearly" because our first full-on creative squabble involved the novel's ending. Our disagreement was strictly professional and didn't extend to our personal lives, even though we argued back and forth about this for some days.

Larry's ending was abrupt. My notion was to sign off with the various characters' points of view about Charley, the last being Charley's son, Dempsey, who, as it turned out, was still alive and in his sixties. In the end, Larry agreed to hear from the rest of our cast as an epilogue. By the time we began our book tour, he had forgotten about the argument, and the tour was without controversy. Mostly.

As some years passed and our collaborative life matured, we switched roles: I began the writing, and Larry worked from my pages, each of us moving the other forward as the days passed.

And so it went. From the day I met him, Larry remained a creature of habit throughout our thirty-five-year friendship. In the mid-1990s, when he was able to leave the house and we started traveling again, he insisted on eating dinner six nights a week at our favorite Italian restaurant, Tavolino, just a few blocks from our Tucson home. The seventh night was spent at Sullivan's Steakhouse only because Tavolino was closed on Sundays.

After *Pretty Boy Floyd,* the novel, was published, we spent most of our time in Texas. The rural and unassuming McMurtry family ranch house outside of Windthorst was a refuge from city life and Hollywood, a place where we could relax and recharge. It was a mere twenty minutes from Archer City and Larry's Blue Pig/Booked Up bookstore. We frequented catfish restaurants and barbecue joints in and around Wichita Falls many nights for dinner.

———

Larry was stubborn and bullheaded. He was, on every level, the most intractable human being I've ever known. I learned early on that whatever position I had on an issue, I had to be prepared for Larry to take the opposite stance randomly and unpredictably because he enjoyed the debate. If I felt strongly enough about the issue at hand and didn't budge, Larry would relent, but not without hours and sometimes days of mulish dissent.

In 1997, when I first read the short story "Brokeback Mountain" in the *New Yorker*, Larry's bullheadedness reared up. He refused to read the story: "I don't read short fiction because I can't write it." I rolled my eyes and stood my ground for over an hour until he finally agreed to read the story. Larry often described me thus: "Diana is eccentric in her relentlessness."

In our personal lives, however, we rarely disagreed. We were in synch during interviews. On our book and film tours, we would finish each other's sentences. Larry was by far my biggest fan and supporter. He bristled when someone tried to minimize my role in or contribution to our work. I never doubted his loyalty and support.

I'm often asked about Larry's ability to write such realistic and authentic female characters. Larry knew and understood all of his characters, inside and out, because they came from his endlessly fertile imagination. Often the follow-up question was whether he had the same insight into and perceptiveness about the women in his real life. Real life, you ask? Larry was just as clueless about the opposite sex as the next hapless male. But he was smart enough to know it. He had very little interest in men or in their opinions. He believed that if one wanted to learn about life and emotion, one had to go to women, which is why nearly all his close friends were female.

Larry married the lovely and appealing Norma Faye Kesey in 2011, and we lived in what Larry described as "an unconventional but chosen family" until Larry journeyed on alone in March 2021.

Larry McMurtry was my best friend. He was my touchstone through the deaths of my contradiction of a father, beloved brother, beautiful son, and perfidious mother, and during the losses of our many companion animals. I stood by him through surgeries, illness, and family crises, and he did the same for me. We were blessed with great good fortune, and exceptional children and grandchildren. We remained loyal and devoted friends for more than thirty-five years. Larry was irreverent, contrary, eccentric, unsentimental, loyal to the extreme, and oh so lovable. There was no one like Larry, and there never will be.

There are many hard days without Larry, and I know there will be many more. He was such an integral part of my life, every aspect of it, that he will remain deeply missed. Sara, James, and Curtis remain a great comfort to me. Trust has been a constant challenge for me, and I trusted Larry more than anyone who has drifted into my orbit. The moments of sadness will diminish, but they'll never disappear. Sometimes I sit at the same window where Larry spent so many months looking out at the Catalinas and feel the sadness wash over me, but also the love and gratitude that I had him in my life and how fortunate I was to be an essential part of his life. I learned so much from him. That's a gift no one can ever take away from me.

I'll miss him forever.

DIANA OSSANA, born in St. Louis, Missouri, left a twenty-year career in law at Larry McMurtry's request to begin their thirty-year collaboration, which included two novels, numerous essays, and more than forty screenplays. They were writers/executive producers on four award-winning miniseries. Ossana read the Annie Proulx story "Brokeback Mountain" in 1997 and convinced Larry to cowrite the screenplay and Ang Lee to direct. They received a Best Adapted Screenplay Oscar, and in her producer role Ossana was nominated for the Best Picture Academy Award. She also received numerous other honors for *Brokeback Mountain*, including two Golden Globes and two BAFTA Awards.

The *Moby-Dick*
of the Plains

IN 1969, Larry McMurtry's name was only vaguely familiar to me. I had not read any of his novels, nor his collection about Texas, *In a Narrow Grave.* I had seen and liked the films made from two of his novels, *Horseman, Pass By* and *The Last Picture Show.* I was reviewing movies for *Glamour* as a sideline, salaries for book editors being what they were then, and no doubt still are. A lifetime horse lover and rider, I had developed an unlikely interest in rodeo. I may have been at the time the only subscriber to *Rodeo News Weekly* in Midtown Manhattan and had ridden in the rodeo in Madison Square Garden, although only as part of the opening parade of riders cantering around the Garden in a figure eight, each carrying a state flag (mine was New Mexico's), to introduce Montie Montana and his Wonder Horse Rex, while the band played *California, Here I Come* over and over again and thousands of people twirled little blinking plastic flashlights.

I had met the book agent Dorothea Oppenheimer a couple of times. She was shy and self-effacing, not at all anybody's picture of a brash ten-percenter. She was not one of the big-time agents with whom it was almost impossible to get a lunch date, like Candida Donadio, or Phyllis Jackson of MCA. I do not remember ever having received a manuscript from her.

So I was surprised when she called me at Simon & Schuster. She explained that she represented Larry McMurtry and asked if I was familiar with his books. I replied that I was not, though I had liked two of the films that had been made from them. There was a slight, embarrassed pause. Larry, she said, had not liked either film much. I said I understood that. Not too many writers *do* like films based on their work, hence the prevailing belief that the best thing a writer can do when it comes to film rights is, in the words of the late West Coast superagent Irving "Swifty" Lazar, "take the money and run."

That was not, as I was soon to discover, an approach that appealed to McMurtry. The movie business fascinated him. He knew almost as much about films as he did about books. He was already becoming a successful screenwriter, a pursuit that would culminate in sharing an Academy Award with Diana Ossana for the screenplay of *Brokeback Mountain* in 2005. Throughout his life he would always have one foot in Hollywood and the other in Archer City, Texas.

The reason she was calling me, Dorothea explained, was that Larry had just completed a new novel and was looking for a new publisher. She had heard through the publishing grapevine that I was interested in rodeo, and if that was the case, I might be the right editor for the book. I acknowledged that I was and that I would very much like to read it.

Dorothea's voice was always a trifle cautious and hesitant. "It's very long," she warned. *How* long? I asked. "Over a thousand pages." I explained that length didn't put me off. I had published Susan Howatch's *Penmarric* and R. F. Delderfield's *God Is an Englishman*, both of them whoppers the weight of a brick, and both had been big bestsellers as well as full selections of the Literary Guild, which in those days was a big deal.

As promised, when the manuscript of *The Country of the Horn* arrived by messenger the next day, it filled two untidy boxes. The photocopy was in pale gray type on a slightly paler gray background. I didn't know then that Larry always typed on yellow paper, which the copying machines of the day didn't like as much as white paper. Every page showed cuts, changes, second thoughts, and amendments, either typed or scrawled in with a thick black Magic Marker. I lugged it home that night in a shopping bag, sat down to start it after dinner, and then stayed up all night reading it.

I just couldn't stop, much to the annoyance of my wife, Casey. It wasn't just that there was a lot of rodeo in it—maybe more than most readers other than myself would want—but that Larry stood out as a natural storyteller. All the things that novelists labor to do he did naturally, seemingly without effort. And more important, he wrote well about women.

Not many male American novelists do. From Herman Melville to Norman Mailer, women tend to appear, when they appear at all, as objects, sometimes of desire (as in *The Sun Also Rises*), sometimes of contempt. Seldom are they fully realized as people by male writers.

Larry had the knack, from the beginning, of writing convincingly about women. At the center of *The Country of the Horn* is Patsy Carpenter, torn between the men who aspire to be—or already are—in her life, and like all of them I fell instantly in love with her.

Like an overambitious meal, the book had too much of everything—too much weather, too many highways, too many descriptions of Houston, too many characters, even too much rodeo. It was the *War and Peace* of the Plains.

As for Patsy, in retrospect, she was the kind of girl who looked sexier than she was, as if she aroused stronger passions than she felt or knew what to do with.

Still, I was bowled over. I took the manuscript back to the office and set about convincing everybody who mattered at Simon & Schuster that we had to buy this novel. Not too many people wanted to read a novel that long. But they were willing to rely on my enthusiasm, or at least resigned to doing so. By the end of the week, I had made an offer to Dorothea, who responded to it with rather more caution than I had expected.

Larry, she explained, had a certain suspicion of East Coast reviewers, and of publishers too. Early on in his career he had been pigeonholed as a "minor regional novelist" and had even had sweatshirts made up with that damning judgment emblazoned on the chest. The prevailing view in New York City (and, for what it mattered, in Boston) was that culture virtually ended once you crossed the Hudson River into New Jersey and that Texas was for all intents and purposes culturally off the map.

The big names among male novelists then were mostly New Yorkers and Jewish—Roth, Mailer, Bellow (the last actually more of a Chicagoan). Small-town Texas life was not something that interested most reviewers and editors. Many of them had fled just that kind of small town to transplant themselves in Midtown Manhattan; they had no wish to see tumbleweeds rolling across the highway again, or to read about them. Larry, on the contrary, loved small-town Texas and was a keen observer of the seamier side of it. (Consider Larry's portrayal of Coach Popper and his wife Ruth in *The Last Picture Show*.)

Larry was the Flaubert of towns with one stoplight, like his own beloved Archer City. When Archer City residents talked about going to "the big city," they meant Wichita Falls. I had not as yet discovered that Larry had a certain taste for the finer things in life. He would go on to cut something of a figure in Hollywood as more of his books were made into movies or television miniseries; in Washington, DC, where he opened a fashionable Georgetown rare-books store; and in New York City, when he became president of PEN and developed such a taste for caviar that he had his own table at Petrossian, with a polished brass nameplate on it.

Larry had a special ability to move from one world to another gracefully, without betraying or rejecting either one. He was as much at home at the Academy Awards in blue jeans, cowboy boots, and a dinner jacket as he was when he slouched in an old sweater in the Archer City Dairy Queen, eating Fritos with a side of chili poured into the bag and drinking a Dr Pepper. I had a lot to learn about him.

Dorothea Oppenheimer thought so too. It might be a good idea, she said, for me to meet Larry before we made a deal for the book, to see if I would be someone with whom he would be comfortable. I divined that Larry didn't want an elitist editor who thought he was a minor regional novelist, or a publisher who would treat him as one.

In those days I was eager to travel and had not spent much time in Texas. A quick visit to meet Larry McMurtry seemed like a good idea, and I did not think it would be difficult to convey my enthusiasm for his book—and for the whole subject of rodeo—or to convince him that I was not some snooty, highbrow fiction editor in a Brooks Brothers suit.

It was swiftly arranged that we would meet a couple of days later in the lobby of a downtown Dallas hotel that, coincidentally, was where my mother was living and which my stepfather managed. I dressed for the occasion in what I thought was the appropriate style to demonstrate my interest in rodeo, wearing a Stetson Open Road hat from Montechristi Hats in Santa Fe, cowboy boots from J. B. Hill in El Paso, and a silver bolo instead of a tie.

The lobby was full of tall, soberly dressed men and tall, attractive women. But I could see nobody who resembled Larry McMurtry until it began to empty out, leaving only myself and a tall, thin, bespectacled young man, dressed like a graduate student in a sports jacket and slacks and staring at me curiously.

I walked over to him and asked if he was Larry McMurtry, and he replied, "Uh-huh." As I was soon to discover, Larry said that a lot, and it could cover a whole range of meaning, in this case some surprise at my getup.

We sat down in the restaurant—this was in Larry's pre-caviar days, when he seemed to live entirely on steak and milk. We talked a bit about rodeo, on which he was knowledgeable but not enthusiastic, and horses, on which he was indifferent. He had seen as much of horses as he ever wanted to see back when he was working on his father's ranch, before he went to college.

Luckily for me, I had read his earlier novels in the past couple of days, so we talked a bit about them, and then we talked a lot about *The Country of the Horn*, about which I managed to convey my enthusiasm, together with a promise not to ask for cuts, as his previous publisher had done. By the end of the evening we had formed the beginning of a friendship that was to last nearly fifty-two years.

Although I was Larry's editor during most of those years, I never edited him in the normal meaning of the word. He did not need line-by-line editing; no matter how fast he wrote, it always came out well. The only change I ever made was when the Simon & Schuster sales force complained, to a man (as they were in those days) that they didn't understand or like the title. Nobody at S&S got what "the Horn" meant, and since we were selling the book on the basis of Patsy, rather than cattle, neither did the booksellers. Even I only vaguely assumed that it had something to do with the horn of plenty, rather than livestock.

At that time Faith Brunson of the book department of Rich's Department Store in Atlanta was our go-to on romantic fiction titles, and
she said we should change it. So, with some embarrassment, I called
Larry and asked him if he would mind changing the title. To my surprise, he wasn't wedded to it, but he didn't have any suggestion for a
new one. My wife, who by then had read the manuscript and loved it,
came up with *Moving On*, which was the title of a country song, appro-
priately enough, and Larry accepted it, though with some reluctance.
That title was the only thing in all those years I ever asked Larry to
change, and looking back, I think I was wrong.

A bigger problem with the book was that Patsy cried too much.
Even Casey thought so, and she was no slouch at crying herself. When
I mentioned this to Larry, he took the criticism philosophically; all the
women in his life had cried a lot, he explained, so maybe it was something to do with Texas. In retrospect, maybe part of the problem was
that we were aiming the book at two different markets: women who
wanted to read about Patsy and her problems, and men who wanted to
read about rodeo.

At the American Booksellers Association meeting in Washington—
in those days a huge book event—we handed out bound galleys of
Moving On and buckets of lapel buttons that read I'M A PATSY. Most of
the booksellers wore one, but many of them also complained that while
they *liked* Patsy, she cried too much. Only Charlie Roberts, our Texas
sales rep, didn't complain. He said that no matter how long the book
was or how much Patsy cried, he would get the book put in the window
of every bookstore in Texas, and he did.

Despite a big printing and a lot of advertising, *Moving On* was a
sales disappointment. The reviews were disappointing too. The *New
York Times* complained about Patsy's crying (and described her as "fastidious, disconsolate and prudish"). John Leonard balanced his dislike
of Patsy by calling the book "a novel of monumental honesty, about as
real as your sister." But how many people want to read a 794-page novel
about their sister?

The S&S sales force was not daunted, nor was I. They liked reading
Larry's books, as did I, and over the next sixteen years, each time I

presented one I promised them that Larry would eventually write "the *Moby-Dick* of the Plains." My promise grew into something like a joke. Some of the books in those years were among his best work, particularly *Terms of Endearment*, a richly satisfying novel. Set in the New West rather than the old one, it was made into a wonderful film (which Larry disliked).

When poor Dorothea Oppenheimer died, Larry unexpectedly became a client of Irving Lazar, who had been handling the movie rights for Dorothea's books. This change coincided with the completion of Larry's immense novel *Lonesome Dove*, for which Lazar demanded what was then a huge advance.

When I read it, I was completely bowled over. *Lonesome Dove* was, to use a favorite publishing term of the day, "un-put-down-able." I devoured it in one night, swept away, and told Dick Snyder, my friend and the president of Simon & Schuster, that this was the big book from Larry we had been waiting for all these years, and then some. We bit the bullet and paid Lazar what he was asking for, then geared ourselves up to make a major publishing effort.

That included a more "commercial" jacket than we had put on any of Larry's books since *Moving On*. This was the one area of publishing about which Larry was difficult. He had hated the jacket for *Moving On*, which he thought was too bright and commercial. I loved it, and still do. After all, we were trying to make the book a big commercial bestseller. Paul Bacon's drawing of Patsy seated in a car with the two principal men in her life leaning on each side of the car talking to each other over the top of it had everything going for it. With one of them wearing a Stetson and the highlight falling on Patsy, the cover seemed to appeal to both male and female book buyers. Larry had finally approved the jacket, with great reluctance, but ever since then we had rather toned down his jackets, anticipating his reaction.

For *Lonesome Dove*, however, we were once again aiming for a big commercial bestseller and had the jacket designed accordingly, with a painting of Gus on his horse and Lorena against the background of a cattle drive, with old-fashioned "Western" saloon window type. Larry hated it, but we dug in our heels and appealed to Lazar, who was no judge of jacket art but told Larry, "Look, kiddo, they paid what I asked them to. Let them put whatever goddamned jacket they want on it."

Right or wrong, the book would become a huge, instant bestseller in both hardcover and paperback. It was made into one of the best and most successful miniseries ever put on television, and the book won Larry a Pulitzer Prize as well. When I presented it at the S&S sales conference, I held the manuscript up—it weighed a ton—and said, "Well, here it is at last, just what I promised you all these years: the *Moby-Dick* of the Plains."

Afterwards, Larry successfully tinkered with the paperback jackets until they looked the way he thought the book ought to have looked in the first place. And at some point he actually had a hardcover copy rejacketed with a jacket, designed by a relative, that showed how *Lonesome Dove* should have looked, in his opinion. It is one of my most prized possessions to this day.

Knowing Larry and publishing him over so many years was and remains the happiest experience of my forty-nine years at Simon & Schuster. His creative energy was boundless—showcased by his stewardship of PEN, which impressed me almost as much as his books.

There is not a day when I don't regret not being able to pick up the telephone and talk to him. We had disagreements—never about the books, only about the jackets—but we never fell out. The publication of *Lonesome Dove* remains to this day the high point of my career, that once-in-a-lifetime feeling when you know you have a masterpiece that will be read for as long as people read books, in whatever form they read them.

As important to me as his literary artistry, Larry was a connoisseur of friendship. Think of Augustus McCrae and W. F. Call in *Lonesome Dove*; the relationship between the two men is more important than Gus's romance with Lorena.

Whenever anything important happened in my life, good or bad, Larry was always the first person on my list to call. He was a patient, sympathetic listener, and deeply nonjudgmental. He had a degree of easygoing affability that concealed his razor-sharp intelligence. Once you were Larry's friend, you were a friend for life.

It is no accident that Larry's novels have such a warm core. There are very few mean-spirited characters in his books (one exception being the oldest of the Suggs brothers). There is an elemental humanity in his work that echoes his own character. Success and fame never went to his head. Larry was the least temperamental of authors.

When he was contemplating writing a book on the best pie in America, I accompanied him to Uvalde, Texas, to sample the pecan pie, and to Ponder, Texas, to sample the lemon meringue pie. (Both were terrific.) I was surprised that everyone he encountered seemed to know who he was, even people who had never met him. "Hi, Larry," they'd say, as if they had known him all their life.

I remember with such pleasure lying in bed in the ranch house in the early hours of the morning, hearing the clattering of Larry typing away while a pound of bacon for our breakfast sizzled on the stove. Memories like these, I hope, help explain why I have such deep affection and admiration for Larry.

When Larry and Diana Ossana won an Oscar for *Brokeback Mountain*, my late wife, Margaret, and I broke open a bottle of champagne to toast them. I thought about that celebratory moment a lot during the days when Larry's health grew worse and his medical bulletins grew grimmer.

Larry's left us. But like Gus McCrae, he will always be my dear friend and partner.

MICHAEL KORDA joined Simon & Schuster as an assistant editor in 1958 and subsequently became managing editor, executive editor, and editor in chief. Over nearly five decades, his authors have included Presidents Carter, Reagan, and Nixon; such stars as Cher and Kirk Douglas; the historian David McCullough; the novelists Larry McMurtry, Jacqueline Susann, and Mary Higgins Clark; and theater figures such as Tennessee Williams, John Gielgud, and Laurence Olivier. Korda is now editor in chief emeritus of Simon & Schuster and is working on a book titled *Muse of Fire*. He makes his home on a farm in Dutchess County, New York.

My Long Trail to
Lonesome Dove

WHEN I CAME ACROSS a headline for an obituary of Larry McMurtry that dubbed him "the Novelist of the American West," I had to smile despite my great sadness. How ironic, I thought, that when I first knew Larry he swore he was not going to write a cowboy epic. At the time he was writing about Houston, where he had settled in as a writer-in-residence at Rice University, and I was an impressionable student. Though he liked to say then, in his wry, ironic way, that he was just a minor regional novelist, he was already a celebrity, at least in Houston, after Paul Newman's star turn as Hud had made it clear that the lanky, laconic author of *Horseman, Pass By* was a writer to be reckoned with.

We had met on the Rice campus, and a dinner date led to what would become a long friendship, at first romantic and then long distance. Larry's reluctant, crooked smile and his seemingly limitless repertoire of quirky stories were irresistible. I was too young then to realize that having one of the nation's greatest storytellers as my first boyfriend would have a deep impact on my life.

Larry gave me a number of books as gifts. He was already collecting a treasure trove of rare travel books, which would become part of his legendary "book ranching," as he called his dealings in the book world. I was puzzled by the first book he gave me, an early and undoubtedly valuable edition of a then-obscure memoir called *Tent Life in Siberia*. It was in pristine shape. It wasn't until many years later that I came to appreciate George Kennan's entertaining 1870 account of a failed expedition to build a telegraph line across the frozen tundra of Siberia—and why Larry had thought it important. He eventually wrote an admiring introduction to a new edition of the book, in which he praised the dark and revelatory comedy of Kennan's tour de force of travel writing.

During the time we spent together I was witness to his daily output of pages, rain or shine. I'm reminded of what Willie Nelson said when asked where he got his songs. "I pick them out of the air," he said. And so it was with Larry, whose words seemed to just pour out of him as though they were dictated by the wind. He would leave the typewritten pages he had finished of the new novel he was working on at the time with me to read when he was out of town. That novel, which he hadn't titled yet, became *Moving On*, the first of what would become known as his Houston series. Horses did make an appearance in the rodeo scenes, though most of the cowboys were of the urban type.

Larry had told me that he was a misfit in the ranching world he grew up in, with little inclination or talent for riding horses or exhibiting the macho cowboy spirit. He preferred reading books. From what I gathered, he related much more then to the girls and women of that world, who, like him, did not fit into the cowboy culture—or who found ways to survive in it. I don't think he minded that some of them were better riders than he was.

Patsy Carpenter, the heroine of *Moving On*, was one of Larry's memorable women characters with whom he clearly sympathized, despite their flaws and bad choices. Patsy, for all her adventurous spirit, does a lot of crying in the novel, and I told Larry I hoped I hadn't been a model for Patsy. But in retrospect, I think many of the women in Larry's life, if not direct models for his characters, became his muses, infusing his work with a rare understanding of the plight of restless, unconventional women in a male-dominated world—not what you might expect of such a vivid chronicler of male bravado in the sundown of cowboy culture. The voices of his women characters ring true. It's not surprising at all that so many of the actresses who played roles in the movies made from his books delivered such striking performances.

I left Texas—I thought for good—after I headed for graduate school and eventually went to New York and then Boston to make my way as a journalist. But I suppose I never really left Texas, as I returned so often to write about it, covering events that I felt would make compelling stories. I had learned from Larry how to look for stories that acknowledge but shake up the mythic dimensions that sustain illusions. And so I was there for the great oil bust that humbled Houston, leaving wealthy folks in River Oaks huddled around cheese balls, as one party giver put it, and I followed the surreal progress and meltdown of the Super Collider project in rural Texas, writing a story called "Howdy Super Clyde." I was there to write about the apocalyptic burning of the armed compound of Mount Carmel. I think it was probably Larry's way of understanding the myths and illusions that drove his characters into trouble that inspired my own insight about David Koresh as a latter-day, would-be Texas outlaw.

What I hadn't expected to have in those years was a quiet and then more urgent desire to return to Texas, not as an observer but as a daughter returning home. Later I thought of this internal turning of the needle of my compass as some kind of genetic imperative, like a salmon obeying a latent urge to return to its spawning ground. Or maybe more like the instinct that kept drawing Larry back to the world he had left behind in Archer City. But in retrospect, I've concluded that the actual trigger for that desire to return was something quite specific: *Lonesome Dove*, the novel as well as the TV series. I couldn't get those characters, those places, out of my mind. Somehow I wanted to be back on the edges of that vanishing world before it was gone for good.

Though I never told Larry, I did tell Bill Wittliff, who had written the compelling screenplay for the TV series, that it was *Lonesome Dove* that brought me back to Texas. Bill nodded, understanding that homing instinct; he had begun writing stories that reflected his experiences as a child in the ranching country around the Devil's Backbone, on the edge of the Hill Country. And so it was that when my husband and I crossed the state line from Arkansas into Texas with our rickety moving van full of mostly books, we both shed a few tears, as we felt that we were being greeted by the spirits of our ancestors and by their stories that had been summoned.

For me, those ancestors included my grandfather, with his beloved prancing palominos that he hitched to the old milk wagon he used for delivery around rural Zion's Rest; my Aunt Muriel, a champion barrel racer in the rodeo, whose horse stepped into a prairie dog hole as she was surveying fence posts on a remote stretch of her ranch, tossing her and leaving her to lie on the ground with a broken leg for days; and my cousin Steve, a burly bull rider who died after an accident at the rodeo. The ancestor greeting my husband was a semi-famous cowboy who had taken part in some of the last cattle drives in Texas and who had also appeared in a couple of books, in one of them trading stories at the bar in the old Menger Hotel in San Antonio.

Nearly three decades later, when I heard about Larry's death, I remembered many endearing things about him as I grieved—his matter-of-fact voice with just a hint of a drawl, his serious poker face with just a hint of a smile as he told a zinger of a story. But I also remembered in particular that first rare book he had given me. Though that old edition had disappeared after many moves around the country, I went back to look at the introduction he had written to the new edition. And I realized what a gift that had been, though it took me so long to understand it. Larry had been so much more than the Novelist of the West. Like George Kennan and like the fabled T. E. Lawrence of Arabia, Larry had been drawn to wild and desolate places far from home. But for Larry, it was sometimes the places in the heart that had grown lonely and desolate. And sometimes the untamed yearnings he harnessed in his books were those closest to home.

I like to think that of all the things I've written, what Larry might have appreciated most would have been not my stories about Texas but my account of my adventures on a horse trek in Mongolia that appears in my latest book, *Wild Surprises*. The oldest rider in the group by far, I galloped in the hoofprints of Genghis Khan across the vast Asian steppes on a half-wild horse I nicknamed James Brown, and yes, during bitter cold nights I slept in tents—and yurts—and survived a close encounter with a pit viper on a forbidding peak called Mount Mandal. I think Larry might have been surprised at how far his influence had reached. And how deeply his stories had been taken to heart.

After a stint in academia, **CAROL FLAKE CHAPMAN** turned to journalism, working as a writer and editor for a number of leading newspapers and magazines. Following the sudden death of her husband on a wild river in Guatemala, she wrote *Written in Water: A Memoir of Love, Death, and Mystery* about her journey of grief and healing. Her most recent book, *Wild Surprises: Stories and Poems about Encounters That Shifted My World*, combines journalistic storytelling, poetry, and impressionistic photography to evoke a sense of wonder about unexpected encounters with creatures in the wild that are not merely gifts but revelations.

An Unlikely Bond

LARRY MCMURTRY WAS never late and always fulfilled his promises.

I did not know that yet on the windy evening in late 1981 when he drove up just barely before start time for a lecture at the institution then known as the Fort Worth Art Museum. I was responsible for inviting him, so I had been nervously awaiting his arrival in the vast parking lot the museum shared with the adjacent stockyards, having last heard from him weeks before. The sold-out audience was waiting inside when he rolled up, got out of his station wagon, and smiled his droll smile at me for the first time.

Larry's car, I remember well, was a rather smelly junker, having crisscrossed the country many times lugging books for his Washington, DC, bookstore. It was a far cry from the many Cadillacs he would later own or lease, and the far back of the car on this evening was occupied by a rather stinky basset hound called Franklin. He had named the dog, Larry told me, for a colleague in the book business to whom, Larry thought, he bore some resemblance. Larry said the human Franklin was not amused by this. Larry clearly was.

This meeting in the parking lot was our first beyond the logistical conversations that preceded Larry's visit. I'm not sure why, but an unlikely and enduring friendship was ignited in that moment. I was at the time a twenty-something art curator looking only to draw a crowd to the museum. I had happened upon Larry's books without much forethought except my love for the movie version of *The Last Picture Show*.

I was also a newcomer to Texas, which I looked upon through my New York prejudices as a foreign land. It was a time of great enthusiasm nationally for all things Texan, in part because of the John Travolta movie *Urban Cowboy*. I was curious about the culture, but still quite ignorant. I'd just co-curated and installed an exhibition about literary visual art and was hoping that inviting Larry to speak might draw an actual literary crowd. It did. The hall was crammed that night, and as with all of Larry's Texas appearances, the anticipation was great. Grabbing the text of his speech, Larry laughed off my anxiety and we went inside.

He had an idea that all hell would break loose that night and was looking forward to it. He had brought with him a piece he'd written—to be published soon after by the *Texas Observer* magazine—that lambasted the perpetuation of Texas's Western literary model. In it he named hallowed names and proclaimed the genre over and done with. He pointed to J. Frank Dobie and called his books "a congealed mass of virtually undifferentiated anecdotage: endlessly repetitious, thematically empty, structureless and carelessly written." He gave Roy Bedichek a weak nod for his well-written, "if minor," books. In fact, he declared none of Texas's writers "major," although he said Walter Prescott Webb was better than the rest, even if, in Larry's opinion, he wrote only two important books. (I can recall this all in detail with the help of the actual diatribe preserved on the *Texas Observer* website.)

Being there was like watching the biblical Abraham in the idol shop—killing gods with abandon. After his skewering of Texas's literary idols had clearly shocked the audience, Larry let loose with the kicker of his piece: he was completing his own Western, a book about a pair of aged cowboys that would be published soon as *Lonesome Dove*. Admitting the hubris of disparaging others while proceeding down their road, Larry smiled and closed his notebook. As he stepped away from the lectern, he invited me to have dinner with him.

In preparation for the night, I had read every one of his prior books, awestruck by his stirring narratives and compelling characters—particularly the women. I was already his fan. That night, witnessing the storyteller onstage, I loved the bravado and his ability to be part of this Texas literary club I knew so little about. I also loved watching him be the wicked child, so blithely willing to denigrate that club.

The blowback that followed his talk was just what Larry was looking for. Texas newspapers and magazines glowered at his impertinence while acknowledging that everyone was nevertheless eagerly awaiting this new novel.

Larry's career had been in a bit of a lull. In fact, that night he told me he thought he'd passed his prime as a writer, though he was clearly wrong about that. At the time Larry was just forty-five and, as always, writing a lot, most recently a novel about a traveling antiques dealer called *Cadillac Jack*. He knew that novel was not one of his greatest hits, although it captured a bit of his own striving and itinerant life in those days.

Between the mid-'70s and the mid-'90s, Larry mostly divided his time between the small specialty used bookshop he ran with Marcia Carter in Georgetown and the somewhat ramshackle small house where he had spent his early years on the family's cattle ranch just outside Windthorst, Texas—an even smaller town than the one-stoplight Archer City he'd made famous in *The Last Picture Show*. He also found time to turn out novels, essays, and screenplays. Nonstop.

Larry and I quickly developed a friendship that would be like no other in my life. It would last more than forty years, never really ebbing.

Larry collected friends as much as he collected books. In particular, he had women friends—mostly platonic but with a commitment to endurance. His ranch house was about ninety minutes by back roads from where I lived in suburban Fort Worth, and I would see him most times he came to town. We'd meet in Archer, or Windthorst, or the tiny town of Ponder, near Denton, which had a small steakhouse serving homemade pies to die for. Larry loved to take me and others there, to show off the vintage Texas he liked best. It was a desolate side of the state, and its people tended to be more than a little grumpy, but they all shared a pride of place.

On our first outing, he took me to a movie set south of Fort Worth, where the Australian director Bruce Beresford was shooting *Tender Mercies* with Robert Duvall. Larry and Beresford were in the midst of discussions about a possible future project—I believe it never got made—and Larry was, I think, trying to impress me with his fancy connections (and, I now also think, aiming to impress Beresford by having a younger woman in tow). I immediately got a migraine, so after lunch we left. Oddly, though I was horrified at my anxiety-induced headache, it turned out to be a bonding experience. Larry too suffered migraines, so he told me about his homemade treatments (ice on the forehead while taking a hot bath), then told me he'd leave me at my home for an hour while he went back to his hotel to write a book review for the *New York Times*. He did write it in an hour—an act that still amazes me.

Our friendship was not always so eventful. We had a lot of fun dinners, and I loved his ranch house and subsequently his mansion in Archer City, a large home that he meticulously restored when he became more affluent. For a time I got to know his family well—mainly his sisters and his mother, who was as frenetic as he was, if not as itinerant. Larry was the type, as we used to say when I was a kid, who had ants in his pants. He never sat still for long, and it still stuns me how he managed to read and write so much despite his perpetual itch to keep on the move.

He always had his typewriter with him, and he carried piles of paper—drafts of whatever he was working on. Food was mostly awful in Archer, but I loved the plainness of the town, and we often ate at the Dairy Queen, usually brimming with a crowd of modern-day cowboys, their lines of pickups parked outside. At the Dairy Queen, immortalized in his 1999 book *Walter Benjamin at the Dairy Queen*, Larry would get nods and casual greetings. He was a celebrity, but not loved much, since he really was not their type. More bookish, nerdier. But still considered a member of the clan.

One time he brought his dear friend Diane Keaton to Fort Worth. They shared a love for collectibles and oddities, and he wanted to show her the water park that had opened between Fort Worth and Dallas. This kind of theme park was new at the time. Larry loved the idea of artificial oceans and beaches amid the Texas plains, and he thought Diane would too. I shared a burger with them at a Fort Worth Dairy Queen. No one recognized either of them.

Larry liked to remind me that I was the one who called to tell him he had won a Pulitzer for *Lonesome Dove*, which happened because I was working at a newspaper when the word came across the wires. It was an earth-shattering moment, really, for a small-town "regional" writer, as he had often mockingly called himself. I knew he was thrilled, but Larry's style was low-key. There was no whooping or hollering.

I was lucky enough to attend his wedding to Faye, and I saw a bit of the expansive book haven he created for a while in Archer. As he became more prominent, both as a novelist and a screenwriter, Larry invested even more in the book trade, amassing what would become a city of books in what was once a largely bookless town. We would share thoughts and tales of family. I met some of his closest friends, most notably Diana Ossana, whose partnership and care would be key to his Hollywood success. I knew his son, James, before he was a prolific singer-songwriter, with his name in lights, and I remember many conversations when Larry boasted of James's accomplishments. Later those same thrills would come to him from his grandson, Curtis, also a songwriter. I have followed both of their careers with great pleasure.

As Larry's health declined through a series of heart attacks and other ailments, I would travel to his other home, in Tucson, to visit him and Faye, whom he married in 2011, when he was seventy-five. I was very glad for Faye's presence, as well as Diana's, because I had witnessed how lonely a writer's life can be, even with the many business transactions Larry kept going in the film and book worlds.

He lived largely in his head, consuming information and reconstituting it into vivid novels and essays. Larry's was a vibrant fiction stemming in part from his youth surviving on the plains of North Texas as a boy bred to be a cowboy who was, nevertheless, inept at riding horses. He never stopped dreaming up new projects, even in his last days. I will forever feel immensely honored that Larry dedicated his final novel, *The Last Kind Words Saloon*, to me. As a journalist, I've seen my name in publications innumerable times, but to see it in his book, to be named in print as a dear friend, continues to be breathtaking.

"Don't lose heart," Larry said in his outgoing message on his old answering machine at the mansion, instructing callers to wait for that familiar beep. As many times as I called there over many years, I never tired of hearing that message, not least because it expressed his own profound impatience with waiting even a moment for anything. Right now I can hear those words in my mind as I struggle to keep him alive in my heart. I frequently miss being able to pick up the phone for a quick call to hear his wry commentary. I miss deeply the opportunity to hang out with him at one of his homes.

To count Larry McMurtry as my good friend for more than forty years is a blessing I continue to find unlikely. I only wish that one time along the way I'd asked him, "Why me?" I say this more out of curiosity than modesty. Although all his women friends were fiercely independent, we were not much alike. Our friendships with him took place in distinct realms and rarely overlapped. But when we have met, there's been a recognition of being part of something special. There must have been some shared spark he discerned.

We were all, admittedly, beneficiaries of his generous nature, though we often found it impossible to return the favors. As one example, Larry validated me as a writer by buying me my first computer (a word processor, we called it then), though he loathed computers and barely used the Mac that much later would sit on his large wooden desk in Tucson. He also once bought me the most beautiful custom cowboy boots anyone could ever imagine. And a pink Stetson and boots for my daughter when she was about five years old. Larry loved to indulge.

Inevitably, as restless as he was, our visits tended to be short—a few hours, and then he'd move on. At the end of each visit, whether I watched as he drove away or he watched me leaving, a smattering of Western sparkle and red Texas dust arose in our wake.

SUSAN FREUDENHEIM is a freelance journalist working in Los Angeles. She began her career as an art museum curator, then worked as an art critic based in Texas. She went on to become a longtime arts editor at the *Los Angeles Times* and executive editor at the *Jewish Journal of Greater Los Angeles*. She has also written articles for the *New York Times* and many other publications. Larry's final novel, *The Last Kind Words Saloon*, is dedicated to Freudenheim.

Scenes from a Friendship

I MET LARRY MCMURTRY in 1978 in the lobby of a big new hotel in downtown Houston, I'm not sure which, maybe the Hyatt-Regency. I had no idea he'd be there, but I'd read his books—from his first, *Horseman, Pass By*, through his new one, *Somebody's Darling*, his seventh—and so I recognized him right off. He was standing at the registration desk, looking toward the door. Maybe we nodded in greeting, maybe not. I figure that, being hospitable folk, we must have. I headed toward the desk to sign in.

We were there to participate in a panel discussion made up of writers whose books had been or would be published in paperback that year. I'd come as a stand-in for Max Apple, whose book *The Oranging of America* had made a big splash. Max was a friend. He'd called a week or so earlier to ask if I'd take his place in the discussion. Though he'd promised to participate, he had to cancel for some reason and had already given the organizers my name as his substitute. The book conference was a big deal. Knowing nothing more than that, I agreed to go.

Put all of that together and there, by chance, we were: Larry, famous and an invited guest. Me, two books in, a second-stringer. But when I gave the registrar my name, I heard him say, quite authoritatively, to somebody behind me, "I'll sit by her."

That he preferred the company of women was well known throughout the world of literature and movies and perhaps beyond. That women often returned the favor baffled a lot of men. A former fiction editor at *Esquire* once told me that every time he saw Larry he had a beautiful woman on his arm. He didn't get it. Larry didn't have the looks for it. The contradiction was too much for the editor. He "hated [Larry's] heart."

Maybe by choosing me as his seatmate Larry was making sure he wasn't trapped between two men, I don't know. He'd also written a favorable review of my second novel, *Emma Blue*—also published that year—in the *Washington Post*. Presumably, then, he recognized my name. Whatever the reason, we walked into the conference room together.

Richard Price was there to discuss his current novel, *Ladies' Man*. Shelby Hearon arrived to talk about *A Prince of a Fellow*. There were others I cannot now remember; I was too dazzled to take mental notes or to remember much about the panel discussion or the lunch and drinks we were served afterwards, other than the conversation I had with Larry.

My husband and I were planning a move to the countryside outside of San Marcos, and we wanted to thin our book collection of some three thousand volumes. Aware of Larry's bookseller reputation, I asked if he had time to come by and take a look. Perhaps he'd want to buy a book or two for one of his stores. Or suggest a plan.

I thought he'd say no, pleading a busy schedule, an impending departure. Instead, he took out a notebook, asked for my address, and said he'd be there early-ish the next morning. And that was that. Sheer *presence* was one of his stellar qualities. He showed up on time and straightaway began to whiz through our floor-to-ceiling shelves, his fingers lightly grazing the titles, occasionally making a selection to open and check for edition status, flipping some of them onto their spines. His pace slowed when he opened one particular book. "I'll give you," he said, "$100 for this one." Published in moderate numbers, Tom Robbins's first novel, *Another Roadside Attraction*, had become a huge best-seller. A first edition, my copy was valuable. I had no idea. He could have offered me $10, or 10 cents, and I would never have known the difference.

In maybe half an hour he chose a hundred or so books. But, he said, he wouldn't take them with him that day. "Writers," he said, "change their minds." I should check through his selections, make sure I was ready to live without them. He'd be back the next morning.

And he was. He packed his choices in thick cardboard boxes and put them in the backseat of his car. We asked him to stay for lunch, but he had a schedule and hit the road soon afterwards. He paid in cash.

Our friendship had begun. It was set, for both of us, for the long run.

―――――――

I moved to San Marcos with my family, and we built more bookshelves. Larry and I kept in touch. Now and then he came to dinners in our new house, perhaps on his way from Houston to Archer City. Once, he brought Leslie Silko, another of his deeply invested women friends. When the conversation drifted to things we were afraid of, Leslie said she was afraid of only two things: lightning and bears. That stuck with me.

I sometimes took a break from my life and drove to Archer City. The first time I stayed over I woke up in the early dark to the unmistakable *clack-clack* of a portable non-electric from downstairs. I checked the clock. It was 4:00 A.M. Larry was up, working. The clacking went on without pause for a time, then stopped. The carriage went *s-rrip* as he rolled one completed page up and out and inserted a blank one. The nonstop clacking resumed. When I got up he looked up, left his work behind, said good morning, and we fixed breakfast. Eggs, bacon, the works.

He was polite, had manners, was infinitely attentive. When asked a question, he had a way of anticipating the heart of the query before it had quite been fully posed, a habit that can be annoying, intrusive. In Larry's case, it wasn't. He was there, he was paying attention, there was just so much information inside his racetrack of a mind, categorized and vast, waiting for the hint of an opportunity to emerge. He couldn't wait. At some point the stories, the information, the life, roared straight out. A patient person simply let it happen. I wonder if this is why he could write all those books. The stories, the characters, the dialogue awaited his attention. Once he focused and sat down at the non-electric, everything was there. Which was why, once he released it, he had no interest in going back to make it better.

He was famously generous. I knew that and didn't want to be a mooch, and so I was careful not to ask for what I considered too much. Others, I thought, took advantage of his generosity. When I said so, he shrugged, smiled, and as if flitting away a fly, brushed the idea of *too much* into the far distance.

In 1989, after he'd been elected president of PEN America, I happened to be in New York when he was there in that capacity. He loved fine hotels and was staying at the St. Regis. I should come up, he said. He'd take me to dinner. We had room service crudités and champagne before walking a few blocks to Petrossian, a tiny restaurant known for its many selections of fine—expensive—Russian caviars. As PEN president, Larry took visiting writers there often enough that he'd earned his own personalized table marker, a wedge-shaped wooden block with "Mr. McMurtry" engraved on its brass-plated face.

"I only accepted the presidency," he told me as we sat at his preferred table, "because I wanted to meet Susan Sontag."

She was a PEN activist. Had he succeeded? He broke into the slight chuckle that often came on him, especially when he was amused at himself, something he had done, seen, or remembered. Oh yes, he said, he had brought her to Petrossian a number of times. Susan, he said, *loves* caviar. She could eat a *lot* of caviar.

Petrossian, at that time, presented no menu and offered only three items: the caviars of our choice, topped with crème fraiche and served with bread or blini; ice-cold Russian vodka in shot glasses; and for dessert, crème brûlée. Oh, we were, without question, a long, long way from Texas.

Sometime during the evening I mentioned a trip I was planning for myself and my young grandson Brandon, who was eleven, and my niece Sarah, who was twelve. A kind of summer learning trip to the nation's capital.

He didn't miss a beat. We should, he said, stay at his Georgetown apartment. He'd be in New York when we planned to arrive, but I'd find the key at Booked Up, his used and rare-books store downstairs in the same building. His business partner, Marcia Carter, would have it. He would let her know right away.

The deal was done. My agreement to it, set.

We arrived on a weekend afternoon the following summer and spent much of that night perched near an open window, listening to college students patrol the Wisconsin Avenue sidewalks below as they made their way from one bar to the next. We went to the Mall, did museums, saw friends. On our last night, Larry returned from New York and took the three of us to dinner at an upscale hamburger restaurant just up Wisconsin.

Brandon was a thoughtful child. He had searing blue eyes and expressive eyebrows that, when he contemplated important questions, folded into a deep frown. In the middle of dinner, pausing over his giant burger and skinny, crisp fries, he turned to Larry. His brows pressed toward his eyes.

"Did you," he asked, "get rich off of *Lonesome Dove*?"

The book had come out five years earlier. It had won the Pulitzer, and the miniseries had run. It was a huge success. I was slightly taken aback by Brandon's boldness, but before I could intercede Larry was addressing his question.

"I would have, Brandon," he said, serious in tone and intention, "if I hadn't been elected president of PEN and wasn't staying at the St. Regis."

Brandon nodded.

We left the next morning.

———

Our friendship lasted through many changes in his life and mine. We both traveled a fair amount, and so there were gaps, the occasional yearlong hiatus. But nothing changed. I saw him in Archer City and DC. Never again in New York. He didn't like it there anyway. When his two-year stint was up, he checked out of the St. Regis and went back home.

One night sometime in 2016, I went with friends to hear his son, James, play a regular Tuesday solo gig at the Gallery, a tiny bar above Austin's Continental Club. I'd met James in Archer City and seen him perform there and later in Missoula, Montana. After his performance, when he was packing up, James motioned me over. His dad, he said, was looking for me. He was writing a book about "his women" and wanted to include me. Did I have his phone number?

I wasn't sure why he couldn't find me, but soon afterward I took a trip to Archer City. By then, Parkinson's was curtailing his life in various ways, but he was as amused by life as ever, viewing his limitations—"they won't let me go downstairs anymore"—as an inconvenient joke he had no right or intention to complain about. I met his wife, Faye Kesey. He told me about their wedding and how they'd met up again after so many years. He, Faye, and his writing partner, Diana Ossana were actually living in Tucson, where he could get expert physical therapy for the Parkinson's. He didn't often make it to Archer City anymore. The drive felt long, and they wouldn't let him fly. He had placed photographs of many women under the glass covering of a long table. Cybill Shepherd was there. Diane Keaton. Leslie Silko. And me. Taken on the front porch of the Archer City "mansion" by my boyfriend of the time.

"There you are," he said.

———————

Late in 2017 I received a letter addressed to me at home in his familiar hand, with an Archer City PO box return address.

I tore open the envelope. On a piece of typing paper, he'd scrawled, "Adios Old Friend. Love Larry." And a couple inches below that, "I'm going." I turned the page over to find a couple of typed lines of something he was writing and had given up on.

I called one of his numbers.

Diana answered. When I asked what was going on and where he was, I'd gotten this letter . . . she said oh she knew and yes he was right there and she didn't know why he had written that letter, he was fine

... and then I heard his voice and she handed the phone to him and he laughed at himself in his amused way and said something about maybe wanting attention and I said well he'd certainly gotten mine. He said I should come to Tucson and I said I would.

We set a date for me to fly there early in 2018.

He was living with Diana, Faye, seven dogs, and a pet rabbit. His manager—also a woman—visited often. There was a female nurse who came by to attend to his meds and general health. He was frail, didn't go out much, had a range of physical problems, and wanted to write the "my women" book James mentioned but wasn't sure he was up to it.

Late one afternoon, while many activities having to do with dogs and that night's dinner were taking place in the house, he and I sat outside in the dry, warm desert air, watching the sky change colors, and I wouldn't exactly say we *talked*; on the other hand, the conversation never slowed down or threatened to quit. Mostly I prodded him about one thing or another and just sat back and listened to his mind work its way through the topic. Books. Movies. Mostly people. Diane Keaton? Her sister lived in Tucson; she visited often. And there'd been a celebration of her career in Hollywood. All her men had been invited. He went. Al (Pacino) showed up. Warren. Woody.

"Jack [Nicholson]," he said, chuckling, "didn't show. He's gotten fat and didn't want the others to see him."

By the time we were called in to supper, I'd barely scraped the surface of what I wanted to hear him talk about, the questions I wanted to ask, the things I wanted to hear him hold forth on, disseminate, chuckle at, expound on. Later, we watched the TV news: Larry, three women, and six of the dogs, the seventh having been banned to the back porch for biting out the eye of one of the smaller guys.

He wasn't well. But he was fine—himself, so far.

Although he covered just about every facet of his native state's oddball habits, histories, and eccentricities, in person Larry wore his Texanness lightly. I'm not sure it even interested him that much, except as fodder for the stories and books he wrote. As a result, I never thought of him as particularly Texan. On the contrary. He had cosmopolitan tastes and a prodigious mind and was probably the most erudite person

I've ever known. I've never met anybody remotely like him, and neither, I expect, has anybody else.

As for the question posed by the former *Esquire* editor, I pass that
one on to Joe Percy, one of the main characters in *Somebody's Darling*,
the book Larry came to Houston to talk about in 1978. Early in the
book, Joe—aging, dyspeptic, gone to fat but nonetheless engaged in
a hot relationship with a twenty-something girlfriend who's asking for
sex in her car—addresses the question:

"I get a certain mileage out of incongruity, but in fact my success
with women . . . is due to nothing more than a capacity for attention.
This capacity is not mysterious, but it is rare, in a man."

BEVERLY LOWRY was born in Memphis and grew up in Greenville, Mississippi. She is the author of six novels and five works of nonfiction, including
her latest book, *Deer Creek Drive: A Reckoning of Memory and Murder in
the Mississippi Delta*. Her writing has appeared in the *New Yorker*, the *New
York Times*, the *Boston Globe*, *Vanity Fair*, *Rolling Stone*, the *Mississippi Review*, *Granta*, and many other publications. She has received awards from the
National Endowment for the Arts, the Guggenheim Foundation, the Texas
Institute of Letters, and the Mississippi Institute of Arts and Letters. Lowry
lives in Austin, Texas.

Not So Silent Women

LARRY MCMURTRY.

I first read that name in 1961 when a friend handed me a copy of *Horseman, Pass By*, Larry's first novel. Since I was furiously writing at that time, working on a novel and a play, I was thrilled to see that a young person my age had published a novel set in Texas. When I finished reading, I closed the book with ardent admiration and respect for its author.

I was encouraged that this contemporary writer, a friend of a friend, had broken through old myths to present a Texas I recognized, one where tensions were building between rural ways and the newly developing patterns of life. Larry's novel was a clear break with the prevailing image of Texas. He knew small towns were destined for "the last picture show"—and he caught the movement of those wrenching changes in his book. For me, his writing had the ringing sound of truth.

When I finished my own manuscript a few months later, I put it in a box, not sure about it, afraid it wasn't worthy of making its debut in the book world. I knew little about the literary scene. But I doubted there would be interest in a story exploring a woman's life during the 1950s in a small Texas town. Pregnant with my second daughter, I turned to my chores as a wife, mother, and part-time employee. This was some years before the women's liberation movement, though I sensed something stirring, something brewing among women, including me.

It took three years and reading Larry's second novel, *Leaving Cheyenne*, for me to work up enough courage to send my manuscript to publishers. *Hannah Jackson* was published in 1966. It got some good reviews and mentions in a couple of women's magazines, won two awards, and sold out the first printing. The award-winning screenwriter J. P. Miller wanted to adapt my novel into a motion picture, but he could not find a producer and the movie wasn't made. The play I had written was published in *The Best Short Plays 1968*, but there were only two productions of it.

While I was encouraged to have my work published, I had to earn a living and I could not see a way to do that with writing as my main focus. I was a young woman from the hinterlands with children to support, and the literary world seemed a masculine bastion. (Thank goodness this is no longer true.) I did not know how to make my way in that world, which I perceived as dominated by male competitiveness.

As a female of my time and place, I was more comfortable with collaboration than competition. So I found myself standing on the edge of the literary arena, watching and listening. Fortunately, I had a number of friends who were focused on books and writing. They often talked about Larry and his work. They included Grover Lewis, who had been a close friend of Larry's at North Texas State, and Jim Brown, a professor who taught both Grover and Larry at that school.

Everyone was awed by Larry's diligence and commitment to writing. For many aspiring Texas writers in the early 1960s, Larry was the shining light, leading the way and setting the pace. His early novels pushed beyond the surface of Texas life to explore the facets, layers, and depths of characters who at first glance might seem straightforward and uncomplicated, but who turned out to be subtle and complex.

Larry created imaginary people who fulfilled William Faulkner's standard for the successful development of fictional characters: they "stand up and cast a shadow." One aspect of Larry's writing that impressed me was his deft portrayal of women. In his novels, the women leap from the page in ways that surprised me.

Larry grew up in a multigenerational household with relatives living close by. So did I. But what Larry wrote about the silent and stoic women in his family was different from my experience. I spent my childhood hearing women talk. In the kitchen, in the garden, at the sewing machine, at the quilting table, washing clothes, ironing them, cleaning the house, tending animals and children, and cooking, cooking, cooking, the women were endlessly talking. Except when men were around. Then they were silent. They listened.

Larry claimed that most of the women he encountered around the ranch or in Archer City were as silent as cloistered monks. Yet the women in his books are anything but quiet. They are vibrant, active, complicated, and multidimensional. Perhaps that's because the women he was meeting in his adult life were complex, intricate, many-layered. And, as always, he was paying attention. Maybe he realized that what the stoic and silent women of his childhood kept quiet about was now being spoken, written, argued, and yelled.

As his novels evolved, I noticed subtle changes in his portrayal of women as they energetically redefined their roles—a transformation that created complications in their relationships. Larry's novels showcase his keen perceptiveness and insights about how societal change affected women's actions, language, behaviors, and choices. He observed how change set consequences in motion for people, often without their knowing. Even as he captured the dynamics of young women and men moving from farms and ranches to cities and suburbs, he marked the fate of those who stayed behind.

In Larry's novels, readers experience the ways in which change tears at the fabric of families and communities. At the same time, Larry conveys the sense of loss and sadness that often accompanies transformation. Still, there is a glimmer of hope in the way his characters—despite turmoil and pain—find ways to sustain themselves and maintain connections, however frail.

In 1967, six years after I first heard his name, I met Larry. I was doing research for an exhibit at HemisFair '68, a world's fair in San Antonio where I had a full-time staff position. I was going to Houston, and mutual friends put us in touch. Larry invited me to stay at his home for the three days I was there.

Upon arrival, Larry invited me into the kitchen for tea, and there we stayed for several hours, talking. We talked about relationships. (Larry was divorced and raising his son, James; I was recently separated and raising my two daughters.) We talked about our children and our lives, about our mutual friends and fellow writers. And we talked about the role that books and literature played in our lives.

Both of us had grown up in a rural home and community where books were not available. Purely by accident, we both stumbled upon some books that fed our hunger for more reading. Yet our obsession with reading and writing would, in some ways, alienate us from our families and communities because they had little interest in our love of literature.

For Larry and me, books were the spine of our lives. They were the organizing principle around which we built our days, each of us in our own way. I was touched when, a year after we met, Larry included me on his short list of young up-and-coming writers "whose light can be counted on to burst upon the world at most anytime," as he wrote in his essay collection, *In a Narrow Grave*.

I saw Larry a few times after he put me on his list of promising Texas writers. Now, all these years later, I regret that I never spoke with him about my shift from writing novels and plays to creating exhibits and public places. I was still telling stories, but through objects and exhibits and buildings and landscapes—not just with words and publications. Most importantly, I found myself in a collaborative work environment with many men and women from various disciplines creating big physical experiences for millions of people from around the world.

I wish I had told Larry that this career path worked for me as a mother with children to raise, support, and educate. With his books, films, and essays, Larry changed, enriched, and enlarged the public's understanding of Texas and the West forever. And during my forty years of placemaking, I could participate in helping shape people's sense of place in projects not only in Texas but in many other places. That made Larry's work and mine deeply satisfying.

Today Larry's luminous literature informs our understanding of Texas and our sense of identity as Texans. That's his legacy. Larry McMurtry and Texas; they are linked forever.

SHERRY KAFKA WAGNER grew up in Arkansas and studied with Paul Baker at Baylor University. She attended the University of Iowa, where her novel *Hannah Jackson* was developed. Her professional occupations include author, urban planner, and historian. A Loeb Fellow at Harvard University, Wagner consults nationally and internationally for museums, aquariums, parks, and urban projects. She has also published a play and several children's books. *Hannah Jackson* was republished in 2020 by Texas Christian University Press as part of its Texas Tradition Series.

Road Trip Tips from Larry McMurtry

THE DETAILS ARE FUZZY all these years later, but one day in 2002, on assignment from *Texas Monthly*, I pulled into Archer City, wandered the aisles of Booked Up, bought a few titles, then checked into the Lonesome Dove Inn, having no idea that within a few hours my orientation in the world would slightly, but permanently, shift.

I was sitting in my room collecting notes when a chatty little girl around four years old marched in and did a headstand. We got to talking, then she skipped out into the hallway, and I took a rest before preparing to go back out on the town. A little while later, there was a knock at the door. Larry McMurtry was standing there with the preschooler and her mother, who introduced herself and asked if I wanted to go out to dinner with them.

Like a lot of writers and readers, I was already a fan of McMurtry's work by my twenties: the novels, the essay collections, the movies, the bookstores. But I was caught a little off guard by the invitation, as I had always heard that in person McMurtry was a crank. Some of my best friends have been cranks; that reputation on its surface didn't scare me. Still, there are different strains of cranks, and some are a real pain in the ass. Now here he was—as enthusiastic as one could be without smiling.

Was there even a real choice? Of course I said yes, and once our foursome piled into McMurtry's car, he started up the highway to a Wichita Falls Tex-Mex restaurant. Along the way I learned he was a gracious and chatty variety of crank, a storyteller in the campfire tradition. He name-dropped to keep the conversation rolling after we got to the restaurant, and the gossip he offered was so captivating, it didn't even matter that many of the stories he offered involved actors and others I'd never heard of.

I kept wondering: *What dream am I having?* Sitting before me was a keen observer known for cutting through the bullshit—a guy who once wrote that some outsiders found Texans "dangerously vulgar, but the majority just find us boring"—and somehow I had not yet been cast out of his sight before the waiter brought in the enchiladas?

I should probably explain here that I was born a painfully shy person. Journalism has been my therapy, the work that forces me out of my safety zone. But in 2002 I was still very much leaning on an impulse to reflect or deflect any attention that came my way. I also wanted to milk this experience. So I searched for some topic that would prompt him to share some expertise.

Luckily, I realized, I had just the thing. Here before me was a road tripper who thought hard about observational writing. So I mentioned my purpose for being in Archer City: I was writing about Texas Highway 281 from Wichita Falls to Brownsville, because I loved the travel writer Jan Morris's travelogue about that highway and I wanted to see the road for myself.

If you can imagine Frank Sinatra showing up in a karaoke bar in some far-flung country where someone asks if he wants to sing a few numbers, McMurtry's response was like that. He took it from there. He told stories about Morris, he offered book recommendations like Eric Newby's *Slowly Down the Ganges*, he lent insight into how to think about a road. (How many writers had thoughts on that?) I would never have anticipated such generosity.

Just as surprising: he radiated acceptance. Rather than expecting me to earn worthiness, which is how most strangers operate—especially strangers of the opposite gender—acceptance seemed to be his baseline. The vibe wasn't leering or lonely or suggestive either. This was more fraternal or avuncular, like he'd known all of us for a long time. Since a few men I knew gave contrary reports, I theorized that maybe Larry McMurtry just loved hanging out with women—a notion I enjoyed entertaining for years afterwards. Occasionally, I would recognize this trait in a man, though it remained rare. I even referred to it with close friends as "that McMurtry thing."

When I got back to Austin, I told a few friends about my encounter—something along the lines of "Good morning, how are you, I had a conversation with Larry McMurtry, and I did not spontaneously combust." I might as well have told them I met a chupacabra and it served me the most delightful orange scones. Did I have a photo? one friend asked. I didn't, though I had dozens of blurry photos of the roadside.

After my story on Highway 281 was published, a few friends asked if I was going to send him a copy. My response was, "Hell no." If his sentiments in his 1968 "Southwestern Literature?" essay still held, he was someone who wanted to post a declaration and let other writers rise to the occasion, but he wasn't volunteering to monitor the situation. I didn't expect to hear from him again, and with the exception of a brief phone interview I conducted with him years later, I didn't.

Still, I suspect he understood how much that invitation and that conversation meant to a younger writer. The interaction was invaluable to my sense of possibility, literary and otherwise, and led me to imagine: *If this is what I can stumble across only 26 miles into a 650-mile route, what other surprises lie ahead?*

KATY VINE joined the editorial staff of *Texas Monthly* in 1997 and became a staff writer in 2002. As a general assignment reporter, she has written dozens of features on a range of topics, including the rocket scientist Franklin Chang Díaz, hip-hop legend Bun B, barbecue pit masters, the cult leader Warren Jeffs, refugees in Amarillo, the Kilgore Rangerettes, a three-person family circus, an accountant who embezzled $17 million from a fruitcake company, and a con man who crashed cars, yachts, and planes for insurance money. Vine's stories have been anthologized in *Best American Sports Writing* and *Best Food Writing*.

CRITIC & CHAMPION

"The Holy Oldtimers," illustration by Ben Sargent. Cover of the October 23, 1981, edition of the *Texas Observer*.

To Hell with the Sunny Slopes

"NOTHING SHORT OF INSULT moves people in Texas," Larry Mc-Murtry once wrote. "Gentle chidings go unheard. In these parts the critical act has never been accepted, much less honored: Literary criticism generally means two writers having a fistfight in a bar."

He came to this wisdom over the course of decades as the Grand Inquisitor of Texas literary criticism, beginning with his 1967 essay "Southwestern Literature?" and continuing fourteen years later with the vehement doubling down that was "Ever a Bridegroom."

This second thunderclap was the more truly comparable to H. L. Mencken's American South–directed "Sahara of the Bozart," a true scouring of a cupboard almost bare. Looking back on the two essays now, the first reads as a gentlemanly shot across the bow of the creaky vessel that passed for Texas literature up to that point compared to the torpedo amidships that was "Ever a Bridegroom."

The first now seems merely a gentle remonstrance of the "Holy Oldtimers," that trinity of Texan scribes whom one simply had to revere at the time to be considered a cultured True Texan: the naturalist Roy Bedichek; the folklorist J. Frank Dobie; and the historian Walter Prescott Webb. (Actually *reading* them was optional; reverence was mandatory.)

McMurtry went out of his way to find something to praise about each of them—Bedichek's prose style, Dobie's sheer energy, and Webb's ability to come up with a major, if not truly great, work of history in *The Great Frontier*—but concluded, presciently, that their works would not stand the test of time. Texas had produced no great fiction, and among Texas poets, only the caged lyric poet songbird of Houston, Vassar Miller, had made lasting work, McMurtry concluded in both of his essays.

"At the time the piece was thought to be harsh, not because I had questioned the existence of a Southwestern literature but because my attitude toward the Holy Oldtimers . . . was less than reverent," he wrote in "Ever a Bridegroom" (the tone of which can be gleaned from its subtitle: "Reflections on the Failure of Southwestern Literature").

"In fact, it wasn't much less than reverent: The books of all three men were given more in the way of praise than they really deserved."

Almost fifteen years after he'd challenged the state to try harder, little had changed. Our fiction was still mired in the state's rural past, in McMurtry's parlance a "country and western" literature, a long and tiresome litany of lessons learned in the hardscrabble fields of yore. It was as if Spindletop had never occurred, dragging Texas behind it into a prominent place in the world economy, or as if the state had not, in the twentieth century, sprouted large, well, *population centers*, if not quite what McMurtry would agree were *cities* in the proper sense of the word.

Texas literature remained yoked to the state's past as the western-most outpost of Dixie, a place of dirt farmers and cotton blights and rigid social structures. The South as "the South" held almost no interest whatsoever for McMurtry. On a rare foray behind the Pine Curtain recalled in *In a Narrow Grave*, McMurtry took in the Old Fiddlers Contest in Athens, one of deep East Texas's most culturally Southern county seats, and after escaping back to the almost-West of a Dallas burger joint, McMurtry dismissed the South as a region for which he "could summon no wonder."

"The South is memories, memories. It cannot help but believe that yesterday was better than tomorrow can possibly be. Some of the memories are extraordinarily well-packaged, it is true, but when a place has been reduced in its own estimation, no amount of artful packaging can conceal its gloom." (He was likewise no fan of its geography—piney woods and hardwood forests alike gave the writer of huge skies and expansive vistas the fantods.)

McMurtry believed that the future of Texas literature was urban and Western, not rural and Southern, and in those two sweeping statements, and in the aftermath of the third, there was an Old Testament process at work. He came first as a prophet in 1967. Fourteen years later, he returned as a vengeful destroyer of worlds, saddened and angered by our (and his own) failure to heed his earlier words. Ever after that day, leading by example if no longer by diatribe, he was a creator of the new, remaking in his own image the world he had twice decried.

Through it all, he remained at bottom the same writer he'd been in the early Thalia novels, written in his mid-twenties: a rattler of cages, a kicker-over of anthills, a squirm-inducing truth-teller. After 1981, his themes came into sharper focus and his prose became even more vivid, the sly humor more pervasive, and the dialogue more sneaky-profound while remaining believable all the while.

Around the time he wrote "Ever a Bridegroom," he was in something of a holding pattern. With only one future sequel between them, neither of the two novels he published around that time—*Cadillac Jack* and *The Desert Rose*—blossomed into the sprawling multivolume sagas that came to define his fiction; in retrospect, they feel like failed, if entertaining, experiments.

And so like many a true genius, he utterly contradicted his prior screeds. As if he'd never preached the gospel of urban and modern, he set to work on an epic Western he believed to be a parody but that instead became the standard.

Only by steeping himself in a past he was uniquely equipped to portray could he drag our literature into the present and guide the way to the future.

"My grandparents were—potent word—pioneers," he wrote in the semi-autobiographical 1999 essay collection *Walter Benjamin at the Dairy Queen*.

They came to an unsettled place, a prairie emptiness, a place where no past was. . . . I spent every day of my young life with [my grandparents] and, consequently, am one of the few writers who can still claim to have had prolonged and intimate contact with

first-generation American pioneers, men and women who came to
a nearly absolute emptiness and began the filling of it themselves.

As those lone prairies had been to William Jefferson and Louisa
Francis McMurtry, so Texas literature had been to their grandson: a
void he came to fill all by himself.

One senses a drive fueled by compensation. He'd been an utter failure as a cowboy. He didn't even know what he should be frightened
of in that dangerous line of work, he once admitted. "Throughout
my cowboy childhood the contrast between what I should have been
afraid of—snakes, bulls, stampedes—and what I was actually afraid
of—poultry and shrubbery—was ignominious," he recalled in *Walter
Benjamin at the Dairy Queen*. "The most frightening factor in my early
childhood, hands down, was poultry, with trees and shrubs a close second. . . . I was a young cowboy who hated his horse and feared almost
every animal on the place."

And yet his mindset remained that of the pioneering rancher. When
he set out to transform Archer City into America's Hay-on-Wye—the little Welsh village that is home to many, many books—he saw himself as
assembling a huge herd on a vast ranch, a Charlie Goodnight or Shang-
hai Pierce of the printed page. He could conceive of books themselves as,
even more than steers, elements of nature—as when the Indian tracker
Famous Shoes of the Lonesome Dove series calls printed words "tracks
in books."

But above all else he saw himself as a pioneer—he pushed the literary line of settlement westward, always westward, literally and figuratively past the chain of forts and deep into the figurative "Indian
Country" where he alone dwelled for generations, and perhaps remains
alone even today.

By 1981, he had learned that it had to be done with at least as much
bile as sugar.

By then, McMurtry felt free to say that the sainted Dobie's works
had come to read like "a congealed mass of virtually undifferentiated
anecdotage: endlessly repetitious, thematically empty, structureless

and carelessly written." Bedichek's *Adventures of a Texas Naturalist* and *Karankaway Country*, while written well, had little to say.

While McMurtry still had praise for Webb, it was qualified with the caveat that Webb's best work still seemed ahead of him when he was killed in a car accident, as he was the unusual writer who improved over time. Webb's historical writing was at its best, McMurtry pointed out, the further he stayed away from sacred cows like the Texas Rangers, over whom he tended to fawn, glossing over their innumerable borderlands atrocities.

"Time has begun its merciless winnowing; today the sheaves these three men heaped up look considerably less substantial than they seemed only fourteen years ago," he wrote. And that winnowing has only continued. Wikipedia is not a scholarly source, but it is a reasonable gauge of the popularity of its entries. While each of the Holy Oldtimers has rated a decent-sized biography, only one out of all their collected works—*Coronado's Children*, Dobie's attempt at a map to lost Spanish treasures—rates an entry of its own, and that one only a terse, two-line description.

His second fusillade complete, McMurtry vanished again to his figurative mountaintop. And then, in 1985, he emerged from the clouds with the great thunderclap that was *Lonesome Dove*, a confoundingly unsuccessful attempt to parody the Texas Rangers. Perhaps he really did set out to portray Call and Gus as the Texan Don Quixote and Sancho Panza, but he wound up giving us a taciturn William Tecumseh Sherman and a gallant frontier Robin Hood. Or maybe Waylon and Willie at the head of a mighty herd. In any event, it quickly became the most beloved work of Texas fiction of all time, a phenomenon, less the parody he intended than an exemplar of what Western historical fiction could be—a narrative peopled with characters whose complex motivations revolve around the eternal questions of mortality, duty, and love, set against the merciless backdrop of a rugged continent in turmoil. And all of this he captured in cinematically vivid prose peppered with alternately humorous and profound dialogue.

In practicing precisely what he did not preach, Larry McMurtry wrote us a new testament. I think the term Great American Novel is a tiresome phantasm: there cannot be only one to last over centuries and across such a wide array of disparate terrain and diverse peoples. There can be American novels that are truly great, however, and I believe *Lonesome Dove* will stand among them so long as people are entertained by amazing and masterfully told stories.

———————

As a fifty-one-year-old man, I am fortunate to have come of age in the post-McMurtry-fied Texan culture. First, as an aside, though an important one, it must be noted that his influence on Texas cinema was enormous. Aside from his own filmed work, especially *The Last Picture Show*, it's hard to imagine the diverse array of films that includes *Lone Star*; *Paris, Texas*; and even *Fandango* getting made were it not for McMurtry. Was *Reality Bites* the bratty Gen-X daughter of *Terms of Endearment*? Would there be a Richard Linklater as we know him, or would he have had to take his talents to Hollywood? In some ways, McMurtry's dream of a sophisticated urban Texan storytelling has been fulfilled more on film than in print.

As for the written word, though my ancestors were friends with Dobie and Bedichek and always spoke highly of them as men, it was not their works my own father passed down to me to read but McMurtry's novels, which I began to not so much read as consume around age thirteen. And so, instead of Bedichek's musings on mockingbirds or Dobie's tales of buried Spanish treasure, as a young teen I read *Cadillac Jack*—whose life on the road and amorous adventures I found extremely appealing as a virgin without a car—and *Texasville*, my out-of-sequence introduction to Thalia.

Neither of these is regarded as among McMurtry's major works today, but I was hooked and well attuned to his prose style, if not his scope, when a copy of *Lonesome Dove* fell my way, luckily on a day when I had a plane to catch. Nothing I have ever read absorbed me so completely. I can't quite remember the exact number of hours it took me to finish it, but I reached the end well within a single day, and I've read it several times more since then and watched the entire miniseries, oh, about ten times. (One of my profoundest regrets was failing, as a freshman at UT-Austin, to answer a cattle call ad in the *Austin Chronicle* for *Lonesome Dove* extras. Maybe, just maybe, I could have been one of the many cowboys to have died on that long drive north.)

Throughout my twenties I was in and out of the McMurtry catalog willy-nilly. While backpacking in Poland, a paperback copy of *All My Friends Are Going to Be Strangers* was pressed into my hand by a very good friend of mine who was not known as a literary sort but nevertheless had been completely won over by this incredible book based in Houston about confused twenty-somethings like us.

The book spoke to my friend, and to me, in a way *Catcher in the Rye* had not in high school—nor ever did—because it spoke our language and employed our landmarks, dialect, and culture. In later years I would learn from North Texas–raised friends that *The Last Picture Show* had played much the same role for those who came of age near the Red River.

Through these works I came to realize that most literature—or art in general—is provincial, that a book like *Catcher in the Rye* was presented to all of America as definitive of adolescence because, and only because, it most closely resembled the adolescences of the nation's most influential critics. The same goes for music—why was it that I, a native Texan, was expected to feel the same resonance with the music and lyrics of Bruce Springsteen when Guy Clark, Steve Earle, and Townes Van Zandt were closer at hand and writing about a world I knew far better than the Jersey Shore or other woebegone Rust Belt dystopias? Again, it was simply because that music spoke to critics who lived a world away but who, blinded by their own more favored provincialism, had come to believe that theirs were the only voices that mattered.

I learned to believe that if something did not speak to me, I should not try to force it to on the say-so of others. As a music critic, I didn't have to worship at the altar of Bob Dylan or the Velvet Underground if I didn't want to, and that was okay: I could prefer Dylan's students, like Van Zandt, Joe Ely, Clark, and Earle. And there was nothing wrong with my failure to connect with the nihilistic poetry and bleak too-cool-for-school rock of the Velvets when it was abundantly plain that the various incarnations of Doug Sahm simply seduced me without making me feel like I'd been assigned homework by cadres of imperious New York critics.

Which is not to say that I became protective of all things Texas. In recent years, our state's regional country music scene has far too often devolved into a place where hit songs that seem to have been penned by the state tourist board predominate, with lyrics that seem like little more than the repetitive chanting of state signifiers, devoid of context save for the twangy music behind them—mindless litanies praising barbecue and beer and "ol' San Antone, the Fort Worth Stock Show and the Houston Rodeo" and name-checking the likes of Waylon and Willie.

There seems to be an enormous amount of insecurity in these constant reminders of the simple pleasures of our state. And in their defiantly Texan, as opposed to American, point of view, this music reflects the narcissism of small differences that also afflicts the Scots. It was once pointed out to me that only Scotsmen and Texans sing songs about yearning to be in Scotland and Texas when that is precisely where they are standing while wailing those laments.

The great failure of these middlin'-to-bad (if often popular) songwriters is their lack of depth. Their songs preach without revelation; you feel like the beer-breathed performers are yelling the lyrics in your face while jabbing a stubby finger in your chest and droning on and on about how Texas is the best. McMurtry encouraged us to write of the land and people as they are. He gave me the courage to unmask the chest-jabbers, repeatedly, from whatever pulpit I occupied at the time, be it that of a full-time music critic or just another aging old man yelling at clouds on Facebook.

It's a cultural milieu I've been fortunate enough to take for granted. For that I must add my gratitude to my continued sense of wonder at the works of our first, and so far only, Great American Man of Letters.

A descendant of the Lomax song-collecting family, **JOHN NOVA LOMAX** was a music critic and staff writer for the *Houston Press*, a staff writer for *Texas Monthly*, and most recently a writer-at-large for *Texas Highways*. In 2008, he was honored at the Lincoln Center for his ASCAP-Deems Taylor Award, garnered by his *Houston Press* profile of the tragic country singer-songwriter Doug Supernaw. He also wrote for the *New York Times* and the *Houston Chronicle*. In May 2023, Lomax, a friend and colleague of many writers in this collection, died at age fifty-three after a long illness.

Writer, Pass By

IN 2001, I wasn't exactly a rising star in the literary world.

When I wasn't working at the Texas Department of Transportation in Wichita Falls, Texas, most of my free time that year was spent printing, cutting, and gluing pages together to make a small paperback book tentatively titled *There's a River Down in Texas*. When I wasn't busy with that, I was mailing out query letters to agents and publishers, hoping someone would take a look at my coming-of-age saga about a thirteen-year-old boy living in a small Texas town in the 1960s and consider publishing it.

At the constant prodding of my sister, Barbara, I finally relented and mailed a copy of my first novel to Larry McMurtry. He and I had never met. Sheepishly, I included a note explaining that I was also from Archer City and would appreciate any thoughts he might have about my book, should he find time to read it. I dropped it in the mail and quickly forgot about it, never expecting to hear back. After all, Larry was an international celebrity. Why would he bother to help me, a wannabe writer who had no literary pedigree whatsoever?

Four days later I received a card in the mail with words of praise and permission to use them. "An excellent first novel—moving, crisply written and the characters are convincing and appealing." Needless to say, I added Larry's glowing review to the back cover of my homemade paperback and all future query letters. Two weeks later I received a reply from a New York literary agent, saying that she would be happy to appraise my manuscript. A month later she phoned with an offer from Penguin.

When I shared the news with Larry, he was quick to remind me that blurbs don't sell manuscripts—they have to stand on their own. Still,

Larry's words had opened a door that had previously been slammed shut on me twenty-nine times. I had a drawer full of rejection slips to show for it. And those very words would eventually appear on the hardcover and paperback editions of my retitled first book, *River Season*.

I received a phone call from Larry soon after I signed my book contract, inviting my wife Lorrie and me to his home. He was having a small get-together for some friends of his and felt it would be a good time to celebrate my first book deal. On a Friday evening, Lorrie and I knocked on the front door of his house straddling the golf course in Archer City.

Larry, dressed in jeans, a white untucked polo, and worn white sneakers, greeted us. We were embarrassingly overdressed, but Larry warmly invited us inside and made us feel at home. He introduced me as a new, soon-to-be-published writer. And he gave Lorrie and me a tour of his stately home, filled with hundreds and hundreds of books on shelves that lined every wall.

During our tour, I was surprised to learn that Larry did not own a computer or even an electric typewriter. A small manual typewriter sat at one end of a large wooden dining table. The table and a scuffed-up wooden chair with a bath towel on the seat for cushioning served as Larry's writing nook. Next to the typewriter sat a stack of paper, face down. With his permission, I removed the top sheet. Lorrie and I read it, and I replaced it.

Two years later, reading a paperback copy of *Boone's Lick*, I came across that page and was reminded of that red-letter day when Larry opened his door to Lorrie and me. Just imagine, after a throng of literary agents and publishers had refused to read my manuscript, how I felt. I remember that evening like it was yesterday.

Being from Archer City, I'm often asked, "Did you know Larry McMurtry?"

"Yes," I say, smiling. "I did." I darn sure did.

A lifelong Texan, **JIM BLACK** was born in Center, Texas, and grew up in Archer City. He is the author of six books and nine stage plays. His first novel, *River Season*, has been assigned reading for classes at both the high school and college level. For the past twenty years, he has been involved in community theater at the Royal Theater in Archer City as a playwright, actor, director, and producer. He and his wife, Lorrie, reside in Wichita Falls.

Loving Gus

THE ONLY TIME I ever met Larry McMurtry face to face I was waiting in a long line of other unpublished, wannabe writers at a large conference in Houston, hoping he would sign a book. I say "face to face," but he was seated and I was standing and I'm not actually sure he raised his eyes to see whose books he might be signing that day. There were just so many of us.

Ten years later he wrote a lovely blurb for the jacket of my second novel, *Promised Lands*, having no discernible reason to do so, given that we had never crossed paths after that conference and I doubt he'd ever heard of me. Our only connection was that we'd both graduated from Rice, although decades apart.

It puzzles me how someone so seemingly remote and indifferent to his nameless fans could be so generous to a beginning writer. Why he even took the time to read my lengthy manuscript when he probably received piles of them from hopeful agents and editors on a weekly basis, or why he even plucked it out of the piles, is a mystery to me.

So not only did I never actually know Larry McMurtry, but I can't explain the one encounter we had. The blurb arrived late, unexpected, and unhoped-for by then, and because the jackets were printed already it was pasted on with a sticker. It was immediately my favorite thing about the jacket, since I disliked the art. His praise was generous and a great gift to me.

But it wasn't the only gift Larry McMurtry ever gave me. It wasn't even the best. Because by then he had already given me Gus McCrae.

The first time I read *Lonesome Dove*, shortly after it was published, I knew the moment Deets died that the Grim Reaper was on the loose

and more death would come. Within a few pages it became pretty clear
who he was looking for.

My brother had already finished reading, so I asked him, "Does
Gus die?" I remember where we were standing when I put this to him.

"Are you sure you want to know?" he asked.

That was all the answer I needed. And it was the end of the book for
me. As much as I loved *Lonesome Dove*, I loved Gus more, and I was
done with it.

I'd like to go on record that I'm not in general a weenie when it
comes to characters dying, having killed off many of my own, and at
times more brutally than was called for. I did once allow Steve Harrigan to kill one of my characters many years ago, when I couldn't stand
to inflict the final sword thrusts myself, but afterwards it felt wrong to
have shuffled the task off, as skillfully as he did it. Since then I've slain
all my doomed characters on my own. This is only right, having been
the one to decree their deaths in the first place.

So maybe it was just the time in my life that made me want to
avoid this particular scene with Gus. More likely, it was Gus himself
who created the problem. He would die honorably, and with humor—I
knew that. He would die well. But then he would just be so utterly
gone.

When the miniseries came out, I got up my courage and blubbered
my way through the dreaded scene. Later, I watched it with my kids.
It was Jake Spoon's death that most impressed my son; he was fourteen
when I walked into his room and found he'd scrawled on the wall in
large letters, with black paint, the words Jake Spoon uttered before
his hanging, "I'd damn sight rather be hung by my friends than by a
bunch of strangers." My daughter was more impressed by Blue Duck's
demise. She was about five when she watched Blue Duck hurl himself
from the jail window and asked me pensively, "Mommie, did Blue
Duck fail his life?" It takes a powerful death to make a family sit and
ponder if a person can actually fail their life.

But for me, the story was never so much about any of those other
characters, or even about Texas, as brilliant as it all was. It was about
Gus. Robert Duvall played that death scene better, and harder, and

sadder, and wiser, than I'd even imagined it. I no longer felt the nagging sense of things left hanging for not having finished the book. He had finished it for me.

So you can imagine how flabbergasted I was, decades later, when Robert Duvall bought the movie option for my novel *The Which Way Tree*. He said he wanted to talk to me on the phone about it. I took beta blockers to get up the nerve for the call. Having never been starstruck by stars, I was, at a very deep level, starstruck by Gus.

Steve Harrigan and I wrote the screenplay for the movie and met with Robert Duvall for dinner at the Worthington Hotel in Fort Worth during the twenty-seventh anniversary of the miniseries, hosted by the Wittliff. By then we had come to know him over the phone from numerous discussions about our screenplay, so the voice was Bob Duvall's to me, not Gus McCrae's. But sitting at the table and seeing him up close, there were moments I felt I was with the character Larry McMurtry had given me so many years ago, as if my cowardly avoidance of his literary death had somehow miraculously kept him alive.

Of course, *Lonesome Dove* isn't the only book Larry McMurtry wrote, and it may not even be the best by some standards. But it's a rare thing when a writer gives you a character you can't bear to lose—when the story carries you right up to the end, and you know the end is going to be great, but you'd rather give up the book than lose the character. You'd rather let your favorite Texas novel be the one you never finished.

ELIZABETH CROOK is the author of five novels, including *The Night Journal*, which received the Spur Award from Western Writers of America; *Monday, Monday*, a Kirkus Reviews Best Book of 2014 and winner of the Jesse H. Jones Award from the Texas Institute of Letters; and *The Which Way Tree*, currently in development as a film. Crook has written for the *Southwestern Historical Quarterly* and *Texas Monthly* and cowrote, with Stephen Harrigan, the screenplay for *The Which Way Tree*. She lives in Austin with her family.

WORKSHOPPER

Larry coaching writers at Booked Up. Kathy Floyd, workshop administrator, standing. Seated from left to right: Bill Marvel, George Getschow, and Larry McMurtry.

Somewhere, a Writer . . .

I HAD QUESTIONS about why my professor and writing coach, George Getschow, taught his literary nonfiction class in Archer City. Surely the University of North Texas had suitable classrooms in Denton. Even though I lived in nearby Wichita Falls—making the Archer City class convenient—I wondered how a writing class in little bitty Archer City was going to make me a better writer.

In the summer of 2013, I was fifty-nine years old—a fossil compared to the other students. My age provided one consolation, though: I received a scholarship from the Bess Whitehead Scott Scholarship Foundation for "older adults" who wanted to further their writing education.

I had no idea what to expect as I waited for George and the other students to arrive at the Spur Hotel. I was scared that I wouldn't fit in with my bushy-tailed classmates. So imagine my anxiety when George and a small convoy of cars finally rolled into town just before dark. The bed of George's silver Ford Ranger pickup was loaded with boxes of books—so loaded that legend has it that the front wheels of the pickup came off the ground at times.

George's books were lined up—double rows of books with books stacked on top of books—across the glass tables in the Spur Hotel dining room, which themselves were lined up to make one long table overflowing with our subject matter: literary nonfiction. Those books, George said, were the shoulders we would stand on to create our own masterpieces of nonfiction. Take one, take several, he said. Study them. Bury yourself in them.

Larry McMurtry's books were not lined up with these books. They were placed on a separate table, away from the rest of our literary inspirations. *Okay,* I thought, *we're in Archer City; George is honoring the hometown boy with a special display of his forty novels and nonfiction books.*

I knew who Larry McMurtry was, of course. You could not live in North Texas in 1970, when *The Last Picture Show* was filmed in Archer City, or in '89, when *Texasville* was filmed there, and not know. My family even got a taste of Hollywood by working as extras. Somewhere I still have their check stubs. Jeff Bridges waved at my son.

I also knew about *Lonesome Dove,* the blockbuster that earned a Pulitzer Prize and transformed the Western genre forever. I had not yet read the book, but I had watched the television miniseries version more times than I could remember. My husband and I watched it every time it aired. And my dad, though legally blind, would sit next to the television screen in his velvety swivel rocker with his head leaned back and his eyes closed, listening to Gus and Call banter back and forth. Daddy said that watching *Lonesome Dove* was as close to "The Real West" as he would ever get.

I'll never forget the day my classmates and I met Larry at Booked Up. He sat at a beat-up table, his Academy Award for *Brokeback Mountain* in a glass case behind his head, answering questions about other writers, literature, television, and the state of publishing. Larry was polite and courteous, addressing our questions about this and that without chastising us for our stupidity. I sensed in him a puzzlement that his thoughts mattered to anyone—a reluctant guru surrounded by followers.

How much do you worry about the fate of Archer City?

LM: Archer City floats on a sea of oil. It's been an oil town since 1905, when the first gusher hit. It's been an oil town all through the thirties, forties, fifties, and sixties, and it has always been a very, very rich land.

You said in your memoir, Literary Life, *that even though the bookstores didn't quite live up to your vision for the town, that it's become kind of a seminar town, is the way you described it.*

LM: Yeah. Here we are.

In the seminar town we now have these writers who have come here thirsty and hungry to become good writers. And they have. Many of them have gone on to produce books and they're writing for magazines and so on, and I was just wondering how much—what—consolation you take in that?

LM: I just don't think about it.

I hovered in the background, well behind the others, straining to hear Larry's weak voice over a noisy air conditioner blowing cool air around us. I finally summoned the courage to move closer. Although I will never forget this day, reading the transcript of our session showed me what panic had blocked from my memory—somehow I got up the nerve to ask Larry about his son, James, and his musical storytelling talent.

"Both James and Curtis. Curtis is James's son, my grandson. Both of them have bands, and they've been very successful," Larry answered. "I'm very happy. Myself, I'm not musical, but I think James is an extraordinary songwriter, and Curtis is going to be just as good. So I'm lucky in having two successful descendants. It's tricky being the child of someone famous. Yet I've been lucky. Both my son and my grandson are doing fine."

Soon after my question, he announced, "Okay, folks, I've got to go to my next job."

Larry stood up to leave. There I was, standing in the same room with this legend of Texas literature. I couldn't just leave without saying anything. Like a spooked camper facing a grizzly bear, I walked up to him and said, "I'm Kathy Floyd. I live in Wichita." Larry looked at me for a few seconds. I could tell he was processing what to do with my awkward introduction. He grunted something I couldn't hear and turned away.

As I headed out the door, I remember thinking: *My first and only encounter with Larry McMurtry was nothing like I expected. No momentous insights. No awe-inspiring advice about the writing life.*

But as it turned out, the week more than exceeded my expectations. Lifelong friendships were forged, and offers came from mentors to help me realize my dream of becoming a competent nonfiction storyteller capable of producing *New York Times* bestsellers. I had worked at small weekly newspapers for eight years—papers so small that I wrote the copy for the entire paper, from sports to hospital board reports. But when I arrived in Archer City, I didn't feel like a writer at all. I was hoping Larry and George would change that. And they did.

George sent us into the town and then out through the wind turbines to the McMurtry place south of Archer City, a windswept bluff known as Idiot Ridge. There was the house and the stirrup—the McMurtry brand—welded onto the top of a gate leading into McMurtry's scrubby cattle ranch. Looking out across the ranch, I saw a red barn rising out of the pasture of native grasses, salt cedars, and mesquites.

I gazed at the steep hill on the western edge of the ranch that, for Larry, was the primordial horizon of his literature of the West. As Larry describes it in *Walter Benjamin at the Dairy Queen*:

> I see that hill, those few buildings, that spring, the highway to the east, trees to the south, the limitless plain to the north, whenever I sit down to describe a place. I move from the hill to whatever place I'm then describing, whether it's south Texas or Las Vegas, but I always leave from that hill, the hill of my youth.

Could that hill do for me what it did for Larry?

I had heard about an Archer City woman who had a lot of birds—so many that she had to keep adding sheds to her yard to shelter them all. I told George, and he told me to write about her not as a piece of journalism but as a piece of literary nonfiction. My story about "the bird lady" changed her life and mine in profound ways.

Just as Larry's love of books began when his cousin gave him a box of books before heading off to serve in World War II, Char Burton's love of birds began when a friend gave her his bird to care for when he went to Vietnam.

And just as Larry's passion for reading grew into collecting books, Char's obsession led to a menagerie of more than 120 birds. She knew the characters and quirks of each bird, just as Larry intimately knew his own books.

Locals call Char "The Bird Lady of Archer City." Char doesn't mind being known as the Bird Lady. She doesn't even mind when some people put the word "crazy" in front of bird lady. She knows that her collection of birds isn't normal. But everything about birds fascinates Char—their brilliant colors and fancy feathers, their personalities, that some have hurts that need healing just as humans do.

For the next few years, I would read my story aloud the first night of a workshop to set the tone for the new attendees before they set out to look for their own stories in Archer County. During one of those readings, a literary agent took special interest in my writing.

For the first time in my life, I sensed that Larry's "seminar town" was slowly transforming me from a mediocre journalist into a creative writer.

Wading through the maze of George's books that had taken over the Spur's dining room, I spotted *Isaac's Storm* by Eric Larson, about the hurricane that destroyed Galveston in 1900. Always fascinated by weather, I picked up the paperback and took it to my room.

"Part 1, The Law of Storms," begins, "Somewhere, a butterfly . . . ," a reference to the butterfly effect, a notion that a slight swirl of air created by a butterfly's fluttering wings can cause a chain reaction in the air currents that results in a violent storm thousands of miles away.

Through the following years of reading, writing, and going back to Archer City to be in the company of writers, I came to understand that my literary awakening would not have happened but for Larry. He was the butterfly that set in motion a fierce storm inside of me—the desire to become a creative writer.

Other wannabe writers who flocked to Archer City also felt the butterfly's wings hovering over them as they sweated over stories about Larry's shrinking hometown and its die-hard denizens, who endured endless challenges just to survive. Once I realized the origins of the storm swirling inside me, I finally understood why George kept Larry's books separate from the rest. That table was a shrine to a writer who created characters and a sense of place that forever changed how Texans and the rest of the world thought about the West. And we discovered that many of Larry's fictional characters and places were actual people and places that we all came to know during our days in Archer City.

Every time I go to Archer City and pass the Spur, or venture out to Idiot Ridge, I remember that summer of 2013 when I did not feel like a writer. Then the wind whips up around me and I think of how far I've come, and I think of Larry.

KATHY FLOYD worked for the US Postal Service for sixteen years, including time as a writer and editor for US Postal Service publications at headquarters in Washington, DC. She has written for several North Texas newspapers and magazines and received Texas Press Association awards for photography. She has twice been honored for essay writing at the University of North Texas's Mayborn Literary Nonfiction Conference. Floyd works in marketing and public information at Midwestern State University in Wichita Falls, Texas, and is the administrator for the Archer City Writers Workshop.

McMurtry's Rebuff

IN MY FORTIES, after a rather lackluster career as a writer, I moved to Texas, a place I knew only from the grainy black-and-white Westerns I watched as a young boy growing up on the island of Oahu, Hawaii. In my fertile imagination, Texas was still a wild frontier filled with granite-jawed cowboys and lawmen riding across the open range, chasing the bad guys in black hats.

It was also a place where I could imagine fulfilling my long-simmering dream of becoming a famous writer, perhaps another Larry McMurtry. So when I found out about a workshop offered for a select group of graduate students and professional writers in Archer City, McMurtry's hometown, I thought maybe, just maybe, my dream could come true.

Even though my portfolio of stories was rather thin at the time, I applied for the workshop and was, much to my surprise, accepted. All I could think about was sitting down at a table with McMurtry as he gave me a crash course on the art and craft of writing epic Westerns like *Lonesome Dove.*

Driving from my well-manicured suburban home in the Dallas metroplex to Archer City in mid-July transported me into a stark and inhospitable terrain I felt I had already experienced from reading McMurtry's novels. The land was blazing hot, dusty, and eerily silent except for the occasional cowboy driving by in a pickup truck, gesturing a *howdy* by lifting an index finger off the wheel. I, driving my little Miata, felt like an alien from another planet in this world. The cattle grazing on the wide-open pastures paid me little mind. But I gawked at each one as if it had something to teach me about the Texas cowboy way of life, something that might inspire a story that even McMurtry hadn't thought of.

As the sun began setting in the west, the prairieland disappeared and the outline of a small town popped up on the horizon. Heading toward the only stoplight in Archer City, I spotted the bright red-and-blue marquee above the hollowed-out Royal Theater, looking exactly as it did in the 1971 film *The Last Picture Show*. Around the corner was the Spur Hotel, another relic, I thought, of the Old West. It was also the location of our workshop.

I stood on the porch of the Spur, drinking in the oddly familiar environs, seemingly unchanged from how they appeared in McMurtry's early novels set around his hometown. It felt like a real-life movie set, and I was one of a cast of characters hoping that the author's staggering storytelling skills would somehow rub off on us. The more I thought about meeting the man whose myth-busting literature inspired a paradigm shift in my romantic notions of the Old West, the more keyed up I became.

Finally the day arrived, July 28, 2011. McMurtry was sitting, somewhat slumped, at a scuffed-up table inside his gigantic bookstore just off the town square. Wearing an ink-stained Dr Pepper shirt and rumpled trousers, the man didn't match my image of the literary lion who laid waste to the myths of the Old West.

But his physical appearance wasn't going to get in the way of what our instructor had promised would be a life-changing encounter with Texas's literary legend. Though McMurtry's voice was weak and his physical stature frail, even us literary greenhorns realized that his written words still roared and bit deep into the flesh, brawn, and heart of Texas, even if his eyes weren't steely and his chin was far from squared and chiseled.

"So, Larry, was *Lonesome Dove*—"

"Naw . . . don't want to talk about that," McMurtry mumbled, waving my question away.

I made a few more stabs at probing McMurtry about the significance of place in his Western fiction; about the inspiration for his stories; about the impact and influence of his iconoclastic Westerns on him; and about the influence of his Westerns—*Horseman, Pass By*; *Leaving Cheyenne*; *Lonesome Dove*; *Comanche Moon*; and all the others—on the genre. McMurtry dismissed every question I asked about his "Westerns" as if he found them distasteful.

I was miffed by McMurtry's sniffy refusals to consider my queries. Why would he wave off questions about the impact of *Lonesome Dove* and his other Westerns on the genre? Why would he dismiss himself as nothing more than "a minor regional writer" when everyone else considered him a treasured American legend?

I desperately wanted to hear McMurtry talk about his place in the literary pantheon and his titanic influence on other Western storytellers, and not just because I was a fanboy of his novels and movies. I also understood that Larry's Westerns were inspired by his own experiences growing up a cowboy on his family's scruffy cattle ranch some twenty miles south of Archer City. I felt that McMurtry could help me figure out how I might go about creating compelling stories out of my own life experiences growing up in a tiny working-class home, one of the *maka'ainana* (commoners) in the old Hawaiian paradise.

I left our hourlong session grumbling to the other writers as we walked back to the Spur about what an utter disappointment meeting McMurtry was for me, especially his refusal to talk about his epic Western *Lonesome Dove* and the television miniseries it spawned. Late that night, sitting on the porch of the Spur with our group, chugging moonshine and a few beers, I worked myself up into a lather. For me, McMurtry was no longer a literary lion. He was an insensitive son-of-a-bitch.

But in the clarity of the morning daylight—suffering from a slight hangover—I remembered an interview McMurtry had given the *New York Times* a few years after his critically acclaimed blockbuster was published in 1985. He said he never intended *Lonesome Dove* to be a traditional Western. "I'm a critic of the myth of the cowboy. . . . I feel it's a legitimate task to criticize it."

McMurtry sounded frustrated that his attempt to demythologize the West with his riveting trail-drive novel had instead reinforced the myths. "People cherish a certain vision because it fulfills psychological needs," he told the interviewer. "People need to believe that cowboys are simple, strong and free, and not twisted, fascistic, and dumb." Most readers, in fact, considered *Lonesome Dove* an homage to the courageous cowboys driving cattle across the savage frontier of the Old West.

Suddenly it dawned on me why McMurtry would balk at addressing the same questions from me about *Lonesome Dove* that he had fielded from a legion of interviewers for more than twenty years. In McMurtry's mind, *Lonesome Dove*, considered by many the greatest Western of all time, was a major disappointment. But how do you explain that to a wannabe writer bewitched by the novel's literary and commercial success?

Still, it took me a few days to get over the sting of McMurtry's snub. It wasn't until I dared to put myself on the other side of the table in McMurtry's place that I began to fully grasp why he refused to address my questions. If I had written a Pulitzer Prize–winning Western novel that reinforced cowboy myths I had set out to debunk, I'd be frustrated too.

Consequently, despite McMurtry's rebuff, I didn't flee Archer City or give up my dream of becoming a notable writer. Each summer I continue to make the annual sojourn to Archer City to attend the writers workshop at the Spur, where we discuss the sort of penetrating questions that McMurtry might ask us: Why do you want to be a writer? Does your work tackle important issues? Does your story advance the form or genre in some way? Does it rise to the level of literature?

At the next workshop in Archer City, I'm planning to step out of my comfort zone. Instead of wearing my customary Hawaiian shirts and shorts, I'll don a pearl snap cowboy shirt and spiffy white Stetson, Wranglers, and Justin boots. As a Texas writer, my new cowboy duds seem fitting attire for when I propose that we writers formally adopt the same philosophy that guided the writing of Larry McMurtry and the cowboys of the Old West: that all things change but truth lives on forever.

ERIC NISHIMOTO is an award-winning writer and artist and a former public information officer and professor at the University of North Texas. He is the author of *Texas Maker: The Heretofore Unknown Legend of Collin McKinney*, about one of Texas's founding fathers. He has won regional and national awards from the Society of Professional Journalists and a Community Service Award from Texas Managing Editors for an in-depth reporting series on health care reform. In 2013, Nishimoto was named a Mayborn Biography Fellow. He has received numerous citations for his role in strategic communications and media crisis response.

At the Intersection of
Aspiration and Asphyxiation

THE ROADRUNNER BUZZED past me like a cartoon.

Next to the blond prairie grasses that a century back were the buffalo's stomping grounds, the Mohawk-wearing bird captivated me.

It tried its best to get the hell out of Archer City, a scrap of a town of 1,848 souls near the northern Texas border with Oklahoma. Maybe the roadrunner was the spirit animal of the writer and native son Larry McMurtry. Maybe it was my spirit animal, my *nahual*, as the Mayans say.

There was no escape, though. The wild bird and I were stuck in this harsh and arid landscape for a while. In July 2009, I voluntarily signed up for a literary nonfiction workshop in McMurtry's hometown, hoping to learn how to transform landscape into a compelling character, and how a rich interior life provides a way for characters to escape their oppressive landscapes.

I wasn't in Archer City for long before I began to understand why McMurtry had developed a love-hate relationship with his hometown. I felt like a foreigner, a dark-haired Mexican American writer from California accustomed to crossing international borders but feeling completely out of place in this stubbornly insular North Texas town. McMurtry's alienation from Archer City had spurred his exodus to the more urban venues of Houston, Washington, DC, and Tucson.

Yet he eventually returned. Then he filled his mansion and the adjoining carriage house with the love of his life: books. As a book dealer in Archer City, he made it his mission to transform what he once called "a bookless town in a bookless part of the state" into a book town featuring four stores stuffed floor to ceiling with antiquarian books.

As I dipped into McMurtry's oeuvre of novels and screenplays, my disappointment with Archer City's famous author sparked and scorched the esteem I had held for his work. Mexican American or Mexican characters were relegated to minor roles or to unsavory stock characters like the bandit Joey Garza in *Streets of Laredo*. And McMurtry's heroes Gus McCrae and Woodrow Call were former Texas Rangers, a law enforcement agency despised by many Latinos and now being reexamined by others for the violence they unleashed on Mexicans on both sides of the border.

With *Lonesome Dove*, I kept recalling my grandfather's second wife, a wise Rio Grande Valley native, and her warning to me about the Rangers, *los rinches*. "You never knew if they would kill you or help you."

Despite my hesitancy about spending a week in an all-white world, I decided I could endure whatever indignities might come my way by spending most of my time outside the workshop wrapped up in the landscape surrounding Archer City—a withering world of ranching and cattle. By planting myself in nature that summer, I felt I had found a refuge and a state of harmony watching cenizo sage burst with lilac blooms.

Yet that harmony evaporated. Whenever I walked past the flashing stoplight at the corner of Center and Main on the way to McMurtry's bookshops, I couldn't help but feel that I was at the intersection of aspiration and asphyxiation.

"Are you Hispanic?" a dark-haired man asked me bluntly.

"Yes."

"Oh, I like the Hispanic people. They have such nice faces."

"Oh, thank you."

I felt like Mexican *artesanía*, even if he was flirting.

My writer-colleague Danny struggled too. He had a natural tan, as we say, and dark brown hair that he wore straight up, porcupine style.

"Texas girls wouldn't appreciate you," said one of the female locals. "You need someone more exotic."

Ah, yes, always the "exotic."

A few days later, Danny was sipping his Coors Light outside the writers' hotel.

"Would you really drink that if you could have any other kind of beer?" I asked.

"No, this is method acting."

The method acting continued. One night at the busy intersection of Center and Main, we broke into a party. Lots of beer, pickups, big indigo sky. And Danny, a fine photographer, hovered on a rooftop looking for a sharp shot of the street scene below. The night felt drenched in sepia.

A glass bottle of beer came whizzing high near his shoulder. It shattered at Danny's feet.

It reminded me of a scene from the 1971 film *The Last Picture Show*, where the two friends, Sonny and Duane (Jeff Bridges), fight over dream girl Jacy Farrow (Cybill Shepherd), until Sonny (Timothy Bottoms) gets bonked on the forehead with a glass beer bottle. They had been best friends.

The movie is Archer City's ghost. It's based on McMurtry's 1966 book of the same name. *The Last Picture Show* is an elegy to a dying town and way of life, with townspeople who are either suffering from asphyxiation of the spirit or are eager to escape. The author's snappy dialogue moves the plot forward.

Consider the character Sam the Lion (Ben Johnson). Sam runs the café, the pool hall, and the Royal Theater (which still stands, with a replica of the original sign in faded blue). Sam the Lion clings to a code of behavior and morality that other residents of Thalia (McMurtry's fictional name for Archer City) seem to have abandoned. He berates Sonny, Duane, and other older teens for taking a younger teen, the gentle Billy, who is mute, to a town prostitute. "Scaring an unfortunate creature like Billy when there ain't no reason to scare him is just plain trashy behavior. I've seen a lifetime of it and I'm tired of putting up with it."

But the trashy behavior continues to fill the pages of *The Last Picture Show*. Racist remarks about Mexican and Asian women sting. Even Sam the Lion takes to trash talk. Go to Mexico for an adventure, he tells the teenage Sonny and Duane. But beware of "the clap." Duane laments that when he heads for the Korean War, "yellow" will be his next "piece of ass."

In the rhapsody of romantic notions about how unromantic McMurtry was about the dying West, why is it that few critics took issue with the overt racism littering some of his early novels? Rereading some of McMurtry's Western yarns, I found myself pining for *Giant*, a retro film based on Edna Ferber's 1952 book of the same name, which captured the Texas I knew. Why was Ferber able to illuminate the cruel realities of racism in *Giant* with fearlessness and clarity through the characters of a wealthy Texas ranching family? Why didn't McMurtry?

Many may excuse such racism on the written page as reflective of the times in which it was penned. But as a writer with Mexican roots, I can't and I won't.

McMurtry shows a deep understanding of women, and the female characters in his books are strong women with nuanced motivations. Most of them are white. His 1975 book *Terms of Endearment* is timeless because of its rich treatment of the strained relationship between a wealthy Houston mother, Aurora, and her free-spirited daughter Emma. "You are not special enough to overcome a bad marriage," the mother tells her only child.

The unraveling relationship winds back tight when the mother must deal with the looming death of her daughter from cancer. Emma's English college prof husband has been busy sparking romances with students. Who will take care of their three kids when she dies? Emma has had an affair too. In a reunion, Emma tells her mother, "That's the first time I stopped hugging first. I like that."

Contrast the heroes Emma and Aurora in *Terms of Endearment* with brown-skinned Juanita of *All My Friends Are Going to Be Strangers*. Juanita is portrayed as a whore in Reynosa, Mexico, a "whorehouse town, just across the river."

In a series of exchanges, the white male narrator, Danny Deck, tries to stop the script of "whore and customer." Could he take Juanita to meet his white female friends back in the city? Would they think he was crazy? Was the point here that writer Danny Deck had lost his way?

I find it intriguing that Archer City, which disowned McMurtry over his dark and lurid portrayal of the town in *The Last Picture Show*, also grounded him. He wanted to give back to Archer City. He meandered back to his hometown after years of living in Washington, DC, and built Booked Up on the cheap real estate of that one-stoplight town. Books are "the fuel of genius," he wrote in his semi-autobiographical essay *Walter Benjamin at the Dairy Queen*. "Leaving a million or so in Archer City is as good a legacy as I can think of for that region and indeed for the West."

When the writers arrived for the annual writers workshop in Archer City, McMurtry graciously instructed staff to keep the stores open all night for us. On the floors one very late evening, under fluorescent lights, I scoured the shelves for books on the border and Mexico and its revolution. I was taken by a poster of a photo by Leland Howard Marmon of a Native American man wearing high-top sneakers. "White man's moccasins," read the title given by Marmon, who grew up on the Laguna Pueblo in New Mexico.

I didn't find books that exactly resonated with me. There were plenty of books by the philosopher George Santayana. There was one fat tome by the grand Mexican renaissance man, Miguel Covarrubias, that I already owned. There were military diaries and sheet music.

Then I spotted shelves devoted to dance, including the highly disciplined world of ballet and its premier choreographer, George Balanchine. That's where I sat. Books were McMurtry's hallowed escape, and sitting on that beige linoleum floor, they were mine as well.

DIANNE SOLIS is an award-winning senior writer at the *Dallas Morning News* and a former foreign correspondent in Mexico for the *Wall Street Journal*. She specializes in immigration and social justice reporting. Solis has covered hot-button issues ranging from immigrant family separations at the border to harsh refugee policies that split Muslim families in US immigration courts. She grew up in California and is the granddaughter of immigrants who fled the Mexican Revolution a century ago. The seeds of her career as a writer were planted by her grandfather, who wrote for a Spanish-language newspaper in California.

Reckoning at Idiot Ridge

I NEVER MET Larry McMurtry. But I go to Archer City because of him. And every time I go I get sloppy sentimental. And I write.

George Getschow, the bolo-wearing genius behind this book tribute to McMurtry, shared Larry's vision of Archer City as a literary oasis in North Texas. McMurtry stuffed the town with books; Getschow brings in writers. Every year in July, Getschow ropes in some published authors to mosey over to Archer City for a workshop to help aspiring writers. ("Rope" is the appropriate word. Nobody wants to be there in the summer.) I met some wonderful authors this way, including Ron Powers, Ben Montgomery, Jason Ryan, James M. Scott, and Julia Flynn Siler.

To kick it off, a dozen or so of us would pile into the ninety-year-old Spur Hotel off Main Street with food, beer, and booze. We'd read manuscripts and talk and commiserate over three days. In between would be lazy breakfasts at Murn's Café across the street and trips across the square to Booked Up, McMurtry's outpost of bookstores that filled a hefty portion of Archer City's downtown real estate.

Most years McMurtry would agree to see Getschow's workshop crew. But by the time I started going to Archer City, audiences with Larry were nearly impossible because of his health. Two events, however, were always Archer City workshop standards. One was a night of barbecue and beer and carousing in the backyard of Jackie Lane, a local McMurtry called "the last real cowgirl." Frankly, girlhood had long since passed Jackie by. The Jackie we knew swore and drank like a man and could read you in a minute. The other event, after two days of nonstop workshopping, started when all the writers—published and wannabes—piled into a truck or two and headed west into McMurtry country. Out in the deep dark, in a field, under the suddenly visible Milky Way, we'd get up on a truck bed and confess how much the whole damn experience had meant to us.

I went to Archer City for years, even after I'd left Texas. Like Mc-Murtry, I have always been ambivalent about my home state. I was born in Dallas and never owned a cowboy hat or boots while growing up. In his book of essays *In a Narrow Grave*—written in 1968, the year I first decamped from Dallas—McMurtry called my hometown one of the "maternity wards of urban Texas." As Larry predicted, my '50s city-born generation would be the nemesis of the Texas he grew up in—"the rural, pastoral way of life." We city kids turned our backs on Texas and couldn't wait to see the world. McMurtry, it should be noted, did much the same thing for a long while.

But as it did for McMurtry, Archer City has a pull on me. One year, tired of looking like a failed writer, I finally brought the preface of my memoir to the Archer City workshop. I droned on and on as I read it, thinking all the while, *Why is the darn thing so long?* I looked up at the end and, lord, thank you, a few people were still awake. They had advice, kind at first, then more brutally constructive. The next year I went back with my first chapter.

I'm five or six chapters into my book now. When I find my worries creeping back, especially about some rather steamy revelations, I pick up *In a Narrow Grave* again and rediscover Larry's chapter about sex in Archer City, or rather the sublimation of sex to the Friday Night Lights of football, the divide between the cowboy and his good woman, and some naughtier bits that make me laugh and embolden me. For a man I never met, McMurtry just keeps giving me good advice.

The last time I went to Archer City, COVID was raging and I stayed at the Spur Hotel with my husband. We were one of just two couples roaming its halls that night. Booked Up was closed by the time we rolled into town. My husband and I got spicy chicken from Lucky's gas station down the street, and we opened a bottle of Western bourbon to chase the indigestion away.

I toasted Archer City and Larry McMurtry. I couldn't wait to get off the road and back to writing.

For that, Larry, thank you.

CATHY BOOTH THOMAS is a twenty-two-year veteran of *Time* magazine who served as a correspondent and bureau chief in Rome, Miami, Los Angeles, and Dallas. Her profiles, on subjects from the worlds of business, politics, Hollywood, and high tech, have covered Steve Jobs, Richard Branson, Elon Musk, Paul McCartney, Tom Hanks, Tom Cruise, George Lucas, and Stephen King, among others. She interviewed Fidel Castro four times in Cuba, twice for *Time* covers. Her story about taking care of a father with Alzheimer's won Clarion and National Headliner Awards. Thomas is the founding editor of *Mayborn Magazine* at the University of North Texas.

"Furthur"

ONE OF MY favorite books is Tom Wolfe's *The Electric Kool-Aid Acid Test*. It's about Ken Kesey and his band of Merry Pranksters on a wildly exuberant—and drug-fueled—cross-country bus tour. The old school bus was painted in psychedelic colors, and the destination sign on the front of the tricked-out bus read, simply, FURTHUR.

At one point in the Merry Pranksters' wild road trip, their bus pulled up in front of Larry McMurtry's home near Houston, where he taught at Rice University. This was 1964, when men wore crewcuts and women sprouted beehive hairdos. It was the year of the sports car—the Ford Mustang and the Pontiac GTO. I imagine McMurtry's neighbors peeking out their windows thinking, *God Almighty, what am I seeing?*, their eyes widening as the bohemian crew of leaping gnomes spilled out of the popsicle-colored bus and a wave of nonconformist energy crashed over the neat, manicured lawns.

Beatniks! Good Lord! Hide the kids!

And what on earth did that destination sign on the front of the bus mean? "Furthur"?

Ken Kesey was an old friend of Larry's and a successful writer who was famous for the bestseller *One Flew over the Cuckoo's Nest*, published two years earlier, in 1962. The two had met at the Stegner Fellowship class in fiction at Stanford University. Kesey left a deep impression on the class, and in particular on McMurtry, as he later wrote in a *New York Review of Books* essay: "So who was this lumberjack, a figure so Paul Bunyanesque that I would not have been surprised to see Babe, the Blue Ox, plod in behind him?"

Kesey was the center of attention, McMurtry wrote, and "we let him get away with it." Rivals, friends, or something in between, the two men respected each other and stayed in close touch until Kesey's death in 2001.

I felt that Kesey's "Furthur" was his way of urging McMurtry to not succumb to the comforts of suburban life and the privileged sinecure of a career as a writing professor.

One night in 2009 in Archer City, our workshop leader, George Getschow, escorted our group of writers on a walk from the Spur Hotel to the American Legion post, a sand-colored brick building with a bar, a cranky jukebox, and a gaggle of locals adorned in dusty cowboy hats and oil-field caps.

Getschow was our teacher and spirit guide whose fiery, pentecostal sermons on narrative both delighted and scared the wits out of us. He plucked me out of the crowd.

I was a midcareer journalist, probably the oldest of the writers in the workshop. I thought he was going to pass on a compliment, maybe say he was glad I was in the workshop to share my own writerly wisdom.

He put his arm around my shoulders and said, yelling over the jukebox, "What the hell are you doing here?"

I felt stumped.

"Why aren't you on the road, hitchhiking?"

The night before, sitting outside on the hotel sidewalk, I'd told the other writers a few tales of my hitchhiking days in college.

"That's your story, dammit! If I were you, I'd start hitchhiking to Alaska tonight. That's your story! That's your book!"

He stared at me. There was no twinkle in his eyes.

That night I decided to go hitchhiking. I thought it was a crazy idea. Hell, I'd never pick up a hitchhiker. Anyone who does must be crazy. But Getschow was right about one thing. What was I doing here?

Was this only about taking another class on my way to a master's degree? I was fifty-three years old. I'd been writing for newspapers since 1981, almost three decades at that point. I was a husband with two kids and a home in the suburbs. I prided myself on being a survivor in the digital age, a time when the ranks of local journalists were being decimated.

But George, my personal Ken Kesey, wasn't having it. It was like he and his group of Merry Pranksters had showed up outside my house, jumped out on my lawn, and yelled "Furthur!"

———————

I didn't hitchhike to Alaska. I'm not that crazy. But swear to God, five minutes after I stuck my thumb out at Main and Center Streets, a car stopped. A young guy, mid-thirties, with a little beard stubble, wearing jeans and a T-shirt, rolled down his window.

A cup of black coffee was cooling in a cup holder, and a lit Marlboro rested in his hand on the steering wheel. As we pulled back onto the blacktop, I told him what I was doing. I was afraid he would think hitchhiking for a story sounded foolish. But he nodded like it made sense.

From my hitchhiking days, I remembered that people who pick you up usually have a story to tell. The Marlboro man's story reminded me of McMurtry's haunting first novel, *Horseman, Pass By*, about a West Texas cattleman's losing battle to hold on to his small ranch. The driver's family had owned a ranch in the area for several generations. But cattle ranching could be precarious. Periodic droughts, spiking costs, and falling prices took a toll. His father finally lost the ranch to the bank. Now, instead of cowboying, his son rode herd as head of a maintenance crew for an apartment management firm in Wichita Falls.

I arrived at my destination in thirty minutes. But I didn't want to turn around and head back yet. I looked at my map and pointed my finger at a town about thirty miles southeast called Windthorst. Again I stuck out my thumb.

Further.

I didn't have long to wait. A man about the same age as the first driver stopped. He had his son in the passenger seat, so I hopped in the back and listened to his story. He'd been laid off, along with millions of others that spring, as the Great Recession hollowed out the economy. He was taking care of things at home while his wife worked. He loved the idea of what I was doing but thought it was unsafe. He dropped me off in Windthorst at the crossroads of US Route 281 and State Highway 25.

After getting a sandwich at a small grocery store and diner, I figured I'd head back. At the rate I was going, I'd be back in Archer City in no time. Two hours later, I was still waiting. The thought crossed my mind to call Getschow to come get me. But what kind of ending would that give my story? I had to finish.

Further.

Finally, a pickup truck pulled up. An old man smiled as his white poodle barked at me through the partly rolled-down window. I squeezed next to the dog and told the man how long I'd been waiting.

"That shirt isn't helping you," the man said, pointing at my black-and-yellow Wildcats T-shirt. "Archer City is our big rival!"

My essay talked about finding stories among regular people in small towns—the sort of people who made McMurtry's poignant and powerful stories so memorable.

Now I'm convinced that it wasn't so much the experience of hitchhiking that changed me as my conversation with Getschow at the American Legion post, where he lit a fire under me.

Further.

I did my best work after Archer City, about an explosion at a fertilizer plant that blew up half the town of West, Texas, and about the families of soldiers broken by repeated tours of duty in Afghanistan and Iraq. These stories received national recognition, and I turned them into a digital book.

I finally felt like I was doing something meaningful as a writer. Even so, I'd wake up at night and ask myself: *Am I really doing my best work?*

Further.

For some writers, "furthur" translates to a kind of neurosis, to never being satisfied with what they've done. To push harder. But I like to think that Kesey's message to McMurtry—just like Getschow's message to me—was more gregarious, brotherly, even fun. Yes, you're doing good work. But don't stop now.

Furthur.

DAVE TARRANT, a veteran of nearly thirty years at the *Dallas Morning News*, contributed to the paper's first Pulitzer Prize in 1986 and won national awards for an investigation into the mistreatment of wounded soldiers at Fort Hood. His passion is writing stories about ordinary people involved in extraordinary events. Tarrant has reported on soldiers returning home from war and the survivors of a deadly explosion in a small Texas town. A native of Pittsburgh, Pennsylvania, he married a native Texan and for the last thirty years has been obsessively curious about Texans and the Lone Star State culture.

LEGACY

A portrait of Larry McMurtry.

Writing Plainly and Unforgettably

"HANDLEABLE."

That odd, ungainly, barely pronounceable word threw me off stride the instant I came across it in the very first paragraph of Larry Mc-Murtry's *Moving On*. I read that book, Larry's fourth novel, in 1970, the year it came out. I was twenty-two, dreaming of a future for myself as a novelist and excited by the idea that this was a feat that had already been accomplished by somebody actually living in Texas. And the novel I held in my hands as I sat there on a ratty couch on the screened-in porch of an Austin crash pad wasn't just some slim and wispy literary object. At 794 pages long, it was a real book, an epic-length novel of the sort that back then I had not only the patience but the real longing to read.

But it had never occurred to me to detach the idea of an epic novel from the goal of an epic style. Literature demanded that every sentence be exquisitely wrought, that no word could ever be casually thrown down in the interest of just getting on with the story. But here was Larry McMurtry, beginning a nearly eight-hundred-page journey and trusting a reader would follow him without any sort of flourish or literary throat clearing: "Patsy sat by herself at the beginning of the evening, eating a melted Hershey bar."

Perhaps he was conscious of the arty resonance of a phrase like "the beginning of the evening," and perhaps he had the deliberate design of immediately undercutting it with a mundane reference to a Hershey bar, but I don't think so. That first sentence of *Moving On*, along with the book's title, is a vivid enough demonstration of Larry McMurtry's working method. He moved on and didn't much worry about anything except what came next. That's how he could describe the Hershey bar later in that opening paragraph as being "too melted to be neatly handleable" and keep his focus on narrative momentum and not, as I would have done and would still do, on that singularly clunky word.

Larry wrote in his memoir *Literary Life* that he owned and had mostly read 160 books about the history and theory of the novel, that he devoured works of abstruse criticism about the form that he practiced for almost all of his adult life. But he wrote novels as if he were the first person to ever do so, as if there were no rules or traditions or caution lights that needed attention. Partly this was just his natural disposition. As the writer and art critic Dave Hickey once observed, "If you leave a cow alone, he'll eat grass. If you leave Larry alone, he'll write books."

But I think it mostly came from a clear-eyed awareness of both his gifts and his limitations, and from the indifference of a born outsider to the expectations of distant literary tribunals. "A writer's prose should be congruent with the landscape he is peopling," he said, and therefore, "I write plainly."

He also wrote fast. *The Last Picture Show* took him three weeks. About *All My Friends Are Going to Be Strangers*, Larry remembered that "I just spewed it out, and never . . . looked back."

Not looking back made for some imperfect books but didn't get in the way of Larry McMurtry writing some great ones. He admitted to losing interest in his books once they were finished, to the chagrin of copy editors who couldn't get his attention when it was time to read proofs. He liked his longtime editor, Michael Korda, for his hands-off approach to line editing and for focusing his attention where Larry thought it belonged—on getting Simon & Schuster behind the book and making sure it came out on time. Meanwhile, he was always on to the next novel, the next pasture.

Occasional potholes and gaps in logic didn't appear to trouble him. *Lonesome Dove* is not only one of the greatest American novels, it's also one of the shaggiest. For instance, Larry himself admitted that he had no idea what lay behind a crucial and heartbreaking motivational thread in the book—why Woodrow Call can't bring himself to acknowledge his son.

I was on the set for a week or so during the making of the *Lonesome Dove* miniseries. After the filming of the scene where the Hat Creek outfit crosses the Rio Grande into Mexico to steal horses, I remember sitting around with Robert Duvall, Tommy Lee Jones, and Robert Urich, who played Jake Spoon. Urich raised a question for the other actors: "How come you guys end up hanging me later for stealing horses when that's what we're all doing together in this scene?" They all thought about that for a moment, but nobody came up with an answer, and after a while nobody seemed to care.

Soon after *Lonesome Dove* was published, Larry gave a talk at the Texas Institute of Letters annual meeting in San Antonio. A friend who had written an authoritative field guide to Texas snakes came up to him afterward, thinking that Larry might appreciate knowing that water moccasins do not gather in big heaving masses underwater and kill people like they do trail driver Sean O'Brien in the novel. Larry's reaction, as I recall, was no reaction. He just looked at my friend as if he were staring at a blank wall.

Grounded as he was in a scholarly awareness of Texas and the West, he would have known that fact about water moccasins already, but he wasn't the sort of writer to let real-world knowledge get in the way of telling a fictional story, just as he wasn't going to second-guess an awkward word like "handleable" if it was what he needed to get a giant novel underway.

I knew him only a little and was handicapped in knowing him better because of the exalted position in which I, as a junior Texas writer, could not help placing him. His life and his work and his example had loomed over my own aspiring career ever since that day on the screened-in porch when I began reading *Moving On*.

And *kept* reading. The discovery I made that day was that some sort of mysterious current in Larry McMurtry's writing pulls you along, and that the occasional infelicitous word or phrase is no less authentic—and no less necessary—than a snag in a river.

"I believe the one gift I had that led me to a career in fiction," he once wrote, "was the ability to make up characters that readers connect with."

But you have the feeling, as a reader, that he didn't make up those characters at all. Gus McCrae, Woodrow Call, Duane Jackson, Jacy Farrow, Emma Horton, Danny Deck, Aurora Greenway, Sam the Lion—all these characters were not so much created and written by Larry McMurtry as already present and alive in his imagination, waiting for their turn to be released upon the page.

He worked hard—he had to work hard to produce all those novels, nonfiction books, memoirs, book reviews, and screenplays. Though he had long stretches of doubt and depression, you would not suspect it from his unflagging lifelong output. He wrote at his own steady pace, five pages a day. He often wrote on deadline, but deadlines aren't frightening to a writer long accustomed to heeding his own internal timetable.

Few novelists have ever been able to match Larry McMurtry's work ethic, let alone his towering popularity and influence. For many Texas writers, particularly those of my generation working as soon as they set out in the shadow of his achievements, his career was both intimidating and inspiring. We could never hope to measure up, but we could dare to press on, because he showed us how.

I've come to understand that I'm a different kind of writer than Larry was. I can be fretful and fastidious with word choices and narrative structure where he was bold and expansive. I'm more attuned to outside expectations, hungrier for approval not just from readers but from the editors and publishers and other gatekeepers I still helplessly think of as authority figures.

But I wonder if I would even be a writer at all without Larry McMurtry. He was the first novelist I read who took Texas seriously but not reverently, who made it possible for me to see my own state as fair game, as a legitimate literary place that I didn't have to feel self-conscious in either writing from or about.

And his unfinicky prose—his defiantly plain writing—unlocked something in me. It made me realize in a way I hadn't admitted to myself yet that the literary style I was always reaching for could sometimes just be a symptom of vanity, that spending a week writing and rewriting the same paragraph might scratch my craftsman's itch but make me forget that my job was to get on with things and tell a story about recognizable people.

Most of all, I learned from Larry McMurtry the obvious but sometimes most elusive first principle of creativity. To become somebody worth reading, you first have to have the courage to be yourself.

STEPHEN HARRIGAN is a writer at large for *Texas Monthly* and the author of thirteen books of fiction and nonfiction, including the best-selling novel *The Gates of the Alamo* and *Remember Ben Clayton*, which among other awards won the James Fenimore Cooper Prize for Best Historical Fiction from the Society of American Historians. *Big Wonderful Thing*, his sweeping narrative history of Texas, was named best nonfiction book of the year by the Philosophical Society of Texas. Harrigan has received lifetime achievement awards from the Texas Institute of Letters and the Texas Book Festival and was presented in 2019 with the Texas Medal of Arts.

Borderlands

A Home for Misfits Like Me
and McMurtry's Danny Deck

I VIVIDLY REMEMBER the first time I stepped into the local public library in South Dos Palos, California. I was fifteen years old, a high school dropout, and a Mexican farmworker who spent all day sweating alongside my family harvesting tomatoes grown by one of the massive farming operations in the Central Valley of the Golden State. Not a single book occupied a shelf of my family's humble home. Books intimidated me, an immigrant whose first language remained Spanish.

I still remember walking into the brown brick building surrounded by tall grass and a huge tree that seemed to be on the verge of falling onto the place. I hesitated before walking in, unsure what to do inside, or worse, what to read. I don't remember seeing anyone else. I was reminded of walking inside the funeral home when my uncle died years earlier—it was so eerily quiet in the same way, silent but for the sound of pages being turned by a gray-haired librarian, who suddenly stopped and stared at me.

"Can I help you?" she asked.

What the hell am I doing here? I thought. *Is this my former teacher's way of punishing me for wasting whatever potential I have and for dropping out of school on her watch? Why did my mother listen to her and push so hard to get me here?*

"I'm just looking," I said as I walked away, unsure of where to even begin to look.

My mother had her heart set on seeing me return to school. Worried sick that I had become the biggest cliché—the son of farmworkers turned high school dropout—she insisted that after toiling in the fields, I follow the advice of my former English teacher, Ms. Epperson, and at least read if I wasn't going back to school. After work, I dragged my butt down Sixth Street, past Jerry's Shoe Repair and Dry Goods, turned left on N Street, then entered a now-abandoned building that served as the public library and a post office. I would spend several hours each day reading English-language books housed inside that spooky place operated and occupied by Anglos.

As it turns out, the library was also the place where my best friend, George, wanted me incarcerated for as many days as possible. George was the closest I ever got to having a mentor, someone who would help shape my perspective on how the world worked and share secrets with me for moving forward without obsessing about the past. A lesson neither one of us quite learned.

George was determined to acquaint me with his favorite writer, Larry McMurtry, hoping I would love his novels and screenplays as much as he did. I wrote about George in my book *Homelands*. We were an unlikely pair. An immigrant from the tiny farming community of San Luis de Cordero, Durango, Mexico, I was filled with wonder about the United States, a country that provided a second chance at reinvention, as my parents, the architects of the experiment, repeatedly told me and my brothers. George, a bitter vet who served in Vietnam with my uncle Jesse and was now a labor contractor, was disillusioned with life in America. He took issue with my views on "American exceptionalism"—a term I later learned—by shaking his head repeatedly whenever the subject came up.

All men are created equal. America is a land of opportunity. A land of immigrants. Land of the free. Home of the brave.

The hopeful America I talked about hovered like a dark cloud over George's jaded spirit. For weeks he and I worked to load bins onto tractors pulling flatbeds on the edge of a tomato field. The massive farm machinery roared as workers harvested the red-ripe fruit, tossing it onto a conveyor belt. Mexican women, standing on a platform over the belt, sorted with nimble fingers hundreds, maybe thousands, of tomatoes an hour into bins. Every now and then, the machine would break down.

The fields would grow quiet. That's when George, my surly coworker, would turn into my sagacious mentor, teaching me about music—Neil Diamond, Creedence Clearwater Revival—and the magic of books, particularly those written by Larry McMurtry.

He raved about *The Last Picture Show* and urged me to read the book, set in rural Texas, and watch the movie. Still not convinced I would ever hold in my hands what he called a "McMurtry classic," George inched closer to my pimply face and whispered in my ear that the book included some steamy sex scenes.

Even though my teenage testosterone levels were running as wild as mustangs, sex scenes didn't interest me much. But when I finally began reading *The Last Picture Show*, I was hooked by McMurtry's clear-eyed narrative, an epic elegy to a time and place. The author's small-town Texas characters—driven by dark, sensual, violent passions—fascinated me. I had never come across anyone like them working in the farm fields of California.

During my daily after-work visits to the library, I read every McMurtry book I could get my hands on. The librarian, whose name I can't remember anymore, would greet me with a new find: *Horseman, Pass By*; *Leaving Cheyenne*; *Moving On*. She'd also point me toward other books—about teenage romance or coming-of-age stories that often included a scene with a first kiss. I read them, but none of them held me in thrall like McMurtry's novels.

The first McMurtry novel I picked up at the library and read at George's insistence was *All My Friends Are Going to Be Strangers*. When I read McMurtry's preface, I realized why George had insisted I read it. During one of the lulls in our tomato-packing operation—probably created by a malfunctioning conveyor belt—I told George that my parents were determined to move to the border, where Mexico's shadow would be cast over us. That was their divine place, a haven for nomads like ourselves.

I wasn't keen on that idea, as we loved living near the Pacific coast, even though we were too busy in the fields to play on the beach.

But George zeroed in on one word: *Texas?*

Read McMurtry, he insisted.

That summer ended, and so did my brief friendship with George. I later realized that I never learned his full name or asked where he was from. Maybe somewhere in the Midwest? Or Texas?

After I dropped out of school, Ms. Epperson showed up at my door. She wouldn't give up on me. She persisted in any way she could, pushing me to return to school and fulfill what she saw as my destiny. I wasn't moved by her prodding. I didn't see brown people like me going off to college, even if they graduated from high school.

But she saw something in me I didn't see. She saw me as a writer. I wrote "with feeling," she said, a trait that I later learned is essential to any wannabe writer. She also shared George's message: read.

My mother witnessed our conversations and needed no translation of what passed between Ms. Epperson and me. It was plain as the winter fog in the San Joaquin Valley. She made sure I went back to school.

I now live in El Paso, and many summers have come and gone. Every autumn when leaves turn brown, the image of George and his exuberance over McMurtry's books returns. I recently reopened *All My Friends Are Going to Be Strangers* and couldn't help thinking of George and about how much I love living on the border, despite feeling like I'm part of a medieval theater show with mercurial politicians hungry for power pulling strings from above the stage.

As I started reading, I was back somewhere between California and Texas, and wondered how reading McMurtry's *All My Friends* perhaps subconsciously prepared me for this life I now live along the border, often wondering where I belong.

McMurtry's hero, Danny Deck, is a man with strong moral feelings—feelings that he can't escape, feelings that torment him as an aspiring writer. In the book's preface, McMurtry makes clear that, as a writer, he and Danny had much in common. "He wasn't me. But there was no large gap between his sensibility and my own: I became comfortable with his voice at once and liked his quirks and his mainly sad appreciation of the absurd."

Like McMurtry, Danny struggles with the dilemma most writers and artists face: "Whether art can be persuaded to allow its artists a little of normal life and common happiness and yet permit them to create."

Danny has written only one thin novel. He recognizes that most writers, "whatever they give up and however hard they strive, are still only able to be minor," as McMurtry writes in the preface. "Is the sacrifice of common happiness worth it if one is only going to be minor? That's one of the animating questions the book asks. Is Danny correct? In his judgment that it is art that's distancing him from happiness?"

Ultimately, Danny becomes convinced that a career in writing can accomplish only one thing: the destruction of his happiness. In an act of desperation, he travels down to the US-Mexican border, gets drunk, and attempts to drown his loathsome second novel in the Rio Grande.

"I had never felt such black, unforgiving hatred of anything as I felt for the pages in my hands," says Danny as he shoves the pages of his manuscript into the depths of the river. His pages refuse to stay submerged until he clutches his novel in his hands and dives into the channel of the river, where the current sweeps the pages away.

While traveling down to the border to drown his novel, Danny realizes how much he longs to stand under the immense sky over Texas. "The sky was what I was missing, and seeing it again in the morning brightness made me realize suddenly why I hadn't been myself for many months. It has such depth and such spaciousness and such incredible compass, it took so much in and circled one with such a tremendous generous space that it was impossible not to feel more intensely with it above you."

Danny's happiness as he stands under Texas's big sky and drowns his hated manuscript in the Rio Grande inspires a profound epiphany: his "true country" is not Houston or Austin or Dallas, but the borderland—"a thin little strip between the country of the normal and the country of the strange."

I often think about what I learned from my English teacher: to be a writer, you have to write with passion. And that means your characters must live life intensely, their feelings influencing their actions and behavior. Just like McMurtry's Danny Deck. As I finished rereading *All My Friends Are Going to Be Strangers*, it dawned on me why Danny Deck made such an impression on me.

Yes, we're all misfits along the border—artists, writers, migrants, all of us trying to lead normal lives under the harsh spotlight of a country wrangling with raw nativist sentiments. Old wounds and doubts resurface: maybe America isn't as exceptional as I once thought. And yet it's here, on the border, where my family's two nations, languages, and cultures blur into one land on the far edges of Texas, New Mexico, and Chihuahua.

Dark shadows still hover over the borderlands of the Rio Grande. These days I have never felt so frustrated in my efforts to convey the critical importance of these two countries to one another. I've spent my journalism career trying to be a bridge of understanding between these increasingly volatile worlds. But the misunderstandings persist: Mexican migrants like those I once worked side by side with in California have been turned into cartoons of scary, evil people seeking to take away American jobs.

Sometimes I feel like a broken bridge, battered by a rushing current of lies masquerading as "alternative facts," fearmongering, and race-baiting. As a writer, I'm fighting for truth, even when I question whether that matters anymore. Or matters for the wrong reasons.

And yet, perhaps Danny Deck, aka Larry McMurtry, was right about the borderlands. There's a silver lining to all the madness roiling the region. For it is here where I see the waters of the Rio Grande on the US side or the Rio Bravo on the Mexican side gently flowing, coming together without having to pick one side over the other. A shared happiness, and a shared agony, in a place where I don't have to choose anymore.

ALFREDO CORCHADO is the Mexico border correspondent for the *Dallas Morning News*. He is a noted expert on immigration, drug violence, and US-Mexico foreign policy and has reported on border topics from the disappearance and murders of women in Ciudad Juárez to the exodus of Mexico's middle class to the United States, the exposure of government corruption, and the reach of Mexican drug traffickers into US communities. The recipient of numerous awards and honors for his courageous journalism, Corchado is the author of *Midnight in Mexico* and *Homelands*.

All My Friends Are
Going to Be Larry

I WAS DRIVING to a sacred place—the Medicine Mounds, which rise above the plains about seventy-five miles northwest of Wichita Falls—when word arrived that Larry McMurtry had died twelve hours earlier in Tucson. I knew the old word wrangler (sorry, couldn't help myself) was nearing the end. His health was shot (congestive heart failure, Parkinson's), and an email death watch had been going on for months among that group of gossips known as the Texas literary community. So his departure from this rock wasn't exactly a surprise. Yet I still felt a little shocked when I read the text telling me about his death while standing in line at the famous kolache joint in West, Texas. My world seemed to be getting emptier in a hurry. The artist Bob "Daddy-O" Wade, my friend and book collaborator, died on Christmas Eve 2019. The author Jan Reid, my best friend and literary mentor as well as the person who introduced me to Larry, checked out the following September. Cancer killed my mother two months after that. And now Larry was gone too.

I left West with an altered set of travel plans. I headed toward Archer City, Larry's hometown. I arrived about three hours later. It was dusk by then. I had no plans. I just wanted to be *there* for a while. I prowled the streets in my SUV and thought about how this place was the compost out of which sprang dozens of books, screenplays, articles, reviews, and essays carrying the byline of Larry McMurtry. It was appropriate that I was behind the wheel. Larry loved driving. Grover Lewis, his North Texas University classmate, reported that Larry

could and would drive and read at the same time, book spine resting
against steering wheel, especially while roaring along all-but-deserted
West Texas two-lanes. Larry sometimes took umbrage with Grover for
fictionalizing nonfiction, and he might well have claimed that Grover
made this up. But I hope it's true. I have a fantasy of Larry navigating
a Plymouth between Hereford and Dalhart while scanning the pages
of Galsworthy's *The White Monkey* or Hardy's *Jude the Obscure*.

I drove from Archer City to Vernon and checked into the Holiday
Inn Express adjacent to US 287. After toting my suitcase to my room,
I walked out to the parking lot, where clusters of nomadic turbine in-
stallers consumed their last beers and cigarettes of the day as semitrailer
trucks, several carrying cattle, rumbled along the highway. I looked
to the southeast. A full moon was rising above Archer City. It seemed
fitting to me, but I can see Larry grimacing at the notion. He wasn't
exactly the sentimental type.

I like to think that Larry and Rendal Hamby crossed paths at some
point. The Hambys were descended from a big-money Lone Star wild-
catter. Somehow Rendal wound up working in Donrey Media Group
management gigs. At least that's what we were told when he showed up
at the Donrey-owned daily newspaper in Guthrie, Oklahoma, where
I worked as a teenage reporter. A gray grimness tended to hang in the
air of Donrey's low-rent offices back in the 1970s, along with cigarette
smoke and the combating stenches of offset press solvent and burnt
coffee. Employees were overworked and underpaid, even by small-
town newspaper standards, and often felt trapped. As the new advertising sales manager, Rendal shattered the bleak mold the morning of
his first day at work in Guthrie. He introduced himself by performing
a tap dance while singing "Camptown Races." He was the proverbial
piece of work.

By his own account, Hamby, who died in October 2019, had been a
varsity football player at Texas Tech during the E. J. Holub period but
was invited to exit both team and university because of an incident at

a Juárez *burdel* that caused him to miss the Red Raiders' game against the University of Texas. Hamby then completed his higher education at Texas A&I in Kingsville, where he may or may not have played football for the legendary coach Gil Stenke. After graduating, he worked at different jobs in Texas and put together enough money to buy a string of Fina gasoline stations. He managed to sell them a short time later for a healthy profit, whereupon he set off for a small town in Chihuahua, where he planned to write the Great American Novel. Instead, Hamby being Hamby, he caroused and drank and devoted little time to pecking out words on his typewriter. He wound up in *la cárcel* for the crime of executing his own 1963 Chevrolet with a .38-caliber pistol in the town plaza. Once free, the crazy gringo returned to the United States and eventually went to work for Donrey. I think all this is true, or at least mostly so. It was Hamby's own story, so I'm sticking to it.

Hamby read constantly, and he read well; I'd guess he was the only person in a ten-county region who'd ever made it through John Barth's *The Sot-Weed Factor*. One day I met up with him in Guthrie at Edna's Lounge, a beer joint that was his favorite place to dispense wisdom. I had a copy of Jack Kerouac's *On the Road* stuffed in the back pocket of my Levi's.

"Let me see that book, young Stratton," Rendal said as Conway Twitty's baritone boomed from the jukebox. He squinted the cover into focus, made a face as if he'd just bitten into a green persimmon, and then shoved the paperback back at me. "Why are you reading that piece of ca-ca?" "Ca-ca" was one of his favorite terms. "It ain't got a story, and Kerouac can't write worth shit. Why waste time with it? You want to read a good book? Go over to the library and check out Larry McMurtry's *All My Friends Are Going to Be Strangers*."

Pun unintended, but I was no stranger to Larry's novels, nor, for that matter, to the early Merle Haggard country-and-Western hit that supplied the title for Larry's fifth novel (and sixth book overall). I'd read *Leaving Cheyenne*, *The Last Picture Show*, and *Horseman, Pass By* before choking on the sheer mass of *Moving On*, which seemed to be maybe a hundred pages longer than the King James Bible. No way you could ever tuck a paperback version of *Moving On* into the back pocket of a pair of Levi's. I'd tried his most recent book, *Terms of Endearment*, and while Larry came to consider it his best novel, it didn't hook me at the time. Then there was *All My Friends Are Going to Be Strangers*. I followed Hamby's advice, which turned out to be the best he ever gave me. I consumed it in two sittings.

Larry never wrote a better novel. Of course, it can be debated whether it is truly a novel. Sherry Kafka Wagner told me over dinner one night that Larry just changed the names in what is a true-life story. Sherry is best known these days as an urban planner and arts supporter in San Antonio. But she began her professional life as a novelist. She and Larry went all the way back to when Larry published his first novel, *Horseman, Pass By*, in 1961. She was around during the events that spawned *All My Friends Are Going to Be Strangers*. She would know. That it is a roman à clef was pretty clear to me upon first reading it, even though I knew very little about Larry at the time.

With *All My Friends*, Larry violated Stratton's Cardinal Rule about Fiction: novels should *never* be written with writers or university professors as protagonists. They are among the most boring species on the planet and tend to be infected with self-importance. Fiction is better off being written by them, not about them. But I'm glad Larry ignored my rule. He once admitted that Danny Deck, *All My Friends'* narrator, was the character he created who was most like himself; to be precise, he said: "There was no large gap between his sensibility and my own." Through Danny Deck, Larry gives us insight into what being a writer—in particular, a writer in crisis—means. From the sixth grade onward, I knew I was going to be a writer. Danny Deck's adventures spoke to me even as a teenage newspaper reporter because I knew even then that books were my destiny.

———————

In his early life, Larry knew no shortage of rough times. He grew up in cowboy culture and was exposed to more than his share of roping, castrating, dehorning, branding, and the other unpleasantries of raising cattle. (I know whereof I speak when I say unpleasantries. I did more than my fair share of that kind of stuff myself.) This way of living gets romanticized on movie screens and in the pages of books. But it's hard, dirty, and at times dangerous work. The people who work on ranches and farms, as well the people who live in small towns dependent on agriculture, are so busy just surviving that they seldom have time to ponder beauty or philosophical questions, let alone read thousand-page novels by nineteenth-century Russian masters.

I tend to think that people with artistic personalities are more hard-wired than programmed by the circumstances of their lives. Daddy-O Wade, for instance, was the son of a nomadic hotel manager who roamed from job to job across Texas. Nothing in Bob's childhood experiences really formed him as an artist. But one day as a kid he decided to customize the paint job on a toy car using his mom's fingernail polish. And thus the artist in him popped out. The inclination to create art was somehow embedded in him. A few decades down the line, his gigantic sculpture of an iguana graced the rooftop of the legendary Lone Star Café in Manhattan. I inferred from our conversations that Bob's childhood was pretty isolated and boring before art came along. I think the same was true for Larry in Archer City. "I don't remember either of my parents reading me a story," Larry said. "Of books there were none. . . . There must have been a Bible, but I don't remember ever seeing it."

For Larry, it was a visit by a relative on his way to enlist in World War II that freed his artistic soul. Cousin Robert Hilburn stopped by the McMurtry place and gave Larry a box of books, "the gift that changed my life . . . In my sixth and seventh years I was often in bed, closeted like a tiny Proust, while I listened to the radio from sign-on until sign-off." Larry said he scarcely knew Hilburn. Why would he choose Larry as the recipient of the books? I'm not religious, but, paradoxically, I do believe there are angels in this world, people who show up out of nowhere to give you direction or other aid when you most need it. Hilburn seems to have been just such an angel.

Long before he considered becoming a writer, Larry was subconsciously preparing himself. I say that because one of his contemporaries from Archer City told a documentary filmmaker that Larry wasn't an actual participant in the events that found their way into books like

The Last Picture Show. He was a quiet guy who stood in the back of a group of locals and listened to the tales that others had to tell about their exploits. Much of what they had to say was exaggerated bullshitting, but it made for excellent storytelling. Larry mentally filed away what he heard, just as he had earlier filed away stories that his grandfather William Jefferson McMurtry told about his time as a Texas pioneer. All successful writers do this. They know how to shut up and listen. They don't feel a need to constantly call attention to themselves, and they happily surrender the stage. When a character like Rendal Hamby stumbles into your midst, you recognize (again, usually subconsciously) that you've been gifted with material. It may sound crass, but it is a precious commodity. You record as much as you can and store it in a safe gray-matter zone.

Around the time he published *Horseman, Pass By,* and in the months thereafter, Larry ran into a number of Rendal Hamby–type people: characters who didn't fit the mold for "normal" human beings you might have encountered in the America of the 1960s. He channeled them into *All My Friends Are Going to Be Strangers*, a novel that sprinted out of him after finishing the marathon, *Moving On.* (The original manuscript of that beast of a book was 2,500 typewritten pages.)

An English poet once told an interviewer that he didn't write verse because he wanted to. The process, he said, was more like that of an oyster producing a pearl, which gets made because the oyster is irritated into it. It has no say in the matter. A true poet is irritated into the creation of a poem. It's not something she or he can control. I think Larry's writing of *All My Friends* was not a matter of choice. It was something he had to write. He called it a "lucky book": "I was quite tired but I had a sort of momentum going, and I thought: *I might just do a quick book.* I wrote it rapidly, and I think it has an un-self-conscious tone that I probably could not have got if I had tried. I'm really happy with it. Every time I pick it up, I'm amazed at how easy it is to read."

It's a funny novel—Larry's mastery of humor too often goes unremarked. It's also Larry's most gonzo-like work. But its underlying message about the life of a writer is a sober one.

"It's true that the better you write," Larry said, "the worse you live. The more of yourself you take out of real relationships and project into fantasy relationships, the more the real relationships suffer." This, I think, is the cautionary takeaway from *All My Friends Are Going to Be Strangers*. Danny Deck marries a beautiful young woman, but the marriage falters even as he achieves his dream of getting his first novel accepted by Random House. The rest of *All My Friends* is a tale of Danny moving through a world of displacement. His wife becomes pregnant, but Danny is cut off from a legitimate fatherhood experience as his wife moves toward divorce and keeps him away from his new-born child. He travels aimlessly from Houston to California to Austin and the ranch country where he grew up. (His crazy uncle who lives on a remote spread is the antithesis of the cattleman Homer Bannon from *Horseman, Pass By*, as well as the ranchers who appear in scores of sentimental Texas novels. Uncle Laredo hates cattle.)

As Danny lives through this pinball-like phase he carries the albatross of other people's expectations for his next book, the Big Texas Novel. He finds himself feeling alienated from his friends. In fact, he betrays two of his best friends, a married couple, by covertly sleeping with the wife. Danny winds up in McAllen. He calls a sympathetic woman he met in California. "I've never known anybody who could screw up as bad as you do," she tells him. "So you see I can't save you. I know exactly how lonely you are. I know exactly how wonderful you are too. But I can't even try to help you." After she rings off, he crosses the river into Reynosa, then comes back to Texas, where he begins driving the highway running alongside the Rio Grande. At Roma, where Marlon Brando's *Viva Zapata* was filmed, Danny sheds the final vestiges of his life as he's known it. In one of the great scenes from Texas literature, he wades into the river and "drowns" the manuscript of the Big Texas Novel, which he never really wanted to write in the first place.

Danny's dilemma, Larry said, was "whether art can be persuaded to allow its artists a little of normal life and common happiness and yet permit them to create. Danny's bleak conclusion is that art won't be persuaded." Larry no doubt went through just such an existential crisis. In opting to follow art, he would produce dozens of screenplays and dozens of published books. I know he had to sacrifice much in the way of common happiness as he projected more of himself into the "fantasy relationships" of his fiction than into real ones. That's why, as his fan Rendal Hamby would have said, Larry never wrote ca-ca. His work was uneven at times: that's true for Joyce Carol Oates or any other writer who publishes in quantity. But Larry at his worst as a writer always told well-crafted stories and had interesting characters. Larry's best books are unbeatable.

One other key takeaway: Larry told interviewer Patrick Bennett that he listened to a lot of country music. The country song that possibly inspired the title for his novel, "(My Friends Are Gonna Be) Strangers," also known as "(From Now on) All My Friends Are Gonna Be Strangers," was penned by Liz Anderson and became Merle Haggard's first top-ten hit. In it, the singer vows to be finished with trusting anyone and claims that his fingers are the only thing he knows he can count on.

That had to resonate with Larry. He was determined to have faith in those fingers that showed up at his typewriter seven days a week, holidays included. He followed his own artistic path, not doing what other people expected him to do. I don't know that he actually plunged into the Rio Grande, but he at least figuratively drowned the Big Texas Novel, full of cowboys and Comanches and so forth, that people thought might be coming in the wake of his first three novels. Instead, he wrote a trio of modern urban novels set in Houston, a Hollywood novel, a road novel of sorts filled with Hambyesque characters, a Vegas novel, and a lot of screenplays. When he was almost fifty, he did write the Big Texas Novel—on his own terms. *Lonesome Dove* won him the Pulitzer Prize and became a massive bestseller.

As I sat in my Holiday Inn Express room in Vernon and looked out the window at the full moon over Archer City, I felt gratitude more than anything else. Larry made hard choices and sacrificed a great deal in order to leave us the literary legacy he did. We should all be happy he drove down his own highways.

WILLIAM KIP STRATTON—friends call him Kip—is the *Los Angeles Times* best-selling author of *The Wild Bunch: Sam Peckinpah, a Revolution in Hollywood, and the Making of a Legendary Film* and eight other books. He was born in Guthrie, Oklahoma, but has lived much of his life in Texas. Both his mother's and father's families had deep roots in the West. His mother's family homesteaded outside Guthrie during the Great Land Run of 1889. His father, a rodeo cowboy as well as a runaway dad, became the subject of Stratton's book *Chasing the Rodeo.*

McMurtry Passes By

LONGING IS A MOOD you always bump into with McMurtry. The first of his novels that I read was *Leaving Cheyenne*, which is one long heartache on the part of two cowboys for Molly Taylor and her yearning for companionship and understanding. McMurtry wrote a sentence that I figured would stay with me the rest of my life: "A woman's love is like the morning dew—it's just as likely to settle on a horse turd as a rose." So true, I thought, as I was nineteen and loveless.

McMurtry worked a seam in those early novels, the fraying edge of the Western frontier, a way of life that was at once antiquated and grudgingly modern. He was ruddering against the idea of the great Texas myth, which glorified a way of life that was mostly stultifying and mean. The dust of the cattle drives was still in the air, and the rumble of a gusher lingered in memory, but the residue of the myth was as vacuous as a discarded faith. McMurtry's characters felt trapped by life, whether they were ranchers or suburbanites or the residents of a despairing village on the precipice of extinction, such as his native Archer City, the fictional Thalia of *The Last Picture Show*. "The aridity of the small west Texas towns was not all a matter of unforgiving skies, baking heat, and rainlessness," he wrote in the autobiographical *Walter Benjamin at the Dairy Queen*. "The drought in those towns was social, as well as climatic." The title of that extended essay was as apt a summation of the confluences that made up Larry McMurtry as we are likely to find.

I ran into Larry in 1997 at a party in Austin. He was standing alone under a live oak in the broad front yard of the governor's mansion. He was a little forbidding, to be honest, with those hawkish eyes behind

big black cheap-looking glasses, which were as much a part of his image as they were for Woody Allen, only on Larry they added to the air
of scholarly disdain. I suppose all Texas writers were a little anxious
around him, as he would periodically pee on the entire enterprise with
unsettling force and accuracy. I had met him once before at a meeting
of the Texas Institute of Letters, after *Lonesome Dove* had established
him in the pantheon of great American writers. His remarks about the
burdens of fame elicited little sympathy among those who had felt the
lash of his judgment.

He was cordial enough as we chatted under the oak, but he bright-
ened when his attractive and interesting partner, Diana Ossana, joined
us. She seemed amused by his morose frame of mind. I gathered that
women were extremely important to him, serving as psychological life
jackets on the ocean of depression that always seemed close at hand.

Diana was in Austin to judge screenplays for a writers' festival that
was underway. As it happened, she and Larry were just beginning to
work together on the script for *Brokeback Mountain*, which would be
such a narrative triumph. It was a perfect McMurtry project, a recast-
ing of the cowboy legend through the lens of two men who fall in love.
The life they might have led together would never happen; they were
captives to the conventions of the culture they lived in, like so many
McMurtry heroes.

Larry talked about his efforts to turn Archer City into a book town,
like Hay-on-Wye in Wales. He was busy buying up much of the vacant
downtown and stocking it with books, shoving them down the throat
of his hometown, as I saw it. "Are you doing this out of revenge?" I
asked. Diana laughed, but Larry looked nonplussed. I may have been
teasing him, but I was also really interested.

I reflected on the child Larry had been, growing up trapped in a
place without books, and his passionate flight into the literary life,
only to circle back to his birthplace with such eccentric intentions.
But he had always been a bookman, wherever he settled long enough,
in Georgetown or Houston. He evidently enjoyed being a shopkeeper,
but there must also have been something grand about having so many
books under his command.

Larry came back to Austin a few months later for the Texas Book Festival, where he delivered the best quote of the event: "It's surprising to see so many people involved in the life of the mind on the first day of quail season."

When I wrote *God Save Texas*, I mentioned that Larry was one of my favorite writers. In return, I received a letter. It was written on a manual typewriter and filled with hard-to-decipher emendations in blue ink, with irregular margins like a poem in free verse. By this time Larry was ailing and living in Tucson with Diana and also with his second wife, Norma Faye Kesey, the widow of his old friend Ken Kesey. Larry had buffered the end of his life with the consolation of powerful women. "I wish we'd ever talked," he wrote, obviously not having that meeting under the oak tree in his mind. It would do him a disservice to re-create the letter itself, with all the misspellings and crossed-out lines, but the obvious struggle to write it made it all the more meaningful to me. It's mainly about the women who had "divided up the literary lions as came in." They obviously had provided fond memories. "Bill Brammer lived with us several weeks as he was descending into the final horror," he wrote, mentioning the author of *The Gay Place*, a hallowed novel of Austin in the 1960s. "I had a big house and my wife had run off. My son James was 6 months old. I thought the town was toxic then—now is better: my son and grandson both have made decent careers."

Larry puzzled over the life he chose. He quoted Walter Benjamin on the difference between a novelist and a storyteller. He thought about the stories of the frontier he heard his relatives tell on the porch in his bookless childhood, and he wondered "how someone like myself, growing up in a place that had just been settled, and a place, moreover, in which nothing of cultural or historical consequence had ever happened, became a novelist instead of being content to worry over an old woman who had been traded for skunk hides, or a dairy farmer who has given way to despair. Does mere human memory, the soil that nourishes storytelling, still have any use at all?" And yet he made a career of writing about people who, like himself, were intellectually starved and imprisoned by the life they were born into. The slapdash quality of some of his work was frustrating for his fans—for me, at least. But he still managed to create some of the most memorable figures in Texas literature.

He was a penetrating and learned critic, and no doubt he turned that critical eye on himself too harshly. That self-mocking sweatshirt he wore when he was a young writer, defiantly emblazoned with MINOR REGIONAL NOVELIST, showed that he saw himself as a part of the same Texas writers' scene that he scorned. He held himself to the same high standards that he insisted we shoot for. He was riding herd on Texas writers, driving us all to exceed our narrow ambitions, while feeling that he himself fell short of the mark. He even described his greatest achievement, *Lonesome Dove*, as "no masterpiece."

And yet, it is.

LAWRENCE WRIGHT is the author of *The Looming Tower: Al-Qaeda and the Road to 9/11*, winner of the 2007 Pulitzer Prize for General Nonfiction and named one of *Time*'s Top 100 Books of All Time. He is a staff writer for *The New Yorker* and winner of three National Magazine Awards. His 2013 book, *Going Clear: Scientology, Hollywood, and the Prison of Belief*, was made into an HBO documentary that won three Emmys, including one for best documentary. Wright is a member of the Council on Foreign Relations, the Society of American Historians, and the American Academy of Arts and Sciences. He plays keyboards in the Austin-based blues band WhoDo.

Image Credits